KIDNAPPED

BY A

CLIENT

THE INCREDIBLE
TRUE STORY OF AN
ATTORNEY'S FIGHT
FOR JUSTICE

SHARON R. MUSE, JD

Skyhorse Publishing

Skyhorse Publishing books may be purchased in bulk at special discounts for sales promotion, corporate gifts, fund-raising, or educational purposes. Special editions can also be created to specifications. For details, contact the Special Sales Department, Skyhorse Publishing, 307 West 36th Street, 11th Floor, New York, NY 10018 or info@skyhorsepublishing.com.

Skyhorse® and Skyhorse Publishing® are registered trademarks of Skyhorse Publishing, Inc.®, a Delaware corporation.

Visit our website at www.skyhorsepublishing.com.

10 9 8 7 6 5 4 3 2 1

Library of Congress Cataloging-in-Publication Data is available on file.

Cover photo courtesy of Kevin Bryan with Visual Poet Studios

ISBN: 978-1-5107-3594-1
Ebook ISBN: 978-1-5107-3595-8

Printed in the United States of America

To my heavenly father, God, for rescuing me time and time again. To my warrior of a dad, Richard R. Muse and my lifelong playmate, best friend and world's greatest brother Richard (Rick) Jesse Muse who both passed before this book was printed. I would have never survived without your influence. And to my Mom, Bonnie L. Muse, who showed me what it looks like to walk in faith—especially when it is hard. My sister Lisa, for being a constant support. I'm blessed beyond measure.

Honorable Robert G. Johnson, Circuit Judge for the 14th JC and later a Court of Appeals Judge, and to my jury. Combined you gave me my life back. There are no words to adequately thank you. Codell and Vickie Gibson and David Roe. Your willingness to intervene in an act of violence quite literally saved my life. Jeff Ballard, your intelligence and strength helped me navigate the most terrifying moments of my life and may have saved my trial. Steve Schroering, your expertise and friendship carried me through. Amy Lusk, you stood in the gap when I couldn't do it myself. God sent each of you to protect me. Thank you for doing it.

Everything good that comes from this story is because of you.

CONTENTS

Introduction   *vii*

PART ONE: THE ATTACK

CHAPTER 1: No?   1

CHAPTER 2: Ma'am, I Don't Know Anything   8

CHAPTER 3: A Big Scene   14

CHAPTER 4: A Dogfight   21

CHAPTER 5: On TV They Always Stop   28

CHAPTER 6: A Harmless Guy, a Bloody Woman,
                and a Long Knife   33

CHAPTER 7: The Green Duffle   39

CHAPTER 8: You Picked the Wrong Woman!   46

CHAPTER 9: Whirling Dervish   53

CHAPTER 10: The Aftermath   70

PART TWO: THE CRIMINAL'S JUSTICE SYSTEM

CHAPTER 11: Circling the Drain   91

CHAPTER 12: Conspicuously Absent   101

CHAPTER 13: The Stairwell   105

CHAPTER 14: Freedom   111

CHAPTER 15: Trial Wear   115

CHAPTER 16: The Plea Offer   119

CHAPTER 17: That's Just What We Do   131

CHAPTER 18: Great is thy Faithfulness   138

PART THREE: THE TRIAL

CHAPTER 19: The Juice Isn't Worth the Squeeze   147

CHAPTER 20: Trial Part I—The Jury's Dilemma   167

CHAPTER 21: Trial Part II—Who Was in Charge?   186

CHAPTER 22: Trial Part III—The Five-Year Wait   200

CHAPTER 23: Trial Part IV—The Doggone Knife   215

CHAPTER 24: Is He Single?   226

CHAPTER 25: Malingering   242

CHAPTER 26: Thirteen Calls   264

EPILOGUE: The Campaign   271

APPENDICES

A Conversation with Sharon R. Muse   275

Topics For Discussion   291

Resources   293

Acknowledgments   295

INTRODUCTION

911 CALL

DATE: April 7, 2006

BOURBON COUNTY

TRANSCRIPT EXCERPT

DISPATCHER: Okay. What's going on?

MALE CALLER: I'm not sure. I just pulled up. There's a woman here—she ran into the road [with her shirt down]. She was screaming and asked for help, said she didn't know where she was. Said she's a lawyer and this guy was a criminal or something. I just pulled up on this.

DISPATCHER: Okay. What's going on out there now?

MALE CALLER: Let her tell you.

MS. MUSE: This is Sharon Muse. Is this . . .

DISPATCHER: This is State Police, honey. [Are you injured?] Do you need an ambulance?

MS. MUSE: I don't know, I don't know.

DISPATCHER: Okay, Sharon. Just take a deep breath for me, okay, honey?

MS. MUSE: I'm so scared—he's going to kill me.

DISPATCHER: I know, honey. You've got other people that are there with you right now, right?

MS. MUSE: Yes. But he is still here, please hurry.

DISPATCHER: Okay. We've got a trooper on his way to you, okay?

MS. MUSE: Do you know how close they are? Please hurry. He keeps trying to get around these people to get to me. I want him away from me. I can't fight him off anymore; he'll kill me if he can get to me. Please hurry! He is getting close to me—

[*Muse to Morrison*] You need to stay away from me!

DISPATCHER: [*in background operator to trooper on radio: "You got an ETA?"*] Okay Sharon. We've got them on their way, okay, honey? There's a trooper who's coming out there to you who's going to take care of all of it. Are there other people there with you still? Sharon? Sharon? Honey, are you there? Sharon?

"It doesn't matter if you get away," he said. "I'm going to kill you. It may be tomorrow, it may be next year, but I'm going to kill you."

I believed him then. I believe him now.

I barely survived the first time he came for me.

Why did he come for me?

I don't know. It isn't possible for the mind of the rational to understand the mind of the obsessed. At no point in this story will you say, "Oh, of course. That's why he planned to kill her. That makes sense."

Crime can be random. Mine wasn't. This crime was born, nurtured, and fed in the depths of the mind of an evil and twisted predator.

I never saw it coming.

I first met Larry Morrison[1] years ago when I successfully helped him navigate a legal matter. Once the case ended, I did not think of him again. He eventually landed in prison for the same charge with a different lawyer. He went in disturbed and came out evil two and half years later. He inexplicably fixated on me, plotting my rape and murder as he obsessed in his prison cell. Which brings me to this case, my case, *The Commonwealth of Kentucky v. Larry Morrison* in which I was not his lawyer. I was his victim.

I take umbrage when I'm labeled a "victim." I will not allow it to become my moniker, though it is my title in this legal drama. But it makes me feel as if I'm weak. My strength is one of many things this man has taken from me, along with my dignity and pride. But I'll take it back.

I've made it my job to make sure he doesn't see the light of day again. No one else is keeping watch. Each day of incarceration for him is a day of life for me. Despite multiple witnesses, plenty of physical evidence, and a terrifying crime scene, Morrison was not charged with a number of crimes that would have added to his potential sentence. He tried to rape me, yet he was never charged with attempted rape. He told me he was going to kill me and did his best to slit my throat, yet he was never charged with attempted murder. After he was arrested, he was almost released due to a clerical error.

Procedural errors, data entry errors, and apathy are just as dangerous as murderous psychopaths, it turns out. If I weren't a lawyer savvy in the institution of law and if I hadn't been relentless in advocating for myself, I'd probably be dead right now. Or he would be, since I embraced something I called proactive self-protection. But we'll get to that later.

---

1 Larry Morrison is not the criminal's real name. I choose not to give him further notoriety.

I was shocked by the reality of how the system works, the system I've spent my life serving. I came to realize the criminal justice system is, in actuality, the criminal's justice system.

My story is a crash course in safety, forgiveness, and criminal law.

I had to learn these things the hard way. It almost cost me my life.

Don't dismiss this. Learn from it.

I, too, said, "This can't be happening to me." I was wrong.

PART ONE
THE ATTACK

CHAPTER 1

<u>NO?</u>

COMMONWEALTH OF KENTUCKY

v.

LARRY MORRISON

DIRECT EXAMINATION OF SHARON MUSE
[BY ASSISTANT COMMONWEALTH'S ATTORNEY, MR. EARLY]

Q: For the record, would you state your name?

A: Sharon Muse.

Q: Are you okay, Ms. Muse?

A: It's hard to be here.

Q: Okay. If you need a break—

A: No—

[Bailiff brings water]

A: *[To bailiff]* Thank you.

Q: Just a few questions so the jury will know who you are, okay? Can you tell us where you're from?

A: Georgetown, Kentucky.

Q: What do you do for a living, Sharon?

A: I'm an attorney there. I have my own office.

Q: Who was at the office that day? Do you have a secretary working for you?

A: I have an assistant, Judy. She was there that day.

Q: That was Friday. Did you have plans for that night or for the weekend?

A: I did. One of my best friends who lives in Louisville had had a lot of difficult things going on in her life and was upset. I promised her I would meet her at her house with another friend at 6:00 so that we could spend some time together.

Q: Sharon, I'm going to have to ask you to speak up a little bit. It's—

A: I'm sorry.

Q: Now, did someone come to visit you in the office earlier that day, before 5:00?

A: Yes. My mom came in between 3:00 and 3:30. She had been having health problems, some things we couldn't get figured out. And that day, she had been diagnosed with a rare form of cancer, and she wasn't sure of treatment. It was a very upsetting afternoon.

Q: Now, Sharon, take your time, but tell me—what happened as you left your office that day?

I'll tell you what happened.

I was unprepared, so I resorted to what I knew: good manners, logic, and words. I acted exactly the way I'd been trained to act since Sunday school. I was uncomfortable, but I was polite. And then I was kidnapped.

* * *

Awkwardly carrying a box of files and my briefcase, I pressed a cell phone between my shoulder and cheek and listened to my boyfriend, Jeff, on the other end as I mouthed goodbye to my assistant, Judy. I stepped out of the office into the hall and caught a glimpse of someone's arm disappearing around a corner.

I turned and pushed the office door shut with my foot, struggled to grip my phone between my shoulder and ear, balance my box of files and tried not to sigh. Jeff was my soon-to-be ex-boyfriend. He was a nice guy, but we weren't in the best place. I didn't really want to talk to him, or anyone, right then. It'd been a tough day. I was still upset about my mom's cancer diagnosis and was on my way to a friend's house to discuss what to do about her treatments and what to do with the men in our lives.

Turning to walk down the hall, I abruptly stepped back to avoid bumping into a man in his forties who looked vaguely familiar. A former client? Yes, that was it, but I had no recollection of who, when, or why.

Built like a fireplug, he was your average Southern redneck with a yellow mullet and muddy green eyes. I squinted, trying to place him. What kind of case was it? Regardless, I was pretty sure it was the same guy who had ducked around the corner a second ago. He was squarely in front of me, eyes locked with mine, filling up the hallway.

I was annoyed. I wanted to leave. *Why was he waiting for me out here? What was wrong with my waiting room?*

"Hello? Hello?" Jeff's voice sounded far away.

"Hey, let me call you back. Someone's here waiting for me," I told Jeff, not breaking eye contact with the man in front of me. His intense stare made me squirm.

I closed my flip phone, opened my mouth to ask questions, but before I could speak . . .

"Sharon," he said, as though we had known each other for years. He leaned into my space, vibrating with urgency. At first glance, he looked like an innocuous blue-collar guy, yet something about him disturbed me. I kept my composure, staying professional and calm and asserting authority—or so I thought. Instinctively, I took a step or two back to create space between us.

His voice was desperate, pleading.

"My grandmother wanted me to come see you since you did such a great job for us before. We need your help."

He blocked my exit. I didn't like it. "I . . ."

"My wife just died. We're scared."

That explained his appearance, his odd behavior. He was in crisis mode. His eyes drilled into mine, then darted around. He clenched and unclenched his jaw, as if his life depended on this conversation.

"We don't know what to do. Her bank accounts are frozen. We don't have any money and need help now." He continued, "You are the only one who can help us."

I deal with people from all walks of life, but this was an unusual experience even for me.

"I am very sorry for your loss." I suppressed a tinge of guilt at the realization that I didn't have the energy to help this man. Normally empathetic, I was too drained by the long, difficult day. My head and heart were still reeling after the intense conversation with my mother. "I can help your family, but it's 5:00 p.m. on a Friday. The courts are closed. I can't get you in front of a judge until Monday morning. There is nothing I can do for you now."

"There will be a lot of money in this for you," he said in a rush, talking over me, not seeming to register a word I'd said.

What was going on?

Something was off—with him and his story. I knew he was telling the truth about my working with him in the past, yet the circumstances eluded me. I saw hundreds of people a year. The way he kept referencing his grandma made me think I must have done an adoption for him since that was the only time I inter-acted with extended family.

I moved again to create distance, but he moved with me. "I'm sorry for the loss of your wife." I peered around, trying to plot a course to maneuver past him. "But that's not how it works. You'd pay me hourly, like any other case. I don't get more money because your wife had money. I'll do a good job for you, regardless. But I can't help you right now. As I said, the courts are closed. Go in my office and make an appointment with Judy. Then come back Monday, and I'll see how quickly we can get you in front of a district judge."

I started walking toward the exit, but he stood in the middle of the hallway blocking my way. He wasn't much taller than I, but he was bulkier.

"You did such a good job last time. We'll pay you really well." Syrup dripped from his words. His cheek twitched.

The guy was under a lot of pressure. But I wanted out of there. I wanted to sit down with my friends and decompress.

Staying between the exit and me, he fidgeted, talking fast, speaking in repetitive phrases. "I miss my wife so much. I know you can help us." His face sagged. "We really need your help." He reached into his jacket pocket and pulled out a giant roll of cash wrapped with a yellow rubber band. The edges of his mouth curled.

Was there something white tucked into the bundle? I tilted my head to see, but he jabbed the bills toward my hand that held the briefcase, trying to get me to grab the wad. Instead, I wrapped my fingers tightly around the briefcase handle, refusing to take the money. I wondered why this man insisted on giving me a thick roll of cash if he was so scared of not having access to money.

"My family really appreciates you," he said, jarring me out of my thoughts. His flinty stare was devoid of the emotion lacing his voice. Maybe he was trying not to cry? He thrust the money toward me again.

I excused his erratic behavior as a result of grief and fear. As his former attorney, a sense of obligation flitted around my conscience, even if I couldn't remember him. My Southern manners told me I should at least take some time to talk with him. My Christian upbringing told me I should serve this man and help an individual in need. Yet I had an inkling I needed to get away from him. I hesitated, unsure what to do.

As I stepped to one side, he edged in front of me. I stepped to the other side, he sidled that way. Whichever direction I moved, he moved, as if we were locked in some kind of bizarre dance. My armload of files made it impossible to angle past him in the hallway.

"We need you. I can pay!" He waved the cash in front of me.

"No, no," I told him, sliding along the wall, trying to move past him. "That's not how it works. Make an appointment with Judy. She'll draft a contract, and you can pay a retainer. You don't hand me cash."

"There's a lot in it for you." His face was panicked, worry wafting off him like sweat. "She was worth a lot of money."

"This isn't a contingency case," I said. "I'll be glad to help you. I'll get you in front of a judge next week. But I can't do anything now. The courts are closed."

He did not respond to me, only repeated, "You did a great job for us before. There's a lot of money in this for you."

I still could not place him. Yes, it had to be an adoption case. Clients can become very attached to their adoption attorneys, and the man clearly had an emotional attachment to me—in a desperate, clingy way. I didn't even know his name, but I did not want to admit to a former client that I couldn't remember him. Especially not this guy.

How could I get around this man? I couldn't seem to shake him.

"I have to go. Walk with me to my car." The words leaped from my mouth before I could filter them. "I'll answer a few of your questions, but then you'll need to go back to the office and make an appointment with Judy for Monday."

That suggestion seemed to appease him. He stepped aside so I could move past, toward the exit. He stayed close on my heels. I quickly walked out the door and down the stairs. My white Accord sat in the middle of the lot. My safe harbor. If I could get there, I would be able to break away and climb inside.

"Did your wife have a will?"

"Yes."

"Do you have the original?"

"Yes."

"Were you named executor?"

"Yes."

I asked questions on autopilot, barely listening as he spoke, focused on getting to my car while trying to determine why I felt eerily unsettled. As we approached the Accord, he seemed to calm down, satisfied with my comments. In a matter of seconds, I'd be free of this man. I lowered my guard.

We reached the rear of the car. "I'm very sorry about what happened. We'll do our best to take care of you." I clicked my car remote, unlocking the doors. He had not moved away, so I pointedly said, "Make sure you see Judy. She will be leaving soon. I'll see you first thing Monday morning."

I unloaded the box of files and my briefcase into the back seat on the driver's side. When I moved to open the front door, I froze and stared in disbelief. He'd opened my passenger door and stood there, looking at me over the top of the car, eager and hopeful.

Just then a crack of thunder boomed, and the sky darkened, threatening a torrent of rain.

"Can you give me a ride to my meemaw's house?" he asked.

My client, who had just lost his wife and trusted me to take care of his family, asked for a ride home in dangerous weather.

What would you do?

CHAPTER 2

MA'AM, I DON'T KNOW ANYTHING

COMMONWEALTH OF KENTUCKY

v.

LARRY MORRISON

DATE: April 7, 2006

EVIDENCE: 911 CALL

DISPATCHER: State Police, Dry Ridge, Dispatcher Fields.

MR. BALLARD: Yes. My name's Jeff. I'm calling from Louisville, but I—I've been on the phone with my girlfriend, who's a lawyer in Georgetown, Kentucky.

DISPATCHER: Okay.

MR. BALLARD: She was in her car with a former client, who had been drinking. She dialed my phone so I could overhear their conversation while they were in the car. He was forcing her to drive somewhere in—out in the country.

DISPATCHER: Okay.

MR. BALLARD: Apparently, she was taking him to a relative's house. His name is Morrison or something. He's been drinking. She kept saying, "Where are we going, where are we going? Why are you making me do this?" He said, "Oh, just a little bit farther up here, turn right, turn left." I could hear him hitting her, and I could hear that they were fighting in the car. She sounded terrified and hurt. Like he hurt her.

DISPATCHER: Do we know where she's at?

MR. BALLARD: Ma'am, I don't know anything.

He watched me while standing between the car and the passenger door he'd just opened. My heart sank.

I paused, unsure how to respond. "How did you get here?"

"I walked," he answered as thunder clapped overhead.

"Can't you walk back?"

"It's only three blocks away," he wheedled.

"Then you can walk back."

"I really need a ride."

"I have to be in Louisville in an hour. I don't think I can."

He half smiled at me, just a client in need of a quick ride. "It's on your way." The intensity in his voice had lightened.

"I can't be late. People are waiting on me." How could I get rid of this guy?

"It won't take a minute."

"I am already late." How many more times did I have to say this? Why wasn't he moving?

"What about the weather?" He looked up at the sky.

"You'll be okay, it's a short walk."

A second clap of thunder cracked overhead, and a gust of wind shook the car. I glanced up to see black storm clouds rolling in. I thought of his wife who had died, how his family was counting on me in their time of need, and asked myself if I could really make him walk home in what was likely to be a deluge.

You can't be rude, I scolded myself. You're being selfish. You need to help him out.

Besides, how was I going to get rid of him? Physically remove him? He outweighed me by a good seventy-five pounds. In that instant, I was confused, not sure how to make this end. The obligation of representing him weighed on me.

"Fine," I relented, frustrated with myself for yielding my will to his when I didn't want to. However, the part of me that felt uncomfortable could not articulate a convincing argument. At least nothing powerful enough to overcome my upbringing, all that "do unto others" business. A client in crisis needed help getting home in what looked to be threatening weather.

What could happen in three blocks?

Without saying another word, he dropped his bulk into the passenger seat.

I slid into my seat and shut the door. I instantly shifted from discomfort to feeling trapped. His presence permeated the car. Something was wrong. What was happening? Why was he in my car after all those no's?

I placed my purse between my leg and the door. My phone was sticking out. I opened it furtively and placed it by my left leg. I knew the battery was almost dead, but there was no way to charge the phone without drawing this man's attention to it. *This man. What was his name?* If only I could remember.

Without looking down, I felt for the redial button. Jeff. He was the last person I'd talked to. My boyfriend was smart and analytical, the type of person who would parse every word in a conversation. He knew I was on my way to Louisville, and if he heard a man's voice in my car, he would definitely perk up, try to hear what we were saying. I prayed I pushed the right button and the battery wasn't dead. And that Jeff would be able to hear me.

I turned the key in the ignition, which kick-started my brain, bringing my senses online. I zeroed in on one objective and one objective only: get this man away from me as soon as possible.

"Which way do I go?" I asked, hoping the phone could pick up what I was saying. If Jeff was even listening. If there was power left in the phone.

"This way," he said, pointing to the right.

Backing out of the spot, I drove the twenty feet to exit the parking lot, but even that short distance was already more than I wanted to be alone with him. I turned right out of the lot, unsettled and vulnerable, relying on this man for directions. Something was terribly wrong.

I was not in control of the situation.

I did the only thing I knew to do, I resumed asking legal questions: "Are you the only beneficiary? Were there two witnesses? Were the witnesses' names notarized?"

He clearly articulated his answers. He seemed to have a solid understanding of his wife's estate. His breathless fast-paced speech filled his voice with desperation. His thick, hairy arm was between us, grazing me every time he rocked back and forth.

"I really want this to work out," he said, fidgeting.

"It doesn't sound like it will be a problem to probate," I said. "It sounds like a valid will."

How had he managed to be sitting next to me? Hadn't I told him no? Five, six, seven times? And despite his words of affirmation and respect, despite how much he said his family knew and loved me and owed me a debt of gratitude, his words didn't match his body language—my gut was telling me something wasn't right, but my mind couldn't define it.

"Which street do I turn onto? We must be almost there."

Without hesitation, he pointed straight ahead. Oddly, he stopped looking at me, keeping his face forward. Everything inside me clicked to high alert. Something was very wrong.

"What's the house number?" I asked, maybe a little too loudly, as I continued driving. "Where does your grandma live?"

He ignored my questions.

Something had been niggling at my nose, and I finally realized what it was. The sour tang of alcohol. "Have you been drinking?" I asked before I could stop myself.

"No," he replied, flipping his hand in annoyance. "I had ribs for lunch."

Ribs? What? I hadn't had much exposure to alcohol, but I'd smelled plenty of Southern barbecue. That wasn't ribs.

Instantly, his demeanor changed. He sat up straight, glared at me with huge eyes that had turned black, Charles Manson–like, wild and terrifying. He mutated—from panicky and helpless into a grinning man completely in control of the situation.

The hair on my neck sprang up. And I knew.

He is going to hurt me.

Every sinew fired into action. My mind was working overtime, repeatedly rejecting what didn't make sense and trying to force the situation to fit a scenario that did. I couldn't accept what was happening which only slowed down my ability to react. My thoughts raced.

I counted the blocks but kept him distracted, continuing to ask him about the estate and let him talk about his wife. When the road ended at a three-way stop, and he made no indication to pull over, heat rushed to my head giving way to numbness and a quickening pulse.

"Turn left," he ordered. "Here, on this street."

"Where is it?" I asked, after making the turn. "Where does she live?"

He did not answer. I couldn't make myself look at him. But I sat up tall, trying to command confidence.

All right, what could I do? Just stop the car in the road and run?

I considered it when we entered an intersection, but then I felt his grip as he said, "Keep going straight." His voice low but deadly. He put his hand on my shoulder and squeezed. The shadow of evil across his face, the determination in his voice, and the strength of his hands told me I wasn't getting out of that car.

"I've only been out a week," he said triumphantly.

Bile shot into the back of my mouth, and I gagged trying to keep from vomiting.

Definitely not an adoption case. He was a felon. I was trapped in the car with a felon.

"Out of . . . prison?" I asked for Jeff's benefit.

"Yeah. I just got out last week."

Larry. His name was Larry. Larry Morrison.

It came to me in a flash, out of nowhere. I'd represented him in district court years ago, when I was fresh out of law school. We'd separated on good terms. Or maybe not.

I needed this to end. Now. My mind swirled, trying to create a plan, but it landed on nothing. Just swirling, lots of swirling with the occasional random thought.

Can you hear me, Jeff? I hope you're listening. He had to know how to find me and who took me because this man was going to hurt me.

"Would you prefer I call you Larry or Mr. Morrison?" I asked, so Jeff would hear his name. I cringed at how stilted my voice sounded as I purposefully worked his name into the conversation. I prayed Morrison would not understand what I was doing, but someone had to know who had taken me. A part of me knew they'd have to come look for me.

He grabbed my right knee and squeezed—hard—drinking in my fear, relishing it.

My heart stopped and then broke into an all-out sprint. "Where is it? Where is your grandma's house?" I asked again, trying to keep the panic out of my voice. My hands shook.

"Well, it's out past Crumbaugh."

I blinked. No. I grew up on Crumbaugh, and it was too far. I couldn't stop myself from sighing heavily, exhaling a breath I didn't know I was holding.

"Oh, now, don't you do that to me," he snarled, his voice gravelly.

There was a flash in my peripheral vision, followed by an explosion of light and pain as Morrison's open hand met my cheekbone.

CHAPTER 3

A BIG SCENE

POLICE INTERVIEW OF LARRY MORRISON

BOURBON COUNTY JAIL

[QUESTIONING BY DETECTIVE MURRELL]

Q: I want you to tell me your version, okay, Mr. Morrison?

A: Maybe I was a little too forward with her, you know?

Q: Let me ask you this. What do you mean by forward?

A: Well, I was drinking. Maybe I was just saying hey, I need you to take care of this. I need you to help me. And she wanted me to get out.

Q: Okay. So she wanted . . .

A: She made a big fucking scene, though.

Q: She wanted you to get out of the car?

A: Yeah.

I reeled in shock and in pain from the blow to my face. The sound of his palm against my cheek cracked like a gunshot. Gripping the steering wheel, I tried to discern reality from nightmare. Did he just hit me for breathing? How long had I been in the car? When was this going to end?

His aggression escalated the farther we drove. My stomach lurched when his hand moved again. But this time, instead of hurting me, he reached over and lightly stroked the back of my neck. He was shifting in his seat, his hands always moving. The schizophrenic shifts kept my mind scrambling.

"I sure do like being in this car with you," he said, pitching his voice low, attempting a seductive tone. He moved his hand to my thigh and rubbed it, as if we were on a date.

He is going to rape me.

The hair on my arms rose to match the hair on my neck. My mind froze. Then spun. I had to get ready. I had to stop this.

Then I sighed.

He jammed his fingers into my side. "Stop acting like that." His powerful hands stroked my neck but harder this time, angrily. I couldn't let my mind linger on the pain as he geared up for more.

I drove in a daze, did what I had to, followed his orders down this path to perdition, stopping at lights, obeying the traffic laws, but it was all by rote. Everything around me—except his hands—were a blur.

He was now openly violent, his moods swinging wildly. Just like the clouds rolling across the sky—it would be beautiful and sunny one minute, and then low dangerous-looking black clouds would darken the sky. It was the same with the emotions on his face, diaphanous as a shadow. His features broadcast agitation one second, then sexual hunger, then sheer rage. His responses were random and impossible to predict. I tried to understand what triggered him, but he wasn't driven by logic. He was an animal, a predator with no moral compass or reason. None of my efforts to de-escalate the situation worked. I was trained to use words, logic, and reason to get what I wanted. A madman doesn't respond to logic.

Every second was terrifying. There were moments when a malevolent expression washed over him, like nothing I'd seen before. The evil attached to his presence was tangible at times. It inhabited the car like a living thing.

"I need to get back," I said. "My friends are waiting for me."

His hand crushed my right knee until I groaned in pain. He moved his hand up, traced his fingers lightly over my outer thigh, and smiled—but not with his eyes.

Grinning, he slowly ran his fingers up and down my leg and looked at me with such intensity that I shifted in my seat.

I wanted to cry and scream, but I stayed quiet, horrified by his touch, hoping if I complied he would stop hurting me. Shrinking into the seat, I made myself as small as possible and choked down the bile that filled the back of my throat again. I had a hard time catching my breath. My chest felt heavy and tight. I took another deep breath—trying to fill my lungs and stop my head from spinning—and sighed, unable to control it. The darkness returned, as he smashed his fist into my arm and then my face. I screamed, squeezing the wheel, trying to stay on the road.

"Stop that!" Gritting his teeth, he thundered, "Do *not* disrespect me!"

I couldn't even breathe without his hurting me. No more sighing, I thought frantically. I have to keep him calm, so I can think.

He became my focus. I have no memory of watching the road, seeing other cars, buildings, or people. It was only him. I have no idea how I drove. From the moment we exited the parking lot until we stopped, I could have passed a lie detector test that I didn't see anyone. In reality, the first five minutes of that drive took us through extremely congested areas, but I didn't process that. Only his powerful hands—where they were and where he might grab me next.

"Why are you doing this to me? Why are you making me drive out here?" I cried out, unable to hold back my own rage. And terror. But primarily, I wanted to make sure Jeff, if he was listening over the phone, knew I was not driving Morrison of my own volition.

He didn't answer, just turned and slapped me again.

Time passed, maybe a few minutes, maybe an hour. Each minute stretched out, destined to go on forever. It was all so confusing. It was a bright sunny day—the rain that threatened never came. Couldn't someone see me? Couldn't someone help me? If I asked about his grandma he'd slap, punch, or shake me. If I asked about his wife, he'd stroke my neck or leg and tell me how much he appreciated my work. Considering the abuse, I should have hurt everywhere, but I didn't register the pain.

He was staring at my chest, so I moved my hands higher up the steering wheel, my nails digging into the leather as I gripped and tried to form a barrier between him and my breasts. I was desperate to keep his hands off me, but nothing seemed to work.

As we approached an intersection, he put his hand on the back of my neck again, moving his fingers as if massaging me. Once again, my body started to respond with a sigh as I became short of breath, but he squeezed hard, his fingertips deep in my flesh. For one fleeting moment, I considered stopping the car, but the grip of his hands and hatred on his face gave me pause. He was not going to let me out of this car.

I had to get out of the car. *But*, I argued with myself, *if I try to stop, he'll feel the car decelerate. He will really punish me then.* I kept going—he had a firm grip on my neck, hurting me. The pain I would experience would be much, much worse if I disobeyed him.

I was still trying to use what I had to keep myself safe. I had my words, and I had the phone. *Please, God, keep the phone working so Jeff can listen. Jeff, please be there, you are my only hope.* If Jeff wasn't there, that meant I was alone in the car with this lunatic.

He took his wad of cash and tried to force it into my front pant pocket. I leaned forward making it impossible to shove it in.

Then he ran his fingers up my inner thigh. His hand was between my legs, brushing up against my genitalia. He leaned in to grope my left leg, rubbing my thigh—and touched the phone.

"What is that?" His curiosity instantly turned to anger. "What are you doing over there?"

Please, God, I can't lose my lifeline. I tried to distract him. "What's the name of your grandma's street? How far now?"

"Is that a recorder by your leg? Don't you do that to me! Are you recording me?"

"No, it's just a cell phone." I decided to act confident. "You know what? This is my car. If I want my cell phone on, then my cell phone will be on." I glared at him. "The cell phone is staying on."

"What do you mean, it's on?"

"It's my boyfriend, Jeff . . ."

He narrowed his eyes and said, "Let me talk to him."

Somehow, I found the courage to bring the phone up to my ear and say, "Jeff, can you hear me?"

Jeff's response was immediate, his voice frantic. "I'm here! Are you okay? Do you want me to call the police?"

Morrison sat there quietly, staring at me. His calm was more disturbing than his mania.

"Not yet," I said to Jeff. "I don't know." What could he say to the police that made any sense? I needed him to hear what was happening to me, to be with me. If Jeff hung up to call the police, I'd be alone with this man.

"Where are you? Call out street names!"

I frantically looked around but the landscape was strange. I couldn't pinpoint where I was. This was my hometown. I'd driven these streets my whole life, but nothing was familiar.

Without warning Morrison ripped the phone out of my hand. "I want to talk to your boyfriend!"

As he put it to his ear, I prayed, *Please, God, don't let Jeff make him mad. Don't let Jeff make him mad. If Jeff makes him mad, I'll be the one to pay for it.* I could only imagine what he was going through on the other end of the phone and what he might say to try to stop this. "There's a lot of money in this for her," Morrison said repeatedly. It sounded as though he was speaking over Jeff.

I couldn't hear what Jeff was saying.

While talking, Morrison rubbed my leg again. "You sure do have a nice girl-friend. She sure is." He stopped and leaned into me, pressing his body against me. "Don't worry, I'm going to take good care of her." Then Morrison hung up the phone. Jeff was gone.

My abductor looked at me and repeated, "Don't worry, I'm going to take good care of you."

No question about it. He was going to rape me.

And Jeff could no longer hear us.

One hand on the wheel, I snatched at the phone and after a brief skirmish, got it away from him. I put the phone between my left leg and the door but not before hitting redial. I was praying the call went through, but I didn't look so as not to draw attention to it again. At this point, it was a miracle the phone hadn't died.

Once more Morrison lurched at me with the wad of cash. I pushed his hand away and spotted white powder rolled in the center. There was a vague sensation clinging to the edges of my mind—something ominous. I thought the white powder was . . .

His hands grabbed my neck so tight I fought to keep my eyes open.

Why hadn't he fought me harder for the phone? How could he not notice I'd redialed? Why did he keep shoving that roll of cash toward me?

"Is this the county line? How much farther is it to your meemaw's?" There was little chance, but if Jeff was still able to hear me, I could give him a clue as to where I was.

"Keep going," he said. "We'll be there soon."

"You know what? You are going to get out here. It's late, I need to get back."

"That's not going to happen, Sharon." His tone was hard and immovable.

A tremor passed through me when he used my name.

I told him over and over I was going to drop him off, that I had to go. I tried to speak with confidence, like I was the one in control, even when he was slapping or shaking me, but it was hard not to cower. At one point, he took the phone away again, but I once again got it back from him and redialed as I tucked it to my side.

The hostility was escalating, our conversations swinging back and forth on a pendulum with an ever-increasing arc. One minute, he'd bark at me to shut up and tell me to stop asking questions, and the next, he'd try to charm me, telling me how much he appreciated my work in the past and that it was just a little farther.

We turned again. "Are we still in Scott County? Is this Bourbon County? I thought you said your meemaw lived in Scott County." Leaving the county felt final. *He will not rape me. I won't let him.* Even still, part of me refused to accept what was going on.

By the time we crossed into Bourbon County and went through the blinking lights, Morrison didn't look human anymore. His eyes bulged with rage.

Again, I asked, "What's the name of her street?"

When he answered, "I just need to get to my aunt's house," I naively responded, "To your aunt's or your meemaw's . . . oh, do they live together?" My mind simply refused to believe Morrison had no family out there.

I was the reason for this trip. There was no aunt or meemaw. Morrison wanted me alone in an isolated area. My breath caught in my throat from the fear that grew in my chest. I was out of my mind with fear, but my logical-self kept trying to find some kind of explanation to make sense of it all.

"I've got to get back to Louisville. How do I get back? I don't know where I am. Where's the road to Georgetown?" I immediately regretted saying that out loud. Now he knew I was lost. I couldn't be lost, I had to think, and I had to fight. He had me drive miles and miles out of town, on a circuitous route. I was trying to drive, pay attention to where I was, and avoid his hands. And his anger.

As I noticed a road sign or building, I would comment on it. He refused to answer, just pointed where he wanted me to go. I turned onto one road, saying, "Is that an airport? I didn't know there was an airport in Bourbon County." As we approached an old brick building, "Is that the old lumber yard?" *Please let Jeff be hearing all of this.* "Oh, it's Hawkins Cummins Road." Sending Jeff clues hoping Morrison wouldn't realize what I was doing felt risky. I really didn't want to get hit again.

I drove up to an intersection, and something in me snapped. We had circled and turned for ages. I was disoriented. He was taking me farther and farther into nowhere. He told me to turn right, but instead of doing what he told me to do, I went into full-blown panic mode, screaming and flailing my hands in the air, no longer trying to keep him calm. "Get out of my car! Walk from here!" I banged my fists on the steering wheel. "I don't care where she lives, get out!"

He shocked me by backing off and becoming peaceful. He didn't get out, but he didn't rage back at me. Calmly, he said, "It's just right down here, Sharon. Three houses down. That's it, just over the hill. It's actually the fourth one down."

Unable to get him out of my car, I made what I had decided was my last turn— no matter what. When we crested the hill on the lonely road and Larry's bulky arm pointed to a crumbling house, I knew.

"That one, there. Pull in behind that barn."

He is going to kill me.

CHAPTER 4

A DOGFIGHT

COMMONWEALTH OF KENTUCKY

v.

LARRY MORRISON

DIRECT EXAMINATION OF JEFF BALLARD

[BY COMMONWEALTH'S ATTORNEY, Mr. Gordie Shaw]

Q: What [did] you hear at that point?

A: [JEFF BALLARD DESCRIBES WHAT HE COULD HEAR OVER THE PHONE DURING THE LAST FEW MINUTES OF THE KIDNAPPING]

And he said, "This driveway, right here; this is the one. This is the driveway; pull in here."

And so [I] hear the car slow. You hear it come to idle. And this is where Sharon decides that she's had enough, and so in a very stern voice she says, "Larry, that gate is closed. That place back there looks deserted. I am not driving down that road. I am turning my car around, and I want you to get out now."

Q: Did you hear him give her any commands either before or after?

A: At that point, I heard nothing from him except as soon as she said, "Get out of my car now," there was instant commotion in the car—like wrestling sounds, grunting. I don't know how to describe it but obvious commotion and violent activity in the car. And then the next thing I hear is—is Sharon's screams. And she yells, hysterical, "Jeff, he's got a gun! Call the police!" And then the line went dead.

"It's there, that's her house," Morrison said and grabbed my arm. "Pull in there, behind the barn." He was pointing to a second barn behind the house down a long drive overgrown with weeds.

"Your grandmother lives there?" Hidden from my view until the last moment by a tobacco barn, the two-story farmhouse—with its dingy white siding hanging off the frame, boarded-up windows and collapsed front porch—sat vacant.

During the drive, different parts of my mind had taken charge at different times. Part did whatever he said to keep him calm, part looked for a way out, part still wanted to believe I was taking him to his grandmother's. Until now.

Assessing the narrow road that disappeared around the barn leading back to the dilapidated house and another barn, I knew exactly what he had planned. I'd been doing what he said, hoping to keep him calm, but now I was done. I would not let him get me behind that barn.

Then I noticed a rusty old farm gate blocking the drive, bearing a bulky padlock. Thank God. I wouldn't be able to drive back there, and he couldn't punish me. It wasn't my fault.

"I can't go back there, the gate is locked. That house looks deserted. I am not driving down that road." I kept driving, slowly rolling past the driveway. "I am turning my car around. Get out *now*."

Before he could respond, I threw the car in reverse and backed into the driveway. Now facing the road with the gate behind us, I quickly shifted back into drive, the engine running, ready to pull back onto the road.

"Get out, get out!" I screamed, stripping my vocal cords.

My right hand was on the gearshift. Morrison dropped his left hand on top of mine, bore down, clutching my hand and the gearshift at the same time, and forced the gear into park.

With lightning speed, he grabbed my hair and bashed my head into the steering wheel. The window. The windshield. Stars exploded behind my eyes. I would have passed out from the pain if there hadn't been so much terror-fueled adrenaline running through me.

I tried to scramble away, but my seat belt had me pinned to my seat.

He rammed my head into the wheel again. I wailed, but nothing was going to stop him. He was at his killing place, it was happening. I screamed again. He reached over with his hand, grabbing my chest. He raked over my breast as if he had claws. His fingernails scraped across my flesh, leaving long open wounds. His fingers caught my bra and the elastic neckline of my shirt, yanking them down, leaving me exposed. He forced my head down, mashing the side of my face into the console between the seats, so that my body was bent in half.

I could do nothing. With my head and right arm trapped, I couldn't move. I watched frozen in terror as his right hand ran down the inside of his right leg. In slow motion, he drew up his pant leg, exposing the black handle of a weapon strapped to the inside of his ankle.

"Jeff, he's got a gun! He's got a gun! Call the police!" I screamed at the top of my lungs.

But I was wrong. As he pulled the weapon out I saw the glint of a long steel blade. My eyes never left the knife as I watched it move closer and closer until I felt it. I heard nothing, not even my own screams. My senses were focused on that blade pressing into my neck, harder and harder, until blood started to flow.

My hearing returned, and my bloodcurdling screams echoed in my ears as I struggled for my life.

"This is for those years in prison!" he raged.

His body twisted, and I could see the muscles in his right arm flex as he sawed at the side of my neck—where my carotid artery pulsed. I could feel the cold of the steel as it cut my neck and the warmth of the blood running down my breasts. This was it, I was dying.

Time stopped. Everything inside me became quiet and calm. Almost peaceful. The bone-crushing pressure of death enveloped every inch of my body, sinking in to my lungs, brain, and heart. I remained remarkably void of feeling. The fullness of peace dominated my mind until all that was left inside me was the waiting. I heard no sounds from the outside world, no cries for help or sounds of rescue. I was alone.

Morrison's presence was gone, with merely my thoughts amplified to their fullest extent and enveloping me. The knowledge, then acceptance, that death was imminent.

I was still, expecting to hear the sucking of air as I struggled to breathe, feel the searing pain of my lungs as they burned from lack of oxygen, and taste the gurgling blood mixed with fluid in my throat as the knife sliced further through my neck. My throat exploded with pain. I waited. I breathed. I waited, and I breathed again.

I am still breathing.

I was confused. I saw him continue to flex his muscles and drive the knife deeper into my neck. My body was still bent at a ninety-degree angle, my head being crushed against the center console facing the radio, the edge of the blade pushing deeper and deeper into my throat.

With his left arm, he put his weight on my head, the muscles and veins on his arm bulging, and came up out of his seat as he leaned on me.

The pressure on my neck was unbearable.

"Take off your pants." His voice was guttural, low, his face impatient as he waited for me to obey.

"No." I responded in such a calm, firm, confident voice that I almost didn't recognize it as my own.

I was done making this easier for him. I'd done enough to help him already. If he was going to rape me, he was going to have to rape my dead body.

Then, abruptly, his weight was jerked off me.

I felt the painful pressure of the blade leave my neck. The knife was drug in an arc across the length of the dashboard with enough force to break my control screen and leave a gouge in the leather dashboard.

I could taste fear—bitter and metallic on my tongue—but I was free to move.

I did just that—but not before catching sight of Morrison, pressed back in his seat as if held there. He seemed as confused as I was at what had just happened. He swung his head wildly from side to side looking around, his eyes panicky. His hands still gripped the knife, but they lay in his lap, rigid and at an odd angle. Almost as if they were tied. This was my chance.

Move. Fight. Get out of the car.

I started clawing at the door, trying to find the handle and force the door open. He pounced, and I responded, each throwing punches, swinging elbows, trying to do the maximum amount of damage. I attacked the door with my left foot while struggling to find the handle and using my right arm to deflect blows and punch back.

He slammed me around like a rag doll even though I was strong. I was probably as fit as I've ever been as an adult—I had been lifting weights at a gym and doing cardio. Still he manhandled me easily, tossing me from side to side the same way my puppy Coby whips his toys around in his mouth. It was a dogfight.

I was trying to force my way out of the car, but Morrison was too strong. My punches bounced off him without effect. I was battling for my life, and I knew I was losing. We violently beat each other, thrusting fists, striking, slamming bodies. He was banging my head into anything he could make contact with. It was like being on a roller coaster with my head violently jerked up and down and side to side without the ability to hold on to any view for more than a fraction of a second. I was trying to keep my eyes on the knife at all times to avoid feeling it shoved into my neck again, but I couldn't focus on anything.

I knew I was going to die, but my life didn't flash before my eyes as you often hear people say. Instead, I saw my parents in the distant future, broken, crushed by grief because I had disappeared and they never knew what happened. Someone had to find my body. I wasn't focused on myself, only on my parents and what their lives would look like if I was never found.

As he grabbed my head again and ground it into the steering column, my eyes zeroed in on the keys dangling from the ignition. The keys suddenly became the focus of my tunnel vision.

I knew what I had to do.

If he left my body behind the barn and drove off in my car, no one would ever find me. Or him. I risked taking my eyes off the knife long enough to glance at the door, to gauge where the handle was, calculating how to reach for it quickly. I was going to open the door and hurl my keys as far into the field as I could. I might die doing it, but if they found the car, they'd find my body, and my parents could at least bury my remains. And maybe he'd get caught.

As I looked toward the door handle, movement on the road caught my eye.

Through the window, I could see a truck in the distance, driving down the narrow road toward me.

Hope. My mindset shifted from praying someone found my body to knowing I could survive. I was going to live through this. I would do whatever I had to do to get in front of that truck.

I kicked the door open two different times. Each time I got my foot on the gravel and thought I could pull away from him, hope erupted. Each time he jerked me back into the car as the gravel skittered and my feet slipped, unable to find purchase. A steely will to survive spiked in me even as he yanked me back by my arm and hair, and large chunks of hair and skin ripped from my skull.

Up to this point, things had moved in triple slow motion. Now, with every glimpse of that truck—knowing if it passed me I was dead—the clock was ticking. Both of us fought, pulled, and worked as hard as we could, moving in opposite directions.

For a third time, I got my foot on the gravel, and it slid around. But this time, I dug my left heel in and leveraged my calf against the door frame. I broke free from Morrison and exploded out of the car like a bullet from a gun.

Somehow, I had grabbed my phone as I catapulted myself into the driveway in front of the barn. The strap of my purse caught on my foot and fell out of the car with me. I dragged it as I sprinted toward the road, scattering the contents.

"I *will* kill you!" Morrison screamed as I pulled away from him. "It doesn't matter if you get away," he continued, fueling my sprint. "I'm going to kill you. It may be tomorrow, it may be next year, but I *will* kill you." Those were the last words I heard as I ran to throw myself in front of an oncoming truck.

I dipped through a ditch that separated me from the road, high grass slapping against me until I popped out on the other side, praying the truck didn't pass me before I got there. Chunks of hair were hanging off my head, my top knot blown apart, my shirt yanked down.

I ran out in front of the red truck and planted my feet, spreading my limbs out like a big X, my arms over my head, bloody red streams running over my bare chest. The driver did not slow down.

I wasn't moving. Either I would be run over by this truck or die behind the barn. I chose the truck.

CHAPTER 5

ON TV THEY ALWAYS STOP

COMMONWEALTH OF KENTUCKY

v.

LARRY MORRISON

DIRECT EXAMINATION OF CODELL GIBSON

[BY COMMONWEALTH'S ATTORNEY, Mr. Gordie Shaw]

Q: Now, Mr. Gibson, I want to go back to April the 7th of 2006. Did something unusual happen on the way home?

A: Yes, sir.

Q: Tell us what happened.

A: We were coming north on Russell Cave Road and we topped a little hill. There's a farm off to the right. And there was a white car sitting in the drive down there, kind of like just out of the road—

Q: Okay. And what happened?

A: Like I say, it was kind of just out of the road. I looked at my wife and I told her—this car is going to pull out in front of me, so I'm really watching the car, I'm getting ready to pass, and the door swings open, and I see the lady trying to get out of the car. Her shirt was kind of, like, down, you know [*witness demonstrates,* *forcefully rips shirt*]—the man was holding her, pulling on her like that, And she just looked really, really scared, really red, and—

Q: You said her shirt was down?

A: Yeah. Like, somebody's got ahold of [her], trying to hold [her] in. Looked like she was being held into the car.

I planted my feet in the middle of the lane while the red pickup headed straight toward me. I said to myself, over and over, "On TV, they always stop. On TV, they always stop." It was almost impossible to stand in front of an oncoming truck, my body fighting to move while my mind knew the only hope of survival lay in forcing this truck to stop. If it didn't, Morrison would stab me to death. Yet I could feel my feet pulling toward the ditch and every part of my body screaming to dive out of the way. My body and mind were at war. I reminded myself, "Either I will be run over by this truck or die behind that barn. I choose the truck."

I stayed. Legs spread wide and firmly planted making myself take up as much of the road as possible. Either he was going to stop, or he was going to run me over.

The truck came to a halt eighteen inches from my face, maybe twelve. Behind the windshield, I could see a man in his thirties or forties, thinning hair, his eyes wide behind a pair of glasses. I ran to the driver's side door, screaming, "Tell them where we are!"

He looked at me but sat frozen. Then he pulled his arm out of the window. His face tried to register what he was seeing—me standing there with my breast bared and covered in blood and chunks of hair hanging off my head. He didn't speak.

"Tell 911 where we are! I don't know where I am!" I pleaded with him through his window. "The guy's got a knife, and he tried to rape me, and he says he's going to kill me . . ."

The driver gaped at me. In an effort to snap him out of his stupor, I tapped him on the side of the head with my cell phone, which surprised me more than it did him. He remained silent.

"Tell them where we are!" I needed 911 to know where to find me before Morrison came at me again.

What I didn't know was that another truck had just passed by, one I hadn't seen because my head was being crushed against the console. As I turned to see if Morrison was on my heels, I saw the black truck, now reversing toward the red truck and me. It stopped. A man and woman got out.

I sprinted toward them and was surprised when I heard Morrison bark more orders for me from the car. "Stop playing! Get back here!"

He wasn't going to stop coming for me, even in front of these witnesses.

The couple exchanged glances, glancing from Morrison in the car to me, partly naked, running down the road toward them. They had no idea what their stopping meant for me. The husband was a gift. He was tall and fit—well built, like a brick wall. He was in his thirties, had short black hair, and wore jeans and a black T-shirt. His posture was strong, and his face was alert.

I shoved my phone in his face. "Please!" I wailed. "Please just tell them where we are! He's trying to kill me. He's got a knife."

The wife, a brunette woman in her thirties, beautiful despite the mixture of concern and fear written on her face, was a steel magnolia. She stood close to her husband, but not out of fear. I could see ideas forming as she assessed the situation. Then she walked toward me. Her stance assured me she wasn't one to walk away from trouble. Thank you, God, you sent the right people.

From the car, Morrison shouted, "Don't listen to her, she's just trippin'!"

I could hear him shouting, but I did not take my eyes off the man standing in front of me, pleading and begging him to help. He might as well have had wings and a halo. Both of them.

"Please don't leave me, please don't leave," I sobbed, trembling. "Tell them where we are, I need help."

The husband reached out his hand for the phone. When he took it and started talking to the 911 operator, I could breathe for the first time.

Then Morrison's sturdy, squat body emerged from the car.

"He's got a knife!" I warned them again.

By that time, the man from the red truck had joined the husband in the road. They faced off with Morrison, putting themselves between him and me. "You better hold up right there, buddy," Husband said while Red Truck grabbed a pipe out of the back of his vehicle.

Though the two men created a barrier, Morrison walked toward us, slow and steady. "I don't have a knife. She's making this up, I don't know why." To me he said, "You shouldn't have tried to steal my money. You stole my money."

I was shaking and crying. "Leave me alone! Stay away from me!"

Wife didn't try to hug me or tell me everything was going to be okay. She just stayed close, to protect me.

"Don't come any closer," Husband said.

Morrison stood still as he screwed his face into a frown and shrugged, listening as Husband gave the 911 operator directions to our location.

"He was going to kill me, he tried to rape me," I said, trying to warn the men how dangerous Morrison was.

As soon as the words left my mouth, he responded, braying over their heads to me, "I wouldn't have given you the pleasure of raping you!" He continued, "You're not . . . you're not going to do this, are you? It's not cool to call the police! You're not going to put me back, are you?" He was building steam again, angry but trying to con my Good Samaritans. "She's my girlfriend, and this is a misunderstanding."

We all paused for a second, stunned by his deranged behavior.

I stood next to Husband, not willing to be far from my cell phone as he gave directions to the operator. I felt a tiny amount of relief—at least now law enforcement knew where I was.

When he finished talking, he handed me the phone and turned back to Morrison, who was significantly smaller. "I don't know what's happening, but the police will sort it out. You just stay over there, away from the lady." He was polite but stern. Then he told his wife to move me back, to get some distance between Morrison and me. She guided me behind the first truck I'd seen, the red one.

Wife stayed with me, keeping an eye on the situation while trying to keep me calm. Much like her husband, she was fit and trim, strong. I begged her not to leave. I pressed a hand to my stomach, trying to catch my breath.

I spoke with the 911 operator, who calmly and professionally asked me for more information. I could hardly focus, though, with Morrison weaving around, trying to get to me. He was relentless. I was terrified, certain he would get past the men and kill me right there on the road.

I was pacing, frantic, yet trying to be as detailed with the 911 operator as possible, the lawyer side of me knowing this recording would be played to a jury one day. I tried my best, but my mind was scattered with only a few moments of clarity. Then my brain would freeze with terror again. I wanted to be thorough to give a future jury the picture of what was really going on.

As I paced, Wife herded me back behind the red truck if I wandered, trying to keep me as far away from the men as possible. She stayed close. Wife had no idea if Morrison had a gun or if the knife was real or if he was insane enough to attack them all, but she never wavered.

She's going to change her mind, though, this is too dangerous. She is going to leave me here alone with him.

I overheard Morrison telling the guys that we were just hanging out. My stomach clenched.

I told the operator how I got to the farm, repeatedly begging her to make them hurry, asking when the trooper would arrive, letting her know Morrison continued to threaten me. I paused only to beg Wife to stay or to tell Morrison to keep away from me.

"Thank . . . you for . . . stopping," I said between gulps of air and sputtering sobs. "Thank you. If you hadn't stopped, he'd have killed me."

CHAPTER 6

A HARMLESS GUY, A BLOODY WOMAN, AND A LONG KNIFE

911 CALL

DATE: April 7, 2006

BOURBON COUNTY

TRANSCRIPT EXCERPT

MS. MUSE: Please tell them to hurry.

DISPATCHER: They've got somebody on their way to you, okay? I just want you to stay on the phone with me. Where is Mr. Morrison?

MS. MUSE: He's—now, he's on the other side of my car. And there's a couple of people who just stopped him and if they hadn't stopped him, he would have killed me.

DISPATCHER: Okay. Did he hit you?

MS. MUSE: He grabbed my shirt and bra and pulled it, and pulled the knife on me.

DISPATCHER: And he ripped your clothes?

MS. MUSE: I don't know. I haven't even looked yet.

DISPATCHER: Okay.

MS. MUSE: He—he's telling that guy that he has a knife now.

DISPATCHER: Somebody took the knife away from him?

MS. MUSE: [*Speaking to someone at the scene*] No! That's—that's evidence. You don't want to touch that.

DISPATCHER: Did somebody else take the knife from him?

MS. MUSE: Yeah. He handed it to [Red Truck]. I just told him not to touch it.

DISPATCHER: Okay.

MS. MUSE: [*Speaking to Morrison at the scene*] You need to stay away from me! [*To dispatcher*] Please tell them to hurry.

DISPATCHER: Honey. The guy was able to give me some pretty good directions on where you're at, okay, so one of the other girls here is getting an officer on his way to you. Do you need an ambulance? [*To dispatcher*] Please tell them to hurry.

DISPATCHER: Okay, Sharon. Just take a deep breath for me, okay, honey?

MS. MUSE: I'm so scared. He's going to rape me!

DISPATCHER: I know, honey. You've got other people that are there with you right now, right?

MS. MUSE: Yeah.

DISPATCHER: Okay. We've got a trooper on his way to you, okay?

MS. MUSE: I'm sorry. I thought that—

DISPATCHER: It's okay.

MS. MUSE: He was—

DISPATCHER: It's okay. I just want you to stay on the phone with me, okay, so I know if anything else happens. If Mr. Morrison leaves, I need you to tell me, okay? What kind of car are you driving?

MS. MUSE: A white Honda Accord. It's reversed—backed into a driveway. He kept telling me his grandma lived there and then he was, like, "Pull back behind this barn." And that's when I really got scared and I'm like, "No, I'm dropping you off on the road." And he pulled this knife out. He bent down and pulled the—then I knew what was going on so I was just trying to get out of my car and he grabbed my cell phone. I was screaming—Did anybody call Jeff?

DISPATCHER: They've already talked to him, okay? He had already called us, okay?

MS. MUSE: Okay.

My mind frantically bounced between what I was trying to convey to the operator, watching Morrison as he kept trying to physically get to me, and begging the wife not to leave me.

Then Husband shouted, "He's got a knife!"

"I don't have a knife, man." Morrison's crooked mouth oozed while he raised his hands in surrender. His version of charming.

"I see it," Husband said.

"What are you talking about, I don't have anything." Morrison opened his eyes wide as if he were innocent, but his voice had a tinge of challenge.

"I see it in your pocket!" Husband got firmer with each response.

"Oh, this little thing?" Morrison said, as he reached into his back pocket and pulled out his very long knife.

I feared he might lunge for my protectors. But instead, Morrison meekly held out the knife, so they could see it, and started walking toward Red Truck.

Husband told Morrison, "What are you doin', man? You back up."

"It's just a filet knife. What could I do with this little thing?" He stuck his arm out, holding the large knife toward Red Truck but not threatening him with it. "I'm just giving this to you."

"I don't want the knife," Red Truck said taking a step back.

But Morrison kept coming. The men stood firm, saying to him, "Real slow. You move real slow, now."

I watched Red Truck reluctantly move to accept it.

"No! That's evidence. You don't want to touch that," I shouted.

Red Truck laid it on the hood of the truck while Morrison backed away. It was impossible to know what he would do next. As for the knife, I could only guess he didn't want to have a weapon when the deputies arrived or he wanted the men to think he wasn't a threat—just a harmless guy out in the country with a bloody woman and a long knife.

Things went from scary to inane. Morrison held out his hands, "Don't you know who I am? Don't you recognize me? I'm Larry Morrison."

The three people who'd stopped to help paused in confusion, looking back and forth at each other, unable to understand this newest approach. None of them knew him, nor should they. They all shook their heads in the negative.

Morrison continued, "Man, I'm Larry Morrison. You all can just go on and leave. She was just out here with me."

It may seem trivial, but Morrison referring to himself as though he was some-one they should know and recognize, was frightening. This break from reality and his increasingly demented behavior made me wonder if he was about to become even more volatile.

I was listening to all of this while pleading with the 911 operator for updates on when the state trooper would arrive. Suddenly, there was no longer a calm voice in my ear, asking for updates.

My sense of security died with my phone. I had no one to help me, and my Good Samaritans could leave anytime. We were in the middle of nowhere with a violent felon intent on hurting me.

"Five minutes until they get here!" I said, loud enough for everyone to hear, repeating one of the last things the operator had told me. I hoped it would keep them from leaving and stop Morrison from thinking he would have time to hurt me and get away. I continued begging Wife, "Please don't leave yet. Please, the trooper is almost here."

She tried to soothe me, but I was inconsolable, knowing we were out here with a man who wanted to murder me. The 911 operator was my lifeline, my source of hope. My Good Samaritans physically put their lives on the line for me, but in that minute, I believed Morrison was capable and willing to go through them to get to me. And my brain kept telling me they were going to leave me. For some reason, it was the operator I clung to as my savior. She was my connection to law enforcement, the guys showing up with guns, handcuffs, and the authority to take Morrison away. I feared the witnesses would flee once they realized I was no longer in contact with the operator, leaving me alone with Morrison.

"Please stay! They're almost here!" I blurted out, shaking, begging. I vacillated from terrified and cornered to thinking about what evidence a jury would need to put this guy away for life. Bouncing from reasonable to distraught.

Then I heard it. The most amazing sound I'd ever heard. Sirens. Bouncing off nearby hills sending echoes across the countryside. I couldn't see any vehicles or emergency lights, but the undulating rhythm grew closer. I was never more grateful in my entire life. The sirens belted out a song of approaching help and safety. Someone with authority was coming to take control of the mayhem.

We all swiveled our heads and scanned the fields, looking for the telltale spinning red light on distant roads. Except Morrison. He put his head down, muttering, and quickly made his way back to the car.

He leaned in the passenger door of my Accord and yanked out a dark green bag. It looked like a tall bowling bag with a long, wide shoulder strap and appeared full.

The outline of duct tape and a hammer pressed against the side of the bag. I thought I also saw rope.

I couldn't catch my breath. Those tools were meant for me. He'd told me he was going to kill me, and he would have used those things on me behind the barn.

Morrison moved back toward us, clearly becoming more agitated, swinging the duffle.

"What's going on?" Wife asked her husband nervously. She took a half step in front of me, as if guarding me.

"I want to leave," Morrison said, stopping to sling the bag over his shoulder.

"We aren't keeping you here," Husband said, folding his arms over his broad chest, maintaining a strong wall between us. None of us knew what Morrison had in the bag. He could have had a gun or another knife. Anything.

He gave me one last, threatening look and in a seemingly indolent walk, headed in the opposite direction from the sirens.

CHAPTER 7

THE GREEN DUFFLE

COMMONWEALTH OF KENTUCKY

v.

LARRY MORRISON

DIRECT EXAMINATION OF VICKIE GIBSON

[BY COMMONWEALTH'S ATTORNEY, Mr. Gordie Shaw]

Q: I'm going to ask you some questions about what happened on April 7th, 2006, the reason why we're all here.

Q: Did she [Sharon] say anything back to him [Morrison] that you recall?

A: She said, "Don't talk to me. You told me you were going to kill me. You told me you were going to rape me. Don't talk to me."

Q: How did the whole situation come to an end?

A: We were behind the truck with—with the lady [Sharon]. I was. And my husband and [Red Truck] were still at the front of the truck and I saw [Morrison] start walking [down the road]—and he had a green duffle bag at that point. My husband said we didn't know what was in the duffle bag and [Morrison] said he wanted to leave, so we told him to go.

Q: Okay. Mrs. Gibson, those are all the questions I have for you. Thank you.

The place where Morrison planned to kill me was a farm with an abandoned house and two big, black tobacco barns. I can picture it clearly, as if I'm standing there now.

There are no crops. The fields are bare and wide open. It has not been farmed in quite some time—mold and high weeds cover bales of hay. The two-story farmhouse is like something from a horror movie: missing chunks of dingy siding with a dilapidated front porch that sags in the middle. Ivy crawls through cracks in boarded-up windows, and high weeds blanket the yard. The mostly dead trees are bare, bent over from years of trying to stand up to wind sweeping across the fields. Wiry branches reach out and curl down to the earth, as if the limbs are propping up the trunks. Hints of rotted leaves and molded hay infuse the air.

He picked the perfect place to kill me. No one would hear me scream, and my body would not be found, not until long after the vultures had picked my bones clean.

On the other side of the field is the tree line where Morrison disappeared. He and his green duffle bag filled with rope and duct tape still haunt me.

Many details of the crime scene didn't sink in while he was attacking me or even after help arrived. I noticed only that the house was abandoned, no one to see or help me. It wasn't until coming back to the crime scene later, walking the grounds with a TV crew, that I got the courage to walk behind the second barn and found a natural, wide impression in the ground, overgrown with weeds and brambles. I knew in my heart this was the ditch where he planned to dump my body. When he was done. Then the animals would have at me. My body, like the house, was meant to rot and decay—ravaged by time and nature. I stood there wondering if maybe years later someone would have stumbled upon the crime scene curious about my remains. Would my parents have lived long enough to find out what happened to me?

That day, Morrison never looked back. The three witnesses and I watched from beside the trucks as he walked away. When we saw the lights from the cruisers bounce off the trees lining the road, Morrison paused for a moment and examined the rickety barbed-wire fence that stood between him and an open field. He headed for a tree with limbs growing into the fence, climbed it, and dropped his square pug body on the other side. He then raced toward a dense cluster of trees.

We could not see him in the tree line as the responders' sirens grew closer. Was he going to circle back around for me?

"I need to use my phone," I said, realizing how badly I needed to speak with someone I knew.

Husband nodded, never taking his eyes off the trees in the distance. He was standing watch. He, too, seemed worried Morrison would come back from another angle.

I got into my car to plug in the phone, trying to ignore the presence of evil that lingered. The witnesses were watching me, watching the tree line, watching the perimeter. These strangers were doing the best they could to help, but I was desperate to speak to a friend. I felt so confused. I needed a familiar voice, someone to be a refuge.

Sitting in the same seat I had fled minutes earlier, tethered to the phone charger, I called Margie, a close friend who worked at the sheriff's department. I told her what was going on, but she already knew. A call had gone out over dispatch asking the Scott County Sheriff Department's helicopter to assist in the search. She said she would meet me at the hospital in Georgetown, but I had to get off the phone—a deputy had arrived.

The first responder was an older, white-haired volunteer deputy. I later learned his name was Tom. He threw his unmarked late-model white Jeep into park in the middle of the road, looked over the scene, and walked carefully—hesitantly—up to me. He asked if I was okay. I nodded. More first responders streamed in, one immediately after the other, sirens breaking the air. Tom asked me to describe what happened. I gave a quick summary. His head reared back and his eyes grew wide as he exclaimed, "Oh, my God, you were abducted!"

What? I was abducted? I squinted at him and turned my head in disbelief, looking behind me as if he were speaking to someone else. What was he talking about, abducted?

I was unable to process what had happened or what was still happening, and I certainly couldn't call it an abduction. My mind was all over the place, and labels weren't making sense to me.

He was compassionate and gentle but got called away, saying he'd be back in a minute.

I knew I wouldn't be left alone for long. The scene was bedlam. Nobody knew what to do, where to start, or who was in charge. The crowd included volunteer sheriff's deputies and off-duty deputies who had heard the call over the scanner. Local law enforcement agencies showed up in droves. It took time for them to get organized which stymied the pursuit. A kidnapping, attempted murder scene—small communities didn't get many calls like this. It was likely a first in their careers. It was a first for all of us.

I called my friend Steve Schroering, a criminal defense attorney who'd also spent years as a prosecutor. He'd know what to do.

"Steve, I need help. The sheriff's deputies are here, I don't know what is going on."

"Sharon, are you okay? Are you safe?"

"I don't know, I think so. Deputies are here. But they are messing up the crime scene, they aren't taking any notes or photos, and they aren't getting information from the witnesses."

Steve immediately understood I was involved in an ongoing crime and knew not to waste time with questions he could ask later, like details about what happened. He went straight for the important information.

"Do you know who did this to you? Is the person who did this still close by?"

"Yes, I know who did it, but he isn't near me. He ran away. They're looking for him. The deputies are coming toward me."

"Sharon, you know who did this, and they will find him. This is going to be okay. The deputies will have questions for you. Talk to them and call me right back."

"Okay."

A small group of deputies gathered around me. They asked me to repeat what happened. I was frantically trying to get necessary information to the deputies so they could start the search. I tried to be succinct yet thorough, but it didn't come out that way. I tried to repeat what Morrison said as I jerked away from him. But then the memory left me.

". . . then he told me to take my pants off, saying 'this is for those years in prison' . . . he tossed me around the inside of that car like I weighed nothing . . . something happened, I don't know what, and I got my foot out the door and miraculously escaped . . ."

Nobody had taken charge yet. At once, I was alarmed by what I was hearing and seeing from the good guys. The responders were in hot pursuit of Morrison and understandably not as concerned with preserving evidence, but the chase didn't preclude one deputy from staying with me and working the scene, maybe getting a quick photo of the car or my injuries, not leaving me alone. Even in my state of mind, I was concerned the mistakes they were making might make it harder for a jury to convict if there was little physical evidence to present.

I leapt from panic to confusion to critical thinking and back again. Three years of law school and seven years of practice had ingrained requirements for preserving evidence that danced around my mind despite the maelstrom of the crime scene.

A jury would not convict Morrison on just my word. No conviction would mean no prison. That was, of course, if they could find him. I shuddered, scanning the tree line. Either way, no capture or no evidence—he would have the opportunity to finish what he started.

I called Steve back.

"Steve, I don't understand what is going on! They told me to move my car! I don't understand why they still aren't taking photos of what it looked like when they arrived. They've been here long enough to do it."

"They don't need to photograph anything because you can tell them who did this. Everything is going to be okay. I know it doesn't feel like it now, but you are safe, they are there, and this guy will go to prison the rest of his life. You are going to be okay."

I moved my car to the side of the driveway, a deputy broke the lock on the gate, and multiple deputies flew past in their cruisers.

Part of my stress came from sitting in the car. The very air was stained with remnants of Morrison. I told Steve I'd call him back, I needed to get out of that space.

I still wasn't sure what had happened to me, and I still did not know where I was. But I did know how to be a lawyer, so that is what I did. I mentally noted what needed to be done: photos of the scene, detailed witness statements with contact information, secured physical evidence. None of those things had happened. Despite Steve's assurances, I knew they had to be done.

In that moment, I fully changed gears from victim to attorney. It wasn't a conscious choice but a survival instinct. Morrison had to be locked up, or he would kill me. He said so.

Just then, in the periphery, a deputy approached the witnesses. No one had really talked to them yet, so I assumed he was getting their statements.

"Can we go?" asked the wife.

"Yeah, you're free to go," the deputy replied.

Fear ramped up in me. "You can't let them just leave!" I yelled, loud enough for everyone to hear. "You have to get their contact information and put it in your report. They are *witnesses*. They'll be called at trial."

The deputy slowed down long enough to take their information before they left.

In the next few minutes, the remaining deputies tore out, focused solely on hunting Morrison. I was left alone.

I hoped once they found Morrison they would return to collect evidence.

Finally, a Kentucky State Police cruiser arrived at the scene, lights flashing, with an ambulance not far behind. The emergency medical technicians backed the ambulance into the driveway, in the same way I had earlier. The trooper had already parked and slid out of his car. He looked young and could not have been on the job long, but I was glad to have him on the scene.

"I'm Trooper Chris Arnett, Kentucky State Police. Can you tell me what happened?" He scanned the fields for the deputies searching for Morrison.

After I gave him a summary of the incident, he asked how I knew Morrison, where he went, and what was happening at the fence line.

During the questioning, the male EMT suggested I get into the ambulance to let them check out my injuries. He was clearly concerned about me, but my focus was on the capture of Morrison and preservation of evidence.

And I was fine—I thought. I couldn't feel anything.

After a few minutes of continued questioning, Arnett finished. Then he stood there, waiting. I stared at him. Why wasn't he doing something? *Take a photo, takes notes, look in my car, look at my injuries, join the search. Do something. Don't just stand there.*

"Don't you want to join the search?" I asked, trying to stay calm.

He didn't speak but remained in place. Finally, he swung into motion when his radio squawked loudly: "Trooper Arnett, we located the suspect!" The deputy at the scene went on to describe how they'd surrounded Morrison after he crawled into some thick brush in the middle of a cluster of trees.

From the driveway, we could just make out the deputies—a line of uniforms and cruisers in a broad circle surrounding a portion of the tree line. Arnett was the officer in charge, so they waited for him to make the actual arrest. The trooper jumped into his car, leaving me with the EMTs. We stood in silence watching the scene unfold.

The trooper's car bumped across the field and stopped by the deputies. He climbed out and strode quickly to the tree line. The others slowly decreased the circumference, tightening the perimeter, and then everyone froze. I couldn't see anything happening, only the deputies, who stood motionless for an uncomfortably long time. My heart raced, imagining all sorts of things. Then they sprinted forward as a group, converging on the center.

CHAPTER 8

YOU PICKED THE WRONG WOMAN!

COMMONWEALTH OF KENTUCKY

v.

LARRY MORRISON

DIRECT EXAMINATION OF TROOPER CHRIS ARNETT

[BY COMMONWEALTH'S ATTORNEY, Mr. Gordie Shaw]

Q: Did you ever have any interaction with Mr. Morrison while [at the scene], Trooper Arnett?

A: While I was interviewing [the victim], I heard on my radio that Guy Turner had found Mr. Morrison lying in some high weeds north of us, in the field.

Q: And what did you do?

A: I drove up to where Guy Turner was and Dusty Bell. I got out of the vehicle.

Q: What did you find with Mr. Morrison, or how did you assist them?

A: Mr. Morrison was laying on his back, with his hands underneath of him. I identified myself as State Police and to get over on his stomach, and he refused to do anything.

Q: Was he looking at you? Was he saying anything? Did he appear to be coherent to you?

A: He didn't say anything. I told him several times to get over on his stomach. That's when I struck him several times in the legs, until he actually rolled over. He put his hands in the small of his back like I told him to, and I handcuffed him. Then he was arrested.

As I watched from beside the ambulance, the deputies fell apart, and everyone scattered to their respective cruisers and headed back to the main road. I prayed Morrison was in one of those cars and not on the loose. He'd promised to come back for me and had already tried to kill me, so I had no reason to wonder what would happen if he wasn't locked up. He would kill me.

"Let's get you into the ambulance," the female EMT directed. "We need to check you out and then take you to a hospital."

I burst into tears, shaking my head. "I don't know, I don't know, I just want to go home. Please let me go home."

"We know, sweetie. Let's take a look at you. When we're done, we'll take you to a hospital in Bourbon County or Georgetown/Scott County, wherever you want to go."

"Georgetown, please." Margie was waiting for me there.

The radio crackled, and a deputy's voice announced they had Morrison in custody. Trooper Arnett drove his cruiser past the deserted house and back toward the gate. Finally, I climbed into the ambulance, believing Morrison was headed to jail.

I sat on the edge of the gurney instead of lying down. The female EMT had just started to ask basic questions when the male EMT opened the back door and told me I needed to step back out. Why were they urging me out of the ambulance when they had so patiently waited for me to get in?

"The trooper needs to talk to you," he said.

I stumbled from the ambulance and walked toward Trooper Arnett. He had stopped his cruiser roughly ten feet from the ambulance, not far from where I had originally parked my car.

Arnett rolled down his driver's side window as I approached, asking me to identify the man in the back seat.

I did what I was told, ignoring the whispers in the back of my mind about how this may not be the proper procedure to identify a suspect.

Morrison's window was rolled up, but I could clearly see him on the back seat, hunched forward, his hands cuffed behind him. There were leaves in his hair, dirt on his clothes. His shoulders slumped, and he had an indignant, self-righteous expression, his lips snarled in anger.

I wanted to go home, take a shower to wash his presence off me, crawl into bed, and hope this was some kind of bad dream. With effort, I kept my eyes on him while he stretched the length of his restraints, forcing his face as close to the window as possible. He leaned toward me, became still, and held his breath as if straining to listen—not quite sure what I would say but knowing his immediate future depended entirely on what was about to come out of my mouth.

I flicked my gaze to the trooper, who was also disheveled. I nodded in the affirmative and choked out, "It's him." Instead of stopping, I walked in an arc past the car and back toward the ambulance.

Immediately, Morrison fought his restraints. I whipped around to see him rocking back and forth aggressively, apoplectic. Like a rabid animal thrashing inside a cage. He shook his head violently from side to side, mouth gaped open, screaming, "Why are you doing this to me?" Rage colored his voice. "Why are you making this up? You can't send me back there!"

Without a thought or a breath, the fear left me as quickly as it had come, replaced with a rage that consumed me, blinded me. It doubled my size. The ground fell away from me. I was floating, suspended where I watched this scene play out.

The only thoughts I had were to make sure this man understood three things: he'd picked the wrong woman, I would spend the rest of my life making sure he never had the chance to hurt me again, and he needed to be more afraid of me than I was of him. And I needed to express these things in a way this lifelong felon would understand.

Threats, profanity, and physical aggression seemed necessary to speak his language. So, that is where I went, and once I started, I couldn't stop. I unleashed a torrent of violence and verbal abuse that caused everyone to freeze, stunned, as the scene grew more outrageous.

I began screaming, beating on the window with my fists, trying with all my might to break the glass and get in that car. I wanted to wrap my hands around his fat neck and squeeze more than I'd ever wanted anything. I wanted to hurt him up close and personal, in an intimate way, face to face, like the way his knife slid over my flesh, his hot breath in my face, and eyes that seemed to bore into my soul.

I continued beating the window, trying to get to him to hurt him. Badly. But he kept rocking, proclaiming his innocence, saying it was my fault—that he was the victim.

I didn't expect him to confess, but blaming me for what had happened ignited a rage in me I didn't know existed.

The more he shook his head asserting his innocence, the angrier I became. I switched from a beaten victim into a raging warrior. I charged at my enemy, screaming, yelling, cursing—I called him every offensive name I had ever heard, consciously and unconsciously, words I had never used and have not used since. I think I may have made some up. But words have power, and my rage was powerful, all encompassing. I could finally fight for myself. I had my voice back, and he wasn't taking it again. He cowed away from the window, pathetic and weak without his knife.

I wanted a piece of him so badly right then, I tried shoving my arm through the trooper's window to get to him. I was hoping Arnett might "accidentally" unlock the door and let me beat the life out of Morrison.

Be warned, if you are offended by foul language, consider skimming over the next few paragraphs because there is a lot of it. I'm not proud, but this is what came out.

"You picked the wrong woman, you piece-of-shit-motherfucker! I won't stop until you're locked in a concrete cell where you'll spend the rest of your life if it's the last thing I do!"

I smashed my face against the window. "Look around, you worthless piece of shit. This is the last time you're going to see green grass, other than through bars, until the day you die, alone, in a six-foot cell. Do you hear me, you coward? How strong are you now, without your knife?"

I felt ten feet tall, powerful. I clawed at the door handle, kicked the door panel. "You want to kill me? Get out of that car and try it now, try it without your knife you half-man, coward, you can't hide behind your knife now. Get out of that car. I'm right here, let's do this right now."

The sound of my voice was unrecognizable. The vitriol poured out of me in one breath. "You picked the wrong woman," I repeated. "I am smarter than you, and I will make sure you die in prison. You better pray to God you stay there because the minute you get out, I'll be waiting for you. You will never see the light of day again, other than through a barred window. I'm going to make sure you die in prison, do you hear me? Do you hear me?"

My body was filled with a power, strength, and rage I have never experienced before or since. I wanted to choke him, to watch the life leave his eyes.

Trooper Arnett sat and stared. My fury was like a projectile, and everyone stayed out of my way.

I wanted Morrison to feel the shame, terror, and anxiety that had overwhelmed me. He'd stolen my sense of safety. I wanted to take that from him, any bit of comfort or happiness. I wanted to beat it out of him. I was determined to make the man feel fear, the kind of fear that rattled him to the core. The kind of paralyzing fear that would wake him up in the middle of the night, drenched in sweat, and keep him awake. I wanted him to hear a sound and wonder if it was me coming for him, to haunt him every day for the rest of his life.

That was what I was trying to do in those moments, to make his skin crawl and shudder when he thought of me, the same way I knew I would feel when I thought about him, for the rest of my life.

Instead, he smiled.

My vision tunneled. My hearing compressed. I thought I heard a distant, muffled voice calling my name, distracting me, but I dismissed it. I slammed my fist as hard as I could on the window, jerking at the handle and continued my rampage.

"Sharon, Sharon!" someone said, little more than a murmur, as I shoved my arm through Arnett's window and behind his head again, trying to get at Morrison.

"Sharon, Sharon!"

"You worthless piece of shit, coward, weak, motherfucker. You don't have to come looking for me, I'll be waiting for you the minute you get out!"

"Sharon!"

But Morrison was the only thing that existed. He needed to understand he picked the wrong woman. I was going to repeat it until he got it. His life was over, I was going to make sure of it . . . but . . . was someone calling my name?

Focused on Morrison, I hadn't realized the male EMT had moved behind me, not until I felt pressure wrap around the middle of my body, squeezing me. I was lifted up and away from the car, my arms and legs thrashing the air in a last attempt to make contact with Morrison. The EMT continued repeating my name.

Even folded into a strong, all-encompassing bear hug, I continued screaming, "You picked the wrong woman!" With limited movement, I clawed again at the door handle.

In an alarmed voice, the EMT said, "Sharon! I can hear that you're not breathing. You're going to pass out." He turned us around, facing away from the cruiser. "Sharon, I need you to breathe. Everything's going out, and nothing's coming in."

I knew he was right. I was empty.

The cruiser started up with a rumble. The tires crunched over the gravel as the trooper eased past the ambulance and then sped away. I went limp, exhausted.

My breathing was erratic. I took in deep breaths, and the EMT gently lowered my feet to the ground and walked me around before taking me back to the ambulance. I sat on the edge of the gurney again. I was weak yet on high alert. My anger kept me upright. I would still not let them touch me, even to clean me up. But they could take me home or at least to the hospital.

I stared out the small window from the back of the ambulance. I had never been out here and had no idea where I was. I could not have given 911 directions to find me. Thank God those people stopped.

As we wound our way through the long country roads, I noticed people out living their lives. People I didn't know, but who were doing the same things I did every day. Taking letters from their mailboxes. Riding their bikes. Mowing their lawns. What just happened? What will happen? Who were these people, walking around, acting normal? Didn't they know the world just caved in?

An intense feeling of isolation washed over me, as if I were in a bubble observing people but unable to interact, watching everyone else but they couldn't see me or feel what I was feeling. I was alone and afraid, small and vulnerable as we sped through the countryside. I knew this world would never be the same for me. How could it be? I'd been living my life cloaked in an illusion of safety which no longer existed. I now knew the world was a different place, a dangerous place, and I was a different person—a broken person. And worst of all, I knew this journey was just starting.

CHAPTER 9

WHIRLING DERVISH

POLICE INTERVIEW OF LARRY MORRISON

DATE: April 7, 2006

BOURBON COUNTY JAIL

[QUESTIONING BY DETECTIVE MURRELL]

Q: Well, here's the problem, man. Here's the problem, Larry.

A: Okay.

Q: She's got cuts, bruises, and knife marks on her, dude.

A: Bruises?

Q: She's beat up and cut up pretty good, and it's new stuff, okay?

A: If she's got bruises, that didn't happen with me—

Q: It's on the right side of her body which would be the side that's closest to you.

A: So, they were right on her arm, then?

Q: Yes, sir, and breast, neck, and all down the right side of her body.

A: I'm telling you, I grabbed her on her arms. If she got a bruise, then I'm guilty of that.

As we circled up the drive toward Georgetown Community Hospital's emergency room bay, I saw a gathering of Scott County Sheriff's deputies lined up outside the entrance. Their expressions disturbed me. My mind still struggled to comprehend what had just happened, that this wasn't a mistake—but their faces reflected the magnitude of what I'd escaped.

We came to a stop, and the driver opened the back of the ambulance and gestured at the gurney. He wanted me to lie back on it. I shook my head no and stood up instead, hunching over so I could walk out. I couldn't imagine having the deputies that I worked with in court see me carted out on a gurney. I already felt weak enough. I did not want to look it, not in front of colleagues. Having become stiff during the long ride, I slowly clambered out on my own.

Margie, my blonde-haired cherub-faced friend who looked as inviting as anyone's mother, her husband, and Deputy Jeff Gardner were waiting. I held my head up, shoulders back, pulled my purse up over my shoulder, and walked to Margie. She opened her arms, and I melted in to her.

I sobbed the ugly cry, the kind where your mouth hangs open and tears pour down faster than you can wipe them away. I wailed, gasped for air, shook from head to toe, and tried to speak but couldn't form words. The EMTs stood back and waited. It was a long time before I was willing to pull away. I can still see the looks on their faces as I struggled to regain my composure. Faces I knew. People who knew me. Cared about me. I must have looked pitiful.

Then Deputy Gardner stepped forward tentatively and cleared his throat. "Sharon? We'd like to get your car for you. Where is it?"

"I . . . I don't know," I blurted out through tears.

The ambulance driver stepped in and explained how to get back to the barn. Someone fished the keys out of my purse, and Margie's husband and Deputy Gardner left to retrieve the car in Bourbon County.

Margie guided me inside, and the ER grew quiet around me. Patients and staff followed me with their eyes as I made my way across the lobby. I was grateful to be put into a private room with a door, not just a sliding curtain, to keep the curious onlookers out. This was a small town and a small hospital in the middle of a big event. The tension in the air was palpable.

In the room, Margie was at my side while we sat waiting for the nurse. I tried to get myself to focus. *Think. Think about your case.*

I'd never seen a room like this in a hospital. It wasn't a patient room. It was large and had a desk, medical equipment, gurneys, and chairs, almost more of an office—maybe a room for criminal cases since it was private, with space enough for law enforcement, medical professionals, and family. How long were they going to keep me? I just wanted to go home.

Someone tapped on the door before it swung open. The nurse, Sherry, was a longtime friend of my mother, who was also a nurse. Sherry had been told it was a crime victim intake but I don't think she was prepared for what she saw. The shock on her face reinforced the seriousness of the incident. Sherry's eyes assessed me: her gaze was intense, dark with pity and compassion.

"Would you prefer another nurse, Sharon?" she asked, knowing I might prefer anonymity.

"No, I am fine with this if you are."

She sat down and began the intake.

In describing my injuries, I considered that everything I said was going to be part of the court record. If I wanted Morrison to go to prison, I needed clarity of thought to articulate the details. The problem was I did not understand what had just happened. So I didn't report his threat to murder me. I still didn't grasp that I'd been kidnapped. I certainly didn't grasp attempted murder. Not yet. I wanted there to be no question of the veracity of my statements, so I stuck only to facts related specifically to my injuries. I couldn't begin to comprehend the rest.

The wounds the nurses and doctors recorded would corroborate my statement. After Sherry finished, she took me to a private examination room.

As I entered, a whirling dervish of health-care professionals swarmed around me. Next came the doctor who introduced himself as Dr. Patel. I had to focus to understand our conversation because my mind was swirling. He kept his distance from me physically. I could sense his apprehension in managing my care. He read over what appeared to be Sherry's notes, assessed my obvious cuts, and spoke to a tech before addressing me.

He asked someone to take me to get an x-ray and CT scan to help determine the extent of my injuries. Then he mentioned having a nurse bring me something for pain and swelling.

"I'll take something for swelling, but I don't take pain medicine, and I don't want any muscle relaxers or anything that will affect my thinking," I said, calmly but firmly.

He nodded in agreement, though his eyes protested.

Another visitor arrived soon after he left.

"Sharon, I'm Anne with the rape crisis center. I'm here to support you in whatever way you need."

"Who contacted you?" I asked, concerned about how many people knew about the incident.

"Someone from the hospital called me. It's standard procedure," she explained. "Do you want to talk about anything?"

"I'm not trying to be difficult, I appreciate what you are trying to do and how you help others, but I don't have the luxury of indulging in my emotions. I have a case to prove, and I have to focus. You're welcome to stay, but I don't want to talk right now." I spoke with an alarming amount of conviction for someone in my position. Or at least it sounded that way to me. I could tell I had moved from victim to advocate—my own advocate. I couldn't afford to devote time to processing feelings. It was a crucial time for my case.

I lay stiffly in my hospital bed, past crying. I'd done that, my red-rimmed eyes attested to it. Instead, I felt determined, no longer afraid. Ready to take action. In some ways, my growing physical pain helped me stay focused. By that point, my joints and soft tissue were swelling. I could not bend my wrist or elbow, and I walked with a limp. But I couldn't let my thoughts linger on my wounds. I might not have been polite to the counselor, but she was professional and didn't show any offense. She remained quiet beside my bed, sitting shiva. Her compassion seemed authentic, not manufactured, which made me wonder if this job was personal for her.

When Scott County Sheriff Bobby Hammons arrived at the hospital, he and his wife waited while a nurse bandaged me. The Hammonses were longtime family friends and rushed to the hospital when the call went out over dispatch. He hadn't come in his role as sheriff but as a friend. He was here to support my parents and me.

I asked Margie to request a female officer take photos of my injuries. A jury would need to see the physical evidence of the wounds, but no one else seemed to be thinking about that. In short order, Officer Teresa Hollon with the Georgetown Police Department entered my hospital room.

I knew Teresa. I had cross-examined her a handful of times when she'd arrested a client. She was smart and capable. How humiliating. Everyone involved was someone I respected and worked with. I didn't want her to witness my vulnerable state, my powerlessness, and the decisions I made that landed me here.

In addition to Sherry, the nurse; Deputy Gardner; and Officer Hollon; I knew the techs processing my medical tests and taking me to x-ray—both former clients. They all wanted to offer sympathy, but I was drowning in shame, thinking this was in part my fault. *Had I let this happen?*

As Teresa prepared her camera, I could barely make eye contact.

"Are you ready to begin?"

"Yes," I said, then immediately, "I can't believe I let this happen!" I thought everyone in the room must be thinking the same thing.

"He was a client, someone you knew, right?" Teresa asked.

I nodded slightly.

She comforted me, saying most people would have given a client a ride. She paused and then said that she may have done the same thing.

I nodded gratefully. She would never have gotten herself in a mess like this.

Despite doubting her response, I felt enormous relief. She was the first person to give me permission to forgive myself, not blame myself, and in the coming days, months, even years, Teresa's words continued to touch me. Every part of me was shaken, even my pride. I'd been outsmarted—worked like a puppet—by a high school dropout career felon, but this distinguished, experienced officer extended grace.

She photographed the areas of my body where Morrison had made obvious contact. My list of injuries was extensive.

Bloody red scratches, perfectly matching the fingers of a hand grabbing my right breast, ran across my chest. Scratches, scrapes, and deep cuts adorned my neck where he had pinned me down with the knife pushing into my throat. Cuts, scrapes, swelling, and bruising covered every part of the right side of my body, from my neck to my ankle. Any part of my body he could physically reach, he beat, cut, punched, pulled, yanked, or jerked. Every joint was out of place. My back was badly bruised from being slammed around the car during the fight of my life. The fight *for* my life.

With Margie's help, we searched my body for bruises, scrapes, blood, knife marks, cuts, and blade entry points.

Teresa continued to take photographs. I was concerned about the "chain of evidence" and how the photos would be maintained until trial—especially since Georgetown Police Department had no jurisdiction over my case and I had been the one requesting the photos, not Trooper Arnett. I had seen how things had already been managed, and I was concerned these photos would get lost between agencies and never seen by a jury.

I thought about what evidence would ensure Morrison spent the rest of his life in prison. He intended to find me again, and only God knew what he would do to me next time. These photos would help.

When Teresa finished taking photos, Sheriff Hammons asked if anyone had notified Dick and Bonnie, my parents.

"I am not going to tell them," I said, stunned he would even suggest it.

Everyone in the room looked at me.

"You can't tell them. They never need to know about this," I insisted.

Margie said, "Honey, don't you think it'll make the news?"

"No. Why would it make the news?"

Sheriff Hammons stepped in. "Sharon, it's going to be on the news. A client kidnapped his lawyer and tried to kill her. I'm sure they are already reporting it."

They didn't understand.

I did not want Mom and Dad to come to the hospital.

I would quietly manage the incident on my own and get it behind me. Maybe I would tell them bits and pieces, once I figured out how to do so without telling the entire story. I never imagined it would become the top news story for a week and hit the Associated Press. At the time I thought I could keep this from them. I had to. Especially my dad. I didn't want him to know Morrison had injured every part of my body he could reach. When my dad saw my black and blue swollen body, he was going to do whatever it took to guarantee this man never hurt me again. My father was not a violent man, but he was a fierce protector of his family and an excellent marksman. He would sacrifice anything to keep his family safe, including going to prison himself.

Our family lived on a horse farm and had a comfort level and appreciation for guns. We used them to protect the horses and saw them as just another tool. There was no emotion attached to them.

For instance, my father used a gun almost daily to deal with our constant nemesis, groundhogs. They burrow underground, creating tunnels that result in holes and unstable topsoil. I've seen a horse racing across a pasture step in a hole and break a leg, resulting in an early demise.

My dad could spot a groundhog hundreds of yards away, pull out a rifle, and line up the tiny beast in his sights. Within a fraction of a second, the chambered round left the barrel. Then, like a short, fat tree being cut off at the stump, the groundhog fell to the ground. It may sound brutal, but the death of every groundhog was the life of one of our horses.

So guns were a normal part of our lives, and I witnessed their usefulness and even necessity. I never worried about anything as long as Dad and our guns were around.

Until the night I was abducted by Morrison. My father had the guns, the skill, and a desire to protect me, no matter the cost to him. And so I would have to lie to him. It would be the only time during or after the incident—from my escape all the way through the end of the trial—that I would lie. But I would do it to protect my dad.

Despite everything that happened—the long drive, the knife, his repeated efforts to get to me—all I could think about was his desire to stab me and leave me behind that barn. I couldn't let my parents know how bad it had been, how scared I was, or that I knew he would return to try to kill me. They needed to see me strong. Especially my dad—the more he saw me hurt, the more driven he would be to take justice into his own hands. Morrison had already taken so much from me. I wouldn't let him take my dad, too.

I had no concept of how this was going to affect me emotionally, and my mind refused to accept what I would endure over the next months and years to survive the legal process. So I thought I could hide it all.

In my mind, I did not understand why everyone wanted to put a label like victim, hostage, or kidnapping on what happened to me. And once I did understand, I still didn't want the label. From the beginning, I resisted being called a victim. And I definitely didn't want to be called that in front of my parents.

"Please don't tell them! I don't want them to know," I begged again.

"Your parents *will* know. They may already know." The sheriff took my hand but politely kept space between us.

Later, I found out my mom already knew. Trooper Arnett had called Gordie Shaw, the Commonwealth's Attorney for three counties—Bourbon, Scott, and Woodford— and the man who would prosecute my case. Gordie called his investigator, Becky, who called her cousin Sue, who was one of my mom's best friends. Down the chain it went. Word of crime in a small town travels fast. By the time Sheriff Hammons got to my dad, mom knew but hadn't known long enough to tell Dad.

"I know Dick. Let me talk to him," Sheriff Hammons said, but it was more like a question.

Bobby Hammons truly did know my dad—who'd actually pulled a gun on the sheriff before.

The sheriff, also a farmer, leased the back forty acres of our farm. Out late one night to check his irrigation, he'd walked past the main gate and poked his head into a barn and then turned to find a gun in his face.

"Dick!" he'd said. "It's me, Bobby."

Dad waited a second before removing the weapon and calmly said, "I didn't know you were on the farm."

Bobby loved teasing Dad that he almost shot the sheriff.

"Sharon," the sheriff said, "I'm going to go notify your parents and bring them here. You understand? I'm also going to ask your dad to surrender his guns."

"Please don't tell him who did this. At least give me that much."

As the Hammonses went to notify my parents, I suddenly became aware of my appearance. I used water from my drinking cup and swiped repeatedly at the blood on my chest. My hair hung in clumps, so I pulled it up on top of my head. I was determined to look as normal as possible when they walked through the door. I didn't want them to see me upset or injured. They definitely shouldn't see any blood. It would be hard enough for them to be brought to the hospital by the sheriff after being informed their youngest child had been kidnapped, but to walk in and see me bloody was not an option. It would be a scene they would never forget.

I didn't know what to say when Mom and Dad got there. How would I handle their pain when they saw me? I loved them so much, so deeply, I would do anything to avoid hurting them.

I locked eyes with them as they entered the room, scanning their faces for emotion. Everyone stepped away from my bed clearing a path. My parents were strong. They were calm, firm, and quiet while taking it in with grace. When recounting the incident, I stayed away from specifics, which seemed easier for all of us. They told me they loved me and were glad I was okay and that my brother and sister were very worried and wished they could be there. My mom reminded me of all their prayers for safety over the course of my life and thanked God for protecting me.

After a few minutes of solemn questions, my dad cleared his throat and said, "Who did this to you?"

The words sucked all the air out of the room as everyone held their breath, waiting for my response.

"I don't know," I lied. I waited and peered into Dad's face, my ears alert for the sound of someone about to speak. I was prepared to talk over, interrupt, or do whatever I had to do to make sure my dad didn't hear the name Larry Morrison. I didn't know if Morrison would be released that night or bailed out soon. But if he was and Dad knew his name, he would be right there, waiting for him.

"Bobby told me you put up a good fight and escaped," Dad said.

I hadn't thought about it that way. Yes, I had shoved him away a few times during the drive, and then kicked, punched, and scratched during our battle at the farm, but I hadn't considered I might have actually hurt him.

The sheriff confirmed Morrison was injured, from reports coming out of the small jail in Bourbon County where they were holding him. It delighted me to think of Morrison sitting in jail with his overcrowded cellmates mocking his obvious wounds and harassing him for getting beaten up by the girl who got away.

Bobby said, "She kicked his ass." Despite the pain on my dad's face, I could see that comment made him feel slightly better.

"Do you remember those tapes I showed you when you were younger? *Street Fighter*?"

I had a vague, distant memory of some self-defense video but didn't recall specifics. I looked him right in the eyes and said yes anyway.

He took a deep breath. "Did that help you?" He stared at me with a desperation I'd never seen in him. His beautiful blue eyes were pleading, a mixture of fear, hope, and helplessness.

"Yes, Dad. That's exactly what I did. I remembered what they did in those tapes and I did it." My second lie. But the emotion reflected on his face was one I'll carry with me the rest of my life: relief that he hadn't failed his baby girl.

I went out of my way to be honest, accurate, and transparent during the course of my case. I didn't exaggerate to obtain a benefit, and I even downplayed things to ensure accuracy. But with my dad, in those two moments, I wasn't honest. And I don't regret it.

Tears flooded his eyes. He believed that he had been a part of keeping me safe. I could see some of the pain he felt for not being there to protect me wane. I wanted him to know he protected me even in his absence. Because he did. But not exactly like he was thinking. He was the reason I was a natural fighter with a strong will. He'd talked to me about self-defense. He'd given me confidence. He helped keep me safe—and that was the point.

Dad and I had a tender moment while my mom appraised the cuts on my neck, assessing them with a skilled nurse's eye. Her voice was low but clear when she said, "This one is deep and very close to your carotid. Thank God he didn't cut your artery." She let her hand rest on me, pouring love onto me without making a fuss, then demanded the doctor come in and make a note of this specific injury in my file. It was apparent I wasn't the only one thinking about my future trial at that moment. Knowing my strong, capable parents were fighting with me and for me brought me enormous comfort.

Just then, Jeff arrived, having made the hour-long drive from Louisville. He was thinking clearly enough to have a friend drive him down so he would be free to drive me back to my home. He rushed in the door, his face intense and anxiety blowing off his six-foot-five frame. He had heard almost everything that evening, the phone dying as I screamed about Morrison having a gun. He had endured his own trauma, believing I was dead, killed at the hands of a madman while he'd only been able to listen.

We had known each other about six or seven months, dated for the last four. My parents knew about him, but they had not met. When he edged up to my bedside, he nodded at them, but I could see he didn't know what to do next.

Dad reached his huge hand across the bed and said, "Jeff Ballard?"

Jeff nodded and shook his hand. I was fixated on how my dad's arm looked so muscular and thick next to his, though Jeff was no weakling. My father was neatly dressed, appearing confident, standing guard over me. Jeff was disheveled, his golf shirt partially untucked.

My father politely broke the ice. "I understand you're a preacher."

"Not tonight," Jeff said, putting a hand on my shoulder.

I had a team around me, I could feel their support. Then the phone built into my bed rang. It was Trooper Arnett, calling to tell me Morrison had been charged with resisting arrest, first degree sex abuse, and kidnapping. I tensed. Kidnapping was difficult to prove. Resisting arrest was a misdemeanor. Sex abuse didn't seem to dignify what I'd been through. My blood pressure spiked, along with my ire.

"You're telling me you're charging him with a misdemeanor and a hard-to-prove kidnapping? He tried to *kill* me, and that's all you've charged him with? How about attempted murder? How about attempted *rape?*" My voice rose with each question.

He started rambling about hard it was to prove those charges, but I pulled the phone away from my ear refusing to listen. I glared at the headset, then started banging the phone against the base, growling, "I–can't–believe–this. I–can't–believe–this!" before smashing the phone one last time into the cradle.

The room went silent.

Nobody made a move.

The first person to speak was Anne, the rape crisis counselor when she leaned over the side of my bed. I held my breath waiting to see what she was about to say, prepared to unload on her, too. She put her hand on the rail and said, "You are right, I can't believe those charges."

I looked at her. Now she had a reason to be here. If she was going to fight with me, she could stay.

"Thank you," I whispered, my vocal cords hoarse from the screaming.

Trooper Arnett showed up in my room not long after that with no acknowledgment of my concerns over the weak charges. It was almost as if I hadn't hung up on him. I'm fairly confident he didn't typically get that kind of response.

The trooper leaned against the wall about five feet from the end of my bed, almost as though he needed the support. As soon as he finished introducing himself to the others, I confronted him with "Tell me again about these charges."

He claimed he charged Morrison with everything he could. He didn't seem defensive, but he didn't seem confident, either.

"Go to your car and get your blue book," I shot back. "Let's walk through the elements of attempted rape and attempted murder. I'll show you that this meets the necessary elements."

I was furious about the weak charges, one a misdemeanor. The only reason they charged him with resisting arrest was to lessen the success of a lawsuit if Morrison tried to sue the Kentucky State Police for brutality. Their defense would be that he resisted arrest, requiring them to use force to detain him. It benefited the Commonwealth, not me. Knowing this made me even angrier. Arnett ignored my comment, telling me he had called Gordie at home. As the Commonwealth's Attorney, Gordie was the chief prosecutor for our circuit. Arnett went further, stating he had never called Gordie at home before but he did because this case was a big deal. He stood his ground, saying the charges were what Gordie said to file.

In Trooper Arnett's mind, that ended the conversation. In my mind, Gordie was wrong. While still leaning against the wall, he continued casually, "Morrison said you were doing drugs together."

"What? Tell me what he said."

"He said you did some lines of cocaine at the farm and while you were driving."

"Great!" I said excited for the first time since this had started.

This is what I'd been waiting for. Something I could easily disprove. There would be no room for confusion. There was nothing in my system—I rarely even took aspirin when I got a headache. I wiggled to the side of the bed, swung my hips around, and dropped my feet to the floor, ignoring the stabs of pain in my right side and back. I shuffled a few steps, moving side to side like a penguin, trying to get out of the room.

"What are you doing?" Jeff asked, aghast, everyone else chiming in, telling me to get back to bed.

The trooper pushed away from the wall. "What are you doing?"

"I'm going to get a drug test."

He asked me why I would do that, confusion crossing his face as he turned to block my path, telling me no one would believe Morrison over me.

I couldn't believe a law enforcement professional was discouraging me.

"If I get the drug screen, I don't have to worry about anyone believing me. They will have objective medical proof Morrison is lying and I am not." He didn't move. I worked my way around him, mumbling in complete disbelief. "Even if all his law enforcement training came from watching *Law & Order* marathons, he would know I need a drug screen."

There was no way I was going to let one more piece of evidence slip away. I had the opportunity to provide scientific proof to the jury to discredit Morrison's claims. Why would I *not* do that?

No one else tried to stop me, realizing the obvious benefit of what I was doing. I hobbled out to the nurse's station, which was bustling with activity. I waited maybe a second before I slapped my hand loudly on the counter and called out, "I need my doctor right away."

He hustled down the hall toward me. "What is this?"

"I need a drug screen. Hair, blood, urine, go back as far as you can go. Test for everything."

The doctor paused, uncertain what to do.

"He said we were doing drugs together," I told him, hoping this would spur action.

"All right, we can do that." But he didn't move.

"I need one now."

As I turned to go back to my room, I noticed a large man standing at the counter near me. He stared at my bruises and cuts, his mouth open. I realized he was someone else I knew, a detective with the police department whom I had cross-examined a few times. Apparently he had not heard the call go out over dispatch that there was an active search for me.

"What happened?" he asked, shocked to see me in that condition.

I said simply, "Larry Morrison."

"Oh," he said from an obvious working knowledge of Morrison's criminal record.

I turned and started hobbling back to my room but stopped.

That was it. That was why Morrison kept trying to shove the wad of cash rolled around what looked like cocaine in my pocket. He wanted it found on me when they found my body. That was his big plan, a drug deal that ended tragically.

So not only was he going to rape and kill me but try to destroy my character, too. Just another tragic casualty of the drug epidemic.

Once back in my room, a nurse drew blood for the drug screen.

Another nurse filled out the request form. "Are you on any medication? Do you drink alcohol?"

"I don't take anything—no alcohol, no drugs, no prescription meds. I rarely take aspirin. I do eat sugar, though—chocolate."

She laughed. "I don't think we need to worry about that."

I've always used humor to bring levity to difficult situations. I was glad to see I was doing it here. It meant I was starting to feel more like myself and not so much like a cornered animal. The feeling didn't last long.

Arnett started talking to me again. I was surprised when he asked me about a small, round Mickey Mouse container.

"Do you have anything like that in your car?" he asked.

"No." Before I could ask why, he came out with another random question.

"Do you have a blue Whitaker Bank pen in your car?"

"No." I'm oddly specific about the pens I use. I sign my name fifty times a day on a good day, and we keep particular pens in our stockroom that I always use. Perfect for signing—no smudge and they come in blue and black. I don't use the free pens businesses gave out, being a bit of a pen snob.

I knew his questions stemmed from Morrison's interrogation because they were too specific. Despite this, I didn't recognize at the time that he was interrogating me while the detective was still with Morrison, so they could compare each version of the incident.

He told me the knife he recovered had the tip missing and asked if he could search my car for it.

"Sure," was my uncharacteristically laconic response. A sign of my losing faith in the trooper.

My dad stood. I don't know if he understood more than I did or if he simply needed to feel like he was helping, but he asked to assist Arnett in the search, and they headed out.

Quiet conversation flowed around the room as a tech informed me she was taking me to x-ray and CT scan. She rolled me out and quickly moved me through the tests. This was a notably different experience than coming to the hospital without a law enforcement escort. Everything moved faster.

When I returned, the doctor entered with the lab results for the blood work in hand. He said, "I need everybody to leave the room except Sharon."

I said, "It's okay, they can stay."

He peered at me with an intense but indecipherable look and said, "No, I need everybody to leave."

That's not good. What can mess up a drug test? Did I eat a poppy seed bagel? Is that even true about poppy seeds? My mind was racing, listing what I knew about drug tests and what could cause them to fail. I didn't have much to draw from. Had I just made a huge mistake, making them give me the test? How could it be anything other than negative?

You could feel the tension in the room as everyone filed out.

Dr. Patel showed me the lab report. Everything was negative. "Completely clean screen," he said.

"What was that all about, then?"

"What do you mean?"

I was relieved but frustrated at the same time. "Why did you clear everybody out? I thought something had gone wrong. You scared me."

"Hospital policy." He sounded surprised it bothered me.

He didn't understand. I didn't get the drug screen because I was a patient—I got the drug screen because I was building my case, piece by piece, making sure

Morrison would go to prison. Now I had scientific proof to impeach his statement that we had done drugs together. I could prove unequivocally that he was a liar. A point for Muse.

The trooper and my father came back into the room with everyone else, unaware of what had just happened, so I informed everyone of the clean results. No one was surprised.

Trooper Arnett demanded a written statement.

I objected and held up my bandaged right arm.

"Can't write."

Then he demanded a voice recording of my statement. I refused. I knew defense counsel would hear this and that I was not calm enough to recount what happened. It would be spotty and easily used against me if I failed to mention something. And I knew I would. It might be hard to imagine you could forget any detail in a kidnapping, but trauma affects the mind in unusual ways, at times shutting down the things we don't want to remember.

He continued demanding the statement. My mom and dad were in the room, my breathing was strained, my mind was swirling, how could I relive the events that had led me here? How to describe an evil so intense that if you looked at it too long, you wouldn't be able to drag your soul back out, that left me with a fear so consuming it saturated me, wrapping itself around my bones? I couldn't, so I stuck to the facts as best I could while still in shock.

My statement stopped and started with raspy breaths while the sound of the wheels turning the tape in the ancient micro-cassette recorder distracted me.

I just wanted to go home.

When the nurse came into the room with my release papers, it was close to four o'clock in the morning. The doctor had a long list of instructions, including advising me to stay calm and avoid stress.

Did he really just tell me to avoid stress? Funny. He suggested medicine to help me sleep, medicine to help with anxiety, medicine to help me wake up from the medicine that helped me sleep. I declined. Repeatedly. I am very sensitive to medication—what is tolerable for others wipes me out. I knew taking those kinds of pills would ease the pain I was feeling and help me rest, but once I stopped taking them, the ugly reality would be waiting for me. I'd rather dig in and push through this than drag it out. I had to be aware of everything going on and stay on top of my case if I was going to make certain Morrison never had a chance to come back for me. I couldn't keep safe in a drug-induced fog.

My parents asked me to come stay with them. They wanted to watch over me, but I wanted to be in my own bed, an hour away from Georgetown. To nestle into the safety and comfort of my small home. I had no idea that sense of safety would take a very long time to come back. And never permanently.

The doctor made sure I understood his instructions, nodded to us, and left. Jeff went to get my car and drove it around to pick me up.

When I crawled in, my chest began heaving, as though someone were trying to pry open my rib cage. Before we made it out of the parking lot, I was gasping for air. "This is where he sat when he tried to kill me." I sobbed with my face in my hands.

I sat in the car with the drive stretched out in front of me. I don't remember much other than the intense desire to get home—and never leave. Evil lingered, still pursuing me.

CHAPTER 10

THE AFTERMATH

911 CALL
DATE: April 7, 2006
BOURBON COUNTY

TRANSCRIPT EXCERPT

DISPATCHER: Where is Mr. Morrison now?

MS. MUSE: I don't know. He's—I want to thank these people. I literally just ran out in the middle of the road and—

DISPATCHER: That's fine, honey. That's fine.

MS. MUSE: He's talking to them. And I usually don't use bad language, but I did say some nasty things.

DISPATCHER: Well, that's okay. That's understandable in this situation, honey. Do you need an ambulance?

MS. MUSE: I don't know.

DISPATCHER: Do you want me to see if—

MS. MUSE: But I need somebody to help me get home.

When we pulled into my driveway a few hours before dawn, I was a different person. I'd left my house that April morning a young woman with a confident stride and an easy laugh. I returned and anxious, fearful woman with haunting questions. How did this happen? How did he outsmart me? When would he return?

Jeff helped me out of the car and into the house. "I think you should try to rest," he said, guiding me to my room. I was physically having problems getting around, every part of my body on fire or aching, and emotionally I was spent.

He stepped out of the room to let me get settled. I got down on my knees next to the bed, elbows on the mattress, folded my hands with finger tips pressed together, and bowed my head—like nighttime prayers when I was a child. I had a conversation with God.

"God," I started, "I can't imagine how awful it must be to live inside that man's head, the way he chooses to live his life. What must have happened to make him who he is? Please help him. Please forgive him." I bent my head further, pressing my forehead into my comforter, shut my eyes harder, and let tears roll off my face, creating a small puddle on the floor. "Help me forgive him, too."

Having been born and raised in the church, attended Sunday school and church camp, and even serving as a missionary in Russia for years, prayer was instinctive. I knew that forgiving Morrison would be important for me. I'd heard it said that holding onto resentment and failing to forgive is like swallowing poison and hoping the other person dies. Forgiveness was normal, even expected. It was how I lived my life—or tried to. Failing often, failing miserably. This was the first step to moving forward and starting to heal. But the subtle transformation of my mind, one small thought at a time, over the next several months was a terrifying example of how the eighteen-inch distance from the head to the heart can be an insurmountable chasm.

Jeff came back into the room as I lay down in my clothes, too exhausted to change. I left my shoes on as it somehow felt safer to be ready to run in an instant. I asked him to stay, and he understood. He was a physically intimidating man, and I needed him between me and the door. The door I was afraid Morrison would burst through.

Jeff lay down on the other side of the bed. We each stared at the ceiling, silent and numb. Neither of us knew what to do or say, but sleep was impossible.

After a while of lying on top of the covers without moving or speaking, Jeff crept off the bed and padded down the hall. The minute he cleared the door frame,

I slid off the bed and silently followed him. He walked around the corner and into the kitchen. I was right behind him like a ghost, too afraid to have him out of my sight.

He turned, saw me, and startled. "Sharon, what are you doing?"

"Following you."

"I'm just getting ChapStick. I'm coming right back, I promise."

"Okay. I'm going with you."

I didn't have the strength to pretend I was okay.

Even in my tiny Cape Cod–style house, I couldn't tolerate being more than an arm's distance from him.

We returned to the bed and waited for light to come. Sleep did not happen for either of us.

SATURDAY, DAY ONE

After a seemingly endless night, the sun finally came out, giving me a little more courage. I'd survived and was here for another day. The world seemed less dangerous in the light. I was kidnapped in broad daylight, yet the light comforted me.

Knowing Jeff had a work meeting that morning, I dreaded his leaving. The thought of being alone in my own home felt unmanageable, so Jeff called his assistant to explain why he couldn't come in—that he needed to be with me.

As soon as he hung up from giving her a short version of my kidnapping, I asked, "What did she say?"

I was nervous, waiting for his answer. I blamed myself for what happened and assumed everyone else did, too. They would think I was stupid or I should have reacted differently or fought back earlier, because I thought that. I had a long list of things I should have done differently. I was sure the rest of the world saw that, too.

Not surprisingly, her response was loving and free from judgment—she told him he needed to be with me and she would be praying for us.

Jeff had made his work-related call. Now I had to make mine.

Kim and Judy were the ladies who ran my office, but they were also my friends—I cared for them and their safety. I called Kim first, then Judy. I told them both briefly what happened and asked them to consider no longer working with me. I'd pay severance, and they could draw unemployment. I did not want to put my employees in danger. Working for me was suddenly a safety concern and definitely a risk.

Neither of them flinched. I was especially worried about Judy. Since her desk was between my office and the door, she was the first person Morrison would encounter if he came back. Thankfully, Judy didn't scare easily. I honestly don't think she scares at all.

They weren't interested in leaving. I told them we had to create a safety plan, train with a weapon they were comfortable with, and add security measures. Within two weeks we would all have completed Carrying Concealed Deadly Weapons training and continued practicing at the range.

After our calls, Jeff and I talked about what we should do about our evening plans. We had tickets for an Etta James concert and reservations at a favorite restaurant to celebrate the birthday of my childhood friend, Heather. I was determined to go.

Heather and Ernie, another friend, showed up at the house, ready for a fun night. We visited for a few minutes before Jeff explained briefly what happened the night before. It was strange to watch their expressions as Jeff spoke. What were they going to say? I was standing right in front of them, otherwise normal, yet we were telling them I'd been kidnapped and almost killed just twenty-four hours before. They couldn't quite process it. They stood in silence, faces contorting in confusion, disbelief, and shock.

I spent the evening pretending to be okay while occasionally fleeing to the ladies room to cry. Dinner ended up pushed around my plate, but the concert was different. Music has a way of soothing my soul. I sat between Heather and Jeff and held their hands most of the night. I tried to focus on Etta James and her smooth, soulful voice but spent most of the evening feeling a pit in my stomach and quietly crying. It was a very long night, but I felt a strong sense of pride that I didn't cancel. As if I was beating this thing.

We filed out the door with the masses, herded like cattle through the small lobby. It was a bottleneck with people shoulder to shoulder. Someone grabbed me—I instinctively turned and hit the person hard. After landing the punch, ready to throw another, I realized I'd assaulted some poor lady who was just trying to manage her way through the crowd.

I felt guilty, knowing I had likely hurt her. She disappeared before I could apologize. I didn't blame her. Maybe it was too soon for me to be in public.

SUNDAY, DAY TWO

Jeff had to teach at church, and he asked Leslie, my friend and neighbor, to spend time with me. Leslie and I went through a lot together, neighbors while I was studying for the bar exam and she for her Series 7 broker exam. We traveled, worked out, and shopped together. Now I needed her more than ever.

Leslie and I sat on the back porch talking while Jeff was gone. Interestingly, we didn't speak much about the incident. We shared and unspoken desire to discuss anything but that. So we spoke of meaningless things. The little amount of time removing me from the incident was helping me feel stronger, so I told her she could go back home. I just wanted to get back to normal, maybe getting out of the house would help. I needed food and didn't want to wait for Jeff to return, so I headed to the grocery store.

As I pulled into the entrance, I instinctively scanned the length of the parking lot and areas near the door to determine which way to approach the store. I wanted as little exposure as possible—exposure meant anywhere I would be an easy target. I drove up and down several rows before I found a spot clearly visible from the main entrance, with surveillance cameras mounted above the door. I made a dash from my car to the entrance. The knowledge that Morrison wanted to show up, violate me, and murder me gave me a new appreciation for security cameras—not because they would stop Morrison, but at least someone would see what happened to me. The thought of being murdered and never found was unbearable.

With my eyes moving back and forth, never resting on anything, I made it through the door. I moved quickly to the produce section, but focused more on the shoppers than on the fruit. I noticed a large man, mid-forties, without a wedding ring on, standing by the apples. He was too big for me to handle, so I avoided the apples. This was apparently my new way of categorizing people: ones I could physically fight off and ones I couldn't.

I could barely focus because I was intent on keeping an exit in my sights and watching the people, my eyes flicking back and forth, back and forth . . . I put a few items in my basket, not really thinking about what I was buying. I wanted some food, but the energy I had to expend to get it wasn't worth it. I checked out and hurried back to my car. Back to my home. I locked myself in. Worn out. It was only day two.

Unpacking my groceries, I felt the pain from the extensive abuse. The right side of my body was swollen, stiff, and hurting. I had to switch over from my right arm to using my left to get the groceries out of the bag. I also had trouble taking a deep breath. Headaches, strained joints, and burning cuts. Everything took longer. I moved slower and had to start learning to use my left arm to brush my teeth, to put my contacts in, to write. My right arm was clearly going to be out of commission for a while.

Jeff returned, and as we sat in the living room, calls started pouring in. People who wanted to show support and pray with me. I was too empty to talk, too worn out from my efforts to keep myself safe at the store. I loved knowing my mom had everyone praying for me, but I didn't feel like talking to anyone.

That night I started a ritual, one I lived by longer than I want to admit.

I locked myself in the house, looked in all the rooms and behind my sectional, anywhere someone could be hiding. I knew in my head that Morrison wasn't in my house, but in order to try to sleep, I checked everywhere so my brain could tell my body to relax, that I was safe. I did all of this even though Jeff was there, sleeping on the couch in the next room. Lastly, I turned the lights on in the hallway and went into my room.

Then I called the Bourbon County jail where Morrison was being held and asked if he was still in custody. I had no idea if he could afford bail or if he could, when he'd be out. After hearing he was still in his cell, down for the night, I crawled into bed and made my best attempt to sleep, but it only came in small spurts, primarily due to exhaustion. I listened for any sound, to assess its threat level. I must have fallen asleep early in the morning hours because I remember waking up— more tired than when I had gone to bed. Sleep became a draining event. I had to do something to stop this. It was barely forty-eight hours since the incident. I wouldn't be able to live without real rest, not for long.

Then I had an idea.

MONDAY, DAY THREE

My friend Kevin, an amateur photographer, agreed to let me use his SLR camera and dropped it off in the morning.

When he left I grabbed a notebook, and Jeff and I headed out the door to Georgetown. Approaching my office building, we were amazed at the number of news vans parked outside. I was not going to go in. I had been the lead story since Friday and hoped something would knock me off the top. There was no way I'd give an interview.

I headed straight to the Sheriff's Department, spoke with Deputy Cannon, and presented him with an idea.

The incident started in Scott County and ended in Bourbon County. The United States Constitution, along with the Kentucky Constitution and case law, prohibits a defendant from being tried twice for the same crime. We all know that to be double jeopardy. They do not, however, prohibit a defendant from being charged with a variety of crimes stemming from one incident.

Both Scott County and Bourbon County had jurisdiction over the crimes committed in their respective counties, so I could swear out a complaint in Scott County with different charges while the kidnapping, sexual abuse, and resisting arrest were pending in Bourbon County. Deputy Cannon filled out a sheriff's report for me. We charged Morrison with wanton endangerment and false imprisonment—first degree, class D felonies, with up to five years each. The point of filing these charges was to place a "holder" on him. If he was able to make bail in Bourbon County for the kidnapping, sex abuse, and resisting arrest charges, the Bourbon County Jail would hold him until Scott County Sheriff's Deputies could pick him up on the charges I filed there. Morrison would then be transferred to Scott County, where he would be held and arraigned and have to make bail for the charges I filed there.

This would prevent him from getting out of jail and showing up at my office before I knew he was released. All of this would slow him down and buy me time to do whatever I had to do to stay safe.

When I finished filing the charges, I met with Sheriff Hammons. He gathered several deputies in his office and placed maps of Scott County and Bourbon County on a large table. We marked the location of my office and where I was found. Jeff shared the "landmarks" I had given him over the phone, and we studied the maps to determine the path I had driven. Once we realized I had doubled back and had gone in a circle, we identified the route. It also helped create a timeline for the incident. We worked backward from my 911 call to when I hung up with Jeff in the hallway at the office.

Jeff and I got into Sheriff Hammons's SUV and slowly drove the path. Jeff sat in the back, taking notes and marking where we turned, road names, and anything to help identify the route.

I didn't believe what I saw. The streets were full of traffic. We passed gas stations and shopping centers with cars and people. We drove through a large intersection—and then we were quickly out in the country.

How had I safely driven so far and failed to see all the activity? I'd been so focused on Morrison, his hands, and trying to anticipate and deflect his next blow that the outside world ceased to exist. That is, until Jeff told me to call out landmarks. But by that time we were so deep in the country there really wasn't anyone or anything around.

After we left the city limits of Georgetown, my cell service kept dropping. Eventually I had no service at all. Just three days ago, my phone with a dead battery worked an additional two hours and never dropped service. Thank God!

When we came to the crime scene, Sheriff Hammons pulled in to the same place I'd parked Friday night. I started taking photos while the sheriff walked up and down the road with Jeff, looking for the duffle bag. Once I was done taking photos, I joined them in the search for the bag.

I was deflated as we continued to look but couldn't find it. I was with a sheriff, so if we found it, he could call it in, and the chain of evidence would hold up in court. I knew I couldn't go out on my own and "find" the bag. Defense counsel would have had a field day with that.

We didn't hop the fence, where I believed the bag must be, but we walked the road and checked the ditch. I was hoping to find something, the roll of cash and drugs, the hammer I saw. Something. We came up empty.

Oddly, I was not afraid that day. I walked the site where I was almost murdered days earlier, and all I could think about was collecting evidence and taking photos that would help tell the jury my story.

We returned to Georgetown feeling relatively productive. It felt great to be trying, to be part of the effort to build a strong case. To be working while the evidence was fresh. Sadly, this would be the last time the case was worked for a very long time. My efforts in collecting and preserving physical evidence and encouraging law enforcement to do so became an exercise in futility and frustration.

I feared a dearth of evidence at trial, and I was right. But I'm jumping ahead of the story—again.

We got back to Georgetown and met my parents.

"What do you have for self-protection?" Dad asked.

"I have a baseball bat under my desk and one at the house, near the door," I said, knowing how that must sound to my dad.

"If you plan on using a bat, you've got to be up close, and I don't like that." He handed me a Beretta 9mm. "I bought you this. We can practice at the range, and I'll show you how to clean it."

I have been around guns my entire life, but for the first time, I felt an emotional weight attached to this one. Not just a tool on the farm—it was a matter of life or death.

"Thank you, Dad. I'll feel much safer with this."

I didn't know how I could use it anytime soon. My right arm was weak, and I could not grip very well. My injuries seemed to be getting worse, not better. I wasn't going to tell Dad, though. He needed to know he was doing everything he could to help keep me safe.

When Jeff and I returned home, I called my friend Fred, a general contractor who had done the remodeling on my home. I asked him to add locks to my doors, add exterior lights, install motion detectors, hang blinds, and install storm windows. Anything to slow down someone from getting into my house. And make it harder to watch me from outside.

I had enjoyed the unobstructed view of my white flower garden in the backyard, but now the uncovered windows made me feel like I was living in a fishbowl.

Then I called the local police station. We had our own small department in my neighborhood, apart from the Louisville police, and I informed them briefly of what happened, gave them a description of Morrison, and asked them to drive by my house as often as they could. Next, I spoke to two of my neighbors and told them to call the police immediately if they saw anyone around my house that fit his description.

I went into my routine of checking around the house, including making sure my cell phone was charged, but now I added something new: I loaded my 9mm, chambered a round, clicked the safety off, and placed it on my nightstand.

Lastly, I called the jail. Morrison was down for the night. Then so was I.

TUESDAY, DAY FOUR

Flowers, cards, phone calls, and emails poured in. Friends showered me with encouragement. My extended family and friends called after hearing my story on the news. I felt grateful for the support but was too wiped out to respond.

Jeff had to return to work, yet he checked on me frequently. I didn't want to leave the house. I didn't have the energy—it was too much work to stay safe outside my home.

My friend Kevin came to visit me and take photos of my car—part of the crime scene. He zoomed in on the knife gouges across my leather dashboard, the broken knobs, the shattered CD player, and other marks. He planned to have prints made of the photos for me to give the prosecutor. While frustrating, it came as no surprise that these were the only photos of my car presented to a jury. No one in law enforcement ever photographed the crime scene—either the farm or my car.

Kevin and I spoke about the knife and tried to work through how I survived. We wondered how I could have pushed Morrison off me. So I called Steve. Steve Schroering was my friend and legal advisor I called from the crime scene. I first met Steve in law school where he was my trial practice professor. He was young, charismatic, and handsome. And I had a crush. Our project for the end of the semester was to participate in mock trials. At one point, I acted as a witness, while Steve sat on the bench along with a federal court judge. Together, they presided over the cases. During a particularly long argument by the attorneys at the bench, I started whispering to my classmates who were acting as jurors. I pointed out that the younger man on the bench as the professor they had heard me talk about all semester, the one I thought was so hot. Wasn't he handsome? Look at those arms! As soon as the words were out of my mouth, the room went silent. My friends on the jury stared across the room toward the bench, their eyes growing wide and their mouths collectively dropping open. I turned to see all the student attorneys, Steve, and the federal court judge grinning at me. At that moment, I remembered that the video at the judge's bench was voice activated. Every word I'd said was heard at the bench. Steve's face was bright red, my face was bright red, and that was the beginning of our lifelong friendship.

I trusted Steve without reservation. I asked him to help figure out what happened in the car. He referred me to a weapons expert, Eric, who agreed to try to determine what exactly happened with the knife. Eric explained that there was no reasonable explanation for me being able to push Morrison off of me. Certainly not with enough force to break the knife tip.

"What about the stories you hear about women lifting cars off their trapped children, saving their lives? Don't we have some extraordinary power as a result of the adrenaline pumping through us?"

He told me there was not enough adrenaline to do that kind of damage to that kind of blade. The position of my body and angle of the damage in the dashboard made it appear something jerked him off of me. The angles were all wrong for a push. It had to be a pull.

An unseen force pulled Morrison off me. I know it, and Morrison knows it. Even law enforcement and the attorneys knew something extraordinary, inexplicable intervened. Everyone avoided asking me about it at the trial. But I knew what happened. In that moment, God showed up Old Testament style, like a fierce warrior saying, "Enough is enough. This is over. You are not taking her today." God protected me when I couldn't protect myself, and he rescued me from certain death. He would do it again in a few months, but that would be from a different kind of death—we will get to that later.

You would think that after God miraculously intervened on my behalf, I would feel invincible, that I was safe. But my human side prevailed, and I wavered back and forth, with fear continuing to haunt me. Part of me lived with the image of being raped and stabbed to death with the last thing I see the sweaty, hate-filled face of Larry Morrison as he presses against me and slices through my throat. Another part thought I must be God's favorite, the way He'd protected me. That Morrison better think twice about coming back for me—he had no idea who he was messing with.

I wish I could have lived in the latter of the two images, but unfortunately fear won out and drowned out the message that would allow me to live with confidence and peace. Instead, I chose to listen to the fear that led me down a destructive path.

Kevin left, and nighttime set in. I went through my routine, but once again, I added something new. That night, Jeff was not sleeping on my couch. After he left and I was done checking around the house, I pushed the dresser in front of my bedroom door. I was alone, so I barricaded myself in my room. Then I called the jail to make sure Morrison was there.

That was the first night by myself. I didn't sleep. At all.

WEDNESDAY, DAY FIVE

I'm not living, not surviving even. Just existing.

I'd asked my assistant Judy to let people know I was out of the office. She kept an eye on the news reporters camping outside my door and told me Morrison's grandmother called repeatedly demanding to speak with me. She wanted me to stop "all this," claiming her grandson had not done anything. She gave multiple news interviews asserting his innocence and blaming me.

I understood, in part, the unconditional love of a grandmother. I had my own amazing grandmother who would have fought for me if she had still been alive, but this was ridiculous. Meemaw crossed a line blaming me for what happened. I would not dignify her with a response.

Jeff came over late that evening to check on me. I was a zombie. I'd had only had a couple of hours of restless sleep since the previous Thursday night.

On Monday, I had visited my general practitioner and talked about what was going on with my body, how I couldn't control the shaking, breathing, crying, or much else. I wasn't able to sleep and overall felt numb. This feeling—unfamiliar but completely overwhelming—was unbearable. I missed the old me and wanted this to end, now.

The doctor suggested Klonopin and explained it was for panic attacks.

Panic attacks? Unaccustomed to anxiety, it took my breath away and confused me. What had happened that I could no longer seem to control my own body and emotions? My mood, my actions, my feelings were entirely up to me, or they used to be.

I would not take medicine that changed any of that. I would not let what Morrison did change my life that much. When would the constant stream of destruction associated with that man end? I'd take the prescription but I wouldn't take the pills.

But now Jeff was concerned about my health and asked me to try the Klonopin.

I was desperate and needed some sleep, so I agreed. I cut the pill in half. It didn't take long for my eyes to feel heavy and my body weak. I lay back on the couch, propping my legs up. Things got strange fast. I was dizzy and couldn't lift my limbs. My whole body went limp. Breathing was hard. I felt myself sliding off the couch, yet I couldn't stop it. I hit the floor and rolled under the coffee table lifeless.

I lay face down, immobile. Jeff moved the table and picked me up. He asked me questions: Could I walk? Could I speak? I could do neither. He carried me to my bedroom and gently laid me down on the bed. He found my cell phone and called my doctor. She advised Jeff to monitor my breathing through the night. Jeff came in periodically, watched my breathing and talked to me. I couldn't say much in return. Hours later, an overall grogginess and cloudy mind remained. Medicine wasn't going to work for me.

FRIDAY, DAY SEVEN

It's the helplessness that keeps you awake at night. Fred had showed up the day before with a truck full of treasures. With each lock, blind, or storm window added, I'd hoped to feel safer. But no matter what precautions I took, no matter how much I trained or prepared, there was a man out there willing, able, and determined to kill me. He had already tried and was planning to come back. How could I live with that?

Not sleeping didn't help. Sleep had become a burden, a job, something I had to work for.

I spent the seventh day after the incident calling counselors, desperate for someone to tell me this new world of mine was a type of normal but it wouldn't last forever. It was like being in the bottom of a deep well, so deep you can't see any light. Not even a pinpoint. Your mind tells you the light is there, but you see no evidence of it, and you can't scrape together enough faith to believe. I had never experienced such hopelessness and fear.

In an effort to gain more confidence in the office that was going to prosecute my case I called criminal defense attorneys in Central Kentucky, questioning them about their experiences with Gordie Shaw, the Commonwealth's Attorney and his assistants.

I was immediately disheartened. "They are easy to work with, like to make deals, and don't like to prosecute sex crimes." Easy to work with was fine. The other two were not. They technically wouldn't be representing me. I was considered just a witness, like any other witness, with no meaningful rights. Gordie represented the Commonwealth of Kentucky in the pursuit of protecting "the people." As a witness/victim, I was forbidden to represent myself or hire an attorney, so that office was my only option. So far, what I was hearing was a defense attorney's dream, which made him a victim's nightmare.

The only thing that kept me from feeling like helpless prey was having a loaded gun with me—in my purse, my car, my bed. The great equalizer.

It seemed the world was divided into wolves and sheep. Predators and the rest of us. Never feeling safe, waiting, seeing his face attached to every creak of the boards in my house, every bark of a dog at night, every time my motion sensor went off. I had to be prepared. He'd bested me already, and it wasn't a silly competition he beat me at. It was my life. I didn't get away from him on my own. I was gifted the chance to get away from him. Without acts of divine intervention, I would be dead. I didn't have the skills to get away from him the first time, but I was determined to be prepared the second time because it was coming. I knew it. I would be ready. I may be a sheep, but a sheep carrying a 9mm with a hollow point chambered.

Jeff and my friends Darin and Jay arranged to take me to the range to practice with my new gun. Darin helped me load my magazine. It was new, and my fingers weren't strong enough to push down the tight springs to load the bullets. I chambered a round, got my sights lined up, and assumed the proper grip and placement of feet. The only thing left was to aim and pull the trigger. All my senses were heightened. I heard the muzzle blasts of other guns around me, brass casings ejecting from the barrels and clanking off the concrete floor, the stiff cordite smell burning my nostrils. These aren't things you notice when you shoot in an open field, but at an indoor range, basically a concrete box, every sound and smell bounces around until it dissipates.

In front of me hung a paper target with a black form against a white background. But I saw only Morrison's face. My hands were trembling, making it impossible to aim.

My eyes flooded with tears. The idea of pointing this gun at Morrison and pulling the trigger devastated me. Even with all he had done to me and planned to do to me, I couldn't imagine having to kill a man. I pulled the trigger, laid the gun down, and ran out of the range.

As I charged into the lobby, Jeff ran after me with Darin and Jay right behind. In a trembling sob, barely understandable, I blurted out, "Everyone else is here to get better at shooting. I am here because I'm being hunted."

Jeff pulled me in for a giant hug. I turned my head to Darin. He looked as if his heart were breaking. He kindly said, "It's okay. It's okay."

Then I saw Jay. Quiet, strong Jay. He said nothing verbally but a thousand words of comfort radiated from his gaze, which said, "Of course you feel this way. It would be unusual if you didn't."

I don't know how to explain the power of my friends' responses other than they comforted and validated me. They weren't trying to fix the situation or stop my crying. They were simply giving me permission to be whatever I needed to be at that moment, with no pressure to fight off the fear inside me. What a blessing.

When I looked at my gun, I knew that one day I'd have to pull the trigger, over and over, until Morrison was dead. How did my life turn into this?

Even though the thought of using my gun scared me, I couldn't sleep at night unless it was beside me.

SUNDAY, DAY NINE

Sundays were for church, working out, eating with friends, napping. Before. On day nine, it was get myself prepared for returning-to-work day. Having decided I'd given up enough time to Morrison, there would be no more sitting in the house, scared to leave, not living, not working, not taking care of the clients who'd entrusted their cases, parts of their lives, to me. That was over.

I was scared, but I would push through it.

I had yet to find a counselor to help me process living while waiting to die. Yes, the worldwide mortality rate is 100 percent, but for me it wasn't some distant reality. I barely escaped it the week before. I could die in an auto accident or in a plane crash, but the likelihood of dying at the hands of a violent felon had become part of my new reality.

Preparing for work, I packed my laptop and picked an outfit. I felt like an actress in a movie preparing to play a role—someone other than myself. I called my friend Rachel and confessed I felt like a coward. Rachel politely but strongly disagreed, saying, "Courage is not the absence of fear. It is moving forward in the face of fear."

That was a defining moment for me. She'd shown me how to re-frame my feelings from weak and broken to brave and courageous which immediately bolstered my confidence. It was amazing the power of the mind, how we perceive things and how it effects our beliefs and actions. Unfortunately, this euphoric emotional peak faded quickly, overrun by fear again at the thought of going to bed.

Like every night that week, I went through my ritual. Checking the house, turning on outside lights, charging my cell phone, placing my gun on my nightstand, calling the jail, and pushing my antique dresser in front of the door.

MONDAY, DAY TEN

I got out of bed early. It didn't matter since I hadn't slept, not really.

I dressed for work, grabbed the files I'd left the office with a week ago Friday, and headed out the door. During the short walk to my car, several neighbors were doing the same. My street looked like a studio back lot of picturesque little homes filled with families. I was on the set of *Leave It to Beaver* while living a nightmare.

This was the first time I had been in my car for any period of time without Jeff. My drive to the grocery took six minutes, at most. I was now going to drive this car, this crime scene, for an hour each direction. Being in that vehicle made me feel dirty, sick, painfully tense, but I couldn't sell it until they processed the car at the crime lab. I was unable to enjoy the long, beautiful drive through rolling hills, over the Kentucky River, past farms with horses and cattle, and under wide-open sky, the stunning display of what my mom would call, "God's handiwork." Instead, I crossed the river and noticed my jaw hurt and my head ached. I mentally paused to focus on the cause and found I was grinding my teeth, to the point my head felt like it was in a vise. My hands were strained from their grip on the steering wheel.

I was livid and didn't even realize it.

Closer to the office, I called Judy to make sure no news reporters waited outside the office. She assured me they had gone. I'd grabbed a coat with a hood on it so I could cover my face if they tried to film me walking into the office. The media was not supposed to use the names or faces of victims of sexual abuse, but two networks had done so all week, sharing my name and photo and the most intimate details of the incident until my friends, family, and I called and complained. I should have been the one to tell people, but I didn't have the option. The media did it for me.

On my way, I stopped at my friend Carolyn's law firm. Carolyn was a mentor to me. A very successful private attorney and a compassionate friend. Her legal acumen and striking beauty combined to make her quite intimidating in the courtroom. She offered to take me to my office, and I quickly agreed.

I'd spoken with a therapist who encouraged me to use visualization to calm the adrenaline that pumped through my body as I resumed my work at the office and in the courthouse. I'd practiced this during my drive. In my visualization Jesus was beside me, about ten feet tall and built like a tank. This was bone-crusher Jesus. No children or lambs around this guy. He was ready to pounce if I needed Him to. It helped. It wasn't easy getting back to work, but this kind of Jesus made it manageable.

Carolyn parked beside me, two spots over from where Morrison had gotten into my car the week before. We walked the same path, the same steps, down the same narrow hallway, and into the office. I locked the door when she left.

One benefit of having the incident broadcast on the news was that opposing attorneys gave me space, so it didn't take long to catch up on the previous week of work. Which was great since I didn't function at my normal speed. I'd been at this desk, looking out these windows, for seven years. I could see the courthouse, the jail, the Sheriff's Department. The office felt safe despite what happened there, but I needed a strategy.

I called the Sheriff's Office and spoke with deputies about an emergency plan. We agreed that if they got a distress call from my office to assume it was Morrison and to come immediately, not to wait for dispatch. The door of my building was about two hundred yards from theirs. It was faster for me to yell out the window than to dial 911. On the other hand, I found out that Morrison's grandmother, the one he'd been living with since his release six days prior to my kidnapping, really did live three blocks from my office.

The sheriff was close, but Morrison would be, too, when he got out.

I left the office that day proud of myself. Proud that I wasn't under the covers, hiding. Proud that I was walking around three blocks from the place Morrison would return the minute he got out on bail. Despite the almost crippling fear, I felt like I was daring him. Living my life right under his nose. I fielded questions from colleagues, clients, and staff that first day: Are you going to close your practice? Are you going to move your office? The answer was the same. No. He doesn't get that much power over me. I've worked too long and too hard to tuck my tail and run. I'm here, and if he wants to come back for me, he won't have a hard time finding me. He got the jump on me the first time, but that wouldn't happen again. I was watching.

Every part of my life was different now. Those differences were just reminders of the time and the sense of safety he'd stolen from me—the weight of a gun always in my purse, the inability to sit on my screened-in porch, needing every door locked. We are all born with limited time, and he had stolen too much of mine. Simply taking out the garbage and checking the mail were different all because of him—both now included a loaded gun.

Each time I felt afraid, the charred black part of my soul grew. And I was constantly afraid. Months later, the black spot had grown exponentially without my realizing it. I'd let it run rampant because I wasn't paying attention. I prayed to forgive him the first night as if forgiveness was a one-time event instead of a repeated choice. I didn't realize every little change in my life and every loss I attributed to him were seeds planted deep inside me with vines that grew, spreading darkness that choked the life out of me as I provided constant nourishment with my fear and resentment.

I didn't realize the damage those unchecked feelings were doing or how far they would push me to protect myself.

I decided I'd rather confront him soon and get it over with than live with the constant waiting and wondering.

PART TWO
THE CRIMINAL'S JUSTICE SYSTEM

Our constitutionally-based criminal justice system places a high value on protecting the innocent. Among its central tenets is the idea that it is better to let a guilty person go free than to convict someone without evidence beyond a reasonable doubt.

—ROBERT SHAPIRO

CHAPTER 11

CIRCLING THE DRAIN

Anyone who kidnaps someone is to be put to death.
> —Exodus 21:16, The Holy Bible, NIV

From the moment Morrison fled the crime scene, I had concerns about my case. No photos taken, and no evidence collected. Same true for my hospital stay, until I requested photos be taken. My clothes were not bagged and labeled, and my necklace—the one with the deep gouge in it—was not preserved. The one valuable piece of evidence, my drug screen, was done at my request—and that was against the advice of Trooper Arnett.

On my drive home from the hospital, I knew I couldn't rely on my case being managed well. I'd already seen that. Over the next few days, I collected as much evidence as I could, though a decent defense attorney would try to exclude it all from the jury based on flaws in the chain of custody. There are strict requirements for the timely collection of evidence—who collects it and how it is maintained until trial—and those are well intended but again, to protect the accused. Those rules also presume diligent investigators. Who would trust a victim to take all the photos of her car, to hold on to the necklace and shirt, or to drive the car without its having been preserved? I could have taken a large knife, lacerated my dashboard and dug a gouge out of my necklace, and then handed it all over to Trooper Arnett, and no one would have known. The apathy in collecting crucial evidence was incomprehensible. The prosecutors' reputation and lack of interest was devasting. I knew winning my case was up to me.

For the first few weeks, I focused on nothing but personal safety and preserving any evidence within my control. I thought through the case as a defense attorney, trying to avoid any mistakes that could discredit me on the stand. I even avoided Jeff. Despite the trauma of the incident forging us together for a while, we did ultimately quit dating. Although I desperately wanted his protective presence, we did not work in a dating relationship. Ultimately our breakup made Jeff's testimony at trial even more credible.

I was also paying for and insuring my crime scene car that I couldn't drive. Not because someone told me not to drive it, but because as an attorney I knew it should be processed for evidence—someday. So after the first week, it sat on my family farm for a year.

Outside the courtroom, no one was actively working to build the case against Morrison, and inside the courtroom seemed the same. Still, multiple experts advised me not to review the court record with the eye of an advocate. If I did, defense would use it to alienate me from the jury, such that they might see me first as an attorney working the case and not a victim. I took their advice.

Mr. Shapiro correctly says that the basic tenet of the Criminal Justice System is to protect the defendant. Ipso facto, the victim is not considered, not even as an afterthought. Hence, my referring to it as the Criminal's Justice System. Any system consisting of human elements, subjective interpretation, little accountability, and almost no transparency will be at great risk for arbitrary and capricious results. The world of criminal justice consists of all of the above, and the victim is at its mercy. As the weeks turned to months, my frustration grew as I saw a lack of interest in working my case and my requests to collect evidence in my possession ignored.

I emailed detailed lists noting witnesses to contact and evidence to gather to the prosecutor's office. I did this for months without response. I spoke with experts in all areas of criminal law. I called a prosecutor in a neighboring town who suggested we contact Morrison's previous prison library, to look for maps or items he checked out related to his planned kidnapping, rape, and murder. It was a great idea, but Gordie wouldn't do it.

As I watched my case circle the drain, I grew more confident it would not end well for me. I continued to contact the prosecutor's office asking questions and seeking updates. I repeatedly requested that they collect my shirt and necklace, find the bag Morrison had with him, take photos of my car, and get the photos taken at the hospital of my injuries. I wanted my car taken to the crime lab, so the knife marks could be evaluated to show the jury how violent Morrison was with me. Nothing happened. I called to report a witness who'd called my office after seeing Morrison's mugshot on the news, saying he had been in the parking lot the night of the incident and he'd seen Morrison hanging around. Nothing happened. The pattern was clear. I would call, email, remind, and ask. No reply. I would wait and repeat. Nothing happened.

Meanwhile, I lived the same frustrating day over and over, working to ensure my future safety. What I needed was hope—hope I would have a chance at a fair trial, one where the jury would be presented with enough evidence to lead them to a guilty verdict and they wouldn't have to rely solely on my testimony. I engaged in the routine of work, home, church, and friends. I dropped my gym membership since I avoided public places with a lot of people. I started walking but only in front of my house, never more than a hundred yards either direction from my front door. My sweet friend Amy went along with my unusual behavior as I had to keep my house in my line of sight while walking. She endured a dizzying amount of turning around as we weaved and crisscrossed my street to create more steps along that very short path. I was trying to make the best of my own sort of prison, even though I remained unable to plan a future, unwilling to spend much time away from my home, unable to sleep, and unwilling to go anywhere without my gun.

I felt like I was constantly fighting. Fighting for my future. Fighting for a voice. Fighting for safety.

* * *

I had heard (not from the prosecutor's office) the District Court set Morrison's bail at $100,000. It was surprising how many unemployed inmates were able to make bail. They could put up 10 percent or use land, houses, or other assets. I didn't know his family or financial situation but I did know if Morrison got released, he would be living three blocks from my office.

I got Trooper Arnett's cell phone number and contacted him in June. He advised me he was scheduled to testify in front of the grand jury. I asked him to call me as soon as it was over. He didn't have to, but he called me while he was still in the courthouse.

A grand jury decides whether or not the prosecutor has sufficient evidence to indict—to bring formal, criminal charges against a person for a felony. The grand jury hears only the prosecution's version of the evidence, so it is easy to get an indictment. That is why it is commonly said a grand jury "will indict a ham sandwich." Gordie was presenting the evidence to the grand jury as I waited to hear the results. Very little could go wrong, but I anxiously awaited Trooper Arnett's call, quite literally staring at my phone and unable to focus on much else that afternoon. He rang, and I grabbed the phone immediately.

"What happened," I partly asked, partly pleaded. I could hear his footsteps echoing through the tiled halls. He didn't have much detail to share other than two things—one frustrating and one terrifying.

He was a relatively new state trooper, and my case was his first big case, presumably his first grand jury appearance on a major crime. He said that after Gordie finished questioning, he was asked one question, from an older female juror. "Why did she let him in her car?" That question struck fear through me like a lightning strike splitting me to pieces. I had to collect myself before I could respond.

"How did you answer that question? What about the attempted rape or attempted murder? What did you say about that?" My questions poured out all at once.

"Nothing," he said. "Gordie didn't ask me any questions about attempted rape or attempted murder." He didn't have a response for the woman's question, he didn't discuss the two most serious charges, and he was the only witness for prosecution before the grand jury. If he didn't talk about it, the grand jury didn't hear it. If they didn't hear it, they wouldn't indict.

The phone call ended as quickly as it began. My mind was reeling. Did they even present attempted rape and attempted murder? They couldn't, not if their only witness didn't testify about it.

I was frustrated and livid about their failure to present such obvious charges. Each charge meant more potential time in prison for Morrison and more time away from me. Beyond my own personal protection, though, I was frustrated by the vast difference in treatment as a victim at the mercy of a state prosecutor as opposed to the client of a private attorney. Private attorneys answer to their clients and the bar association. Prosecutors don't have that kind of accountability. They answer to the voters who elect them. I wasn't the client. Just the victim.

I had no recourse.

The scariest part of the conversation was the question that haunted me for years. I doubt that woman had any idea that her question struck such lasting fear and self-doubt. Of all the questions to ask, why that one? Did she really have reason to believe that if I hadn't *let* him in the car, he would have abandoned his plans? She couldn't seriously think that. He would have dragged me behind the tree line at the back of the parking lot and done it all there. Or waited for me in the building one day until Judy left and then raped and killed me there. That one isolated moment, his getting in my car, seemed to carry an unduly significant amount of weight—weight that pointed fault back to me.

I understand there is a victim-blaming mindset out there, but the comment that was innocuous to her was paralyzing to me. What if the jury agreed? What if they focused on my actions? Why did she do this or that? Why didn't she jump out of a moving car into traffic and hope that she'd survive getting run over? Or maybe they'd ask what Trooper Arnett asked me at the hospital: "Why didn't you drive your car into a tree?"

I already knew from research that a life sentence was statistically unlikely from a Bourbon County jury, even with the best of evidence. The prosecution's missteps further decreased my odds, and now I realized I would have to combat potential victim blaming within the jury. My fear of a not guilty verdict had just increased exponentially, along with my desire to protect myself.

Being hunted wasn't all that made life difficult. Watching the system that was designed to protect the defendant repeatedly betray me was brutal. My case appeared to be an epic failure from the beginning. I scrambled to find any semblance of hope from the system—the system I was a part of. I understand it is called the *practice* of law for a reason. The human element guarantees error. Memories fail. Well-intended but overworked law enforcement officers, attorneys, and judges are subject to mistakes and failures of judgment. Yet, even as I watched all this, I had to trust my life to it. Maybe ignorance truly is bliss. If I hadn't known how my case should be handled, maybe the mistakes wouldn't have been so obvious, and I wouldn't have felt as pressed to protect myself. People assume I had an advantage because I knew the system, but that knowledge showed me what wasn't happening, and that terrified me. Which in turn forced me to admit I was willing to go further than an otherwise polite society might deem acceptable. But I am getting ahead of myself.

My next call was to Gordie's office. I got an answer, and that was unusual.

"Why didn't you present attempted rape and attempted murder to the grand jury?" I decided to bluff a little and act like I knew with certainty. I withheld my conversation with Arnett since Arnett was doing me a favor and I wanted to keep that line of communication open.

"We did," he said. "The grand jury didn't indict."

My heart sank. I couldn't believe it. *Was I so blinded by my emotion that I lost all objectivity? Was my case that weak?* I hadn't seen the evidence and certainly didn't know what I know now—that Codell and Vickie Gibson gave strong statements that supported a charge of attempted murder.

I hung up and called Steve in a full-blown meltdown. When he answered, I started speaking rapidly to the point of nonsense.

"Sharon, you are swirling. I can't understand you." Steve was calm and trying to direct me.

I kept going. "Grand jury . . . no indictment . . . attempted rape . . . attempted murder," came out in bits and pieces with bursts of sobbing in between.

"Where are you?" Steve asked.

"At home," I managed to say.

He said, "I'll be over in a bit."

I hung up and knew I'd feel better after I talked to Steve. I trusted his expertise, and I could count on his honest appraisal of the case. Still, as I waited for him, I became angrier and angrier. How could this happen? A grand jury doesn't decide guilt or innocence. It is just a procedure to ensure a prosecutor has sufficient evidence before indicting someone.

They could indict a ham sandwich but not Morrison?

I walked into the backyard, pacing back and forth. While my mind raced and tears flowed, I picked a fight with God. I'm sure God was shaking in his boots—or whatever footwear God dons.

"What are you doing? You are God, nothing is too hard for you, yet a grand jury outmaneuvered you on this? You really don't want him getting indicted for attempted rape? Attempted murder? You can't be serious. I've never asked why, why me? Now I am. Why, why are you doing this? Why are you letting this happen? I'm so sick of this. If this is the best you've got then I'm better off without you. Just leave me alone."

Even as the words came out, part of me felt sick. I was raised not just to believe in God but to have a personal relationship with him, to make life decisions after prayerfully seeking God's wisdom. I genuinely loved God and knew He loved me, so this was a bold turn. It was drastic. It was stupid. I expected to feel empty, but I already felt so empty it seemed there was nothing left inside of me.

I turned and headed up the steps to the back porch. As I opened the door, a tiny voice inside me couldn't help but make some small plea. *I really didn't mean what I said. Please don't leave me, God. You're all I've got. But I am furious with you.*

Sitting on the porch I tried to prepare for a meaningful conversation with Steve. What were the next steps? What could I do to increase Morrison's possible sentence? If the jury thought I wasn't kidnapped because I "let him in" my car, then he could walk. How would I help them understand what happened?

I must be living someone else's jacked-up life.

When Steve got there, I caught him up on what I knew. When I told him they couldn't get an indictment on attempted rape or murder, he confirmed the case was clearly being mishandled. Having my friend near calmed my thoughts. He said he would write Gordie a letter, offering his assistance in any way needed. When he did, there was no response. Steve later called Gordie's office, but he was ignored too.

As we continued to talk, I asked Steve something I'd wanted to ask but wasn't sure if I wanted the answer.

"Do you really think Morrison was going to kill me?"

Steve is not dramatic. He sees all the angles and stays objective. He paused. I really thought he was going to say no. Or maybe "There is no way to know, Sharon." Part of me died inside when he finally said, "Yes. And I think he will try again."

That was all I needed to hear. No more doubt, no more telling myself I'd over-reacted. A man out there tried to kill me and still intended to do so. And this prosecutor's office had just made that much more likely.

I refused to believe Morrison had not been indicted on attempted rape or attempted murder. There was physical evidence of a violent, sexually motivated attack, more than enough for charges. Some prosecutors avoid such cases, though, believing them hard to prove and a threat to their win-loss ratio. All I wanted was to put Morrison away for a long time so I could go to bed at night without pushing a dresser in front of my bedroom door. None of this made any sense, and after another few weeks, I'd had enough. I called Gordie's office and requested a CD of the grand jury hearing. I was put on hold.

Gordie got on the line.

"I want to listen to the recording of the grand jury," I said confidently.

"You can't." Gordie said.

I didn't trust this. I decided to push. "Yes, I can. Morrison and his attorney can listen to it, and so can I. I want a copy of the CD as soon as possible."

"Wait a minute," Gordie said, and I was on hold again.

He returned to the phone explaining there had been some confusion and his office had *not* presented evidence on attempted rape and attempted murder. He said he would do so and let me know. I never heard anything more about this.

I called the Commonwealth of Kentucky Attorney General's Office and asked for a new prosecutor. That didn't go anywhere.

I called the post commander for the Kentucky State Police and asked why no evidence had been collected. I called repeatedly.

Finally, months later, Trooper Arnett showed up at my office. He walked in and took a seat across from me.

"Good to see you. Are you here to pick up my shirt and necklace and take my car to the crime lab?" I asked as I stood to gather the items I was hoping he would finally collect as evidence.

He was quite proud and explained he had stopped by on his way to receive an award of some sort relating to the amount of citations he had written.

My mouth dropped open. "So you aren't here to move my case forward, collect evidence, or do anything along those lines? But you're here to tell me you've been busy writing speeding tickets on I-75?"

"No. I was asked to stop by. I can't do anything unless Gordie tells me to." He seemed to believe he was not free to work my case without detailed and specific instruction from the prosecutor.

I stood up and opened my office door for him.

"Thank you. I need to get back to work."

As he made his way to the door, I dialed the post commander to lodge another futile complaint.

Having zero results trying to work within the legal system, I was on the lookout for any outside sources of help. I found it in an unexpected place: a news reporter. When reporters first crashed the scene en masse, they turned my world upside down by sharing my name and sordid details of my kidnapping with the world. The worst moment of my life had become a spectator sport with front row seats for everyone. So when a reporter from a major network affiliate called, I almost hung up.

She quickly introduced herself as Leigh and apologized for how my story had been treated in the media, exposing my name as a victim of a sex crime.

"Thank you, Leigh. I appreciate it." Good move, Leigh. Endearing yourself to me in hopes of getting something back.

She continued by explaining TV stations typically withhold the name of sex crime victims.

"I mentioned that when I spoke with the stations' general managers and their attorneys," letting her know I wouldn't tolerate any shenanigans from the media.

She understood my frustration and said she was willing to continue to develop my story.

This was what I had been waiting for. "As long as your coverage allows me to maintain dignity and privacy, I will help you tell a better story. I'm obviously limited in what I can share, but what I can share, I will."

This was a mutually beneficial deal. She was getting a more detailed story than her competitors, and I could shape how my story developed, which meant I could influence the perception of the populace. Future jury members.

Over time she earned my trust. After I shared several details with Leigh, she interviewed Morrison in jail. She produced a powerful segment on the kidnapping, creating an incriminating piece of evidence. Morrison tried to evade her questions but because she knew details she was able to corner him. Finally he blurted out, "I'm sorry for what I done but I've served enough time for it." She'd gotten an admission of guilt out of him that, if shown to a jury, would help give them confidence in a guilty verdict. I was thrilled. I contacted the prosecutor's office asking them to subpoena it. No response.

More evidence circling the drain.

CHAPTER 12

CONSPICUOUSLY ABSENT

The system. This system that I longed to be part of since I was a child. That I worked so hard to gain admittance to. Preparing for the LSAT while living in Russia, getting recommendations, going through three years of voluminous reading, mock trial, moot court, writing, studying international law in Russia and at the Sorbonne in Paris. Studying for the bar and taking the exam after being in a car wreck with my neck and right arm in a brace. That was just to get licensed to practice. Then years of building a practice and all the work and sacrifice that came with it.

My first trial came long before all that work. It happened the summer before my fourth-grade studies began. It was grueling, with a brutal opposing attorney who would stop at nothing to win. He was about to enter eighth grade and possessed a world of knowledge I wouldn't gain for years to come. He was clever, quick thinking, and always a few steps ahead of me. Who was this wily opponent? Rick, my older brother. What was the case? Theft by unlawful taking. Who was the criminal? Excuse me, alleged criminal? The very same Rick. He chose to represent himself.

CAMELOT FARM COURT

Muse v. Muse

Honorable Dick Muse presiding

My friend Beth and I had been outside playing an intense game of Charlie's Angels. We'd just solved the mystery and closed the case when we decided to move our fun inside the house out of the summer heat. Our Kentucky farmhouse dining room, filled with antiques and loads of glasses, crystal, and china from previous generations, made the perfect place to set up a little store to sell items to Beth. I organized all my "inventory" and awaited customers. I didn't have to wait long. Beth walked in and was looking around when who else entered my store, but Rick. I was immediately suspicious. He was up to something. He was my big brother, my best friend, and my hero. Still is. But I knew him. He was going to do something to interfere with our game.

I turned my head for a second to speak to Beth and out of the corner of my eye I saw a quick motion, Rick bolted out of the room laughing. A crystal vase had gone missing. The hot pursuit began. I accused him of stealing, and he denied it. Dared me to prove it. We decided to resolve our case in court. Muse court.

When Dad came in from work, we agreed that he would preside over our case—we waived a jury trial. Moving forward with my dad as judge was fair. We each made our arguments, presented our evidence, and I called Beth as a witness. Rick tried to shred her on cross-examination. We waited as the judge took a short recess to review the evidence.

Although Dad—wait, Judge Muse—agreed something was amiss with Rick, he ruled that I had not presented enough evidence to convict. Rick was free to go. I was devastated. How could I lose? Truth was on my side.

What I didn't know as a child and didn't realize until decades later, was that truth isn't relevant in a courtroom. Truth is not the deciding factor in a court of law. What the jury hears is filtered through layers of rules of evidence, criminal procedure and constitutional protections for the defendant. So much so the whole truth is often conspicuously absent from the courtroom.

*   *   *

That "trial" was a fun game as a fourth grader but one that fed my deep-seated desire to fight for justice for anyone, including myself. Justice may look like many different things. While I lived in Russia, justice looked like my starting a nonprofit to help orphanages by shipping medical supplies, shoes, clothing, toys, educational supplies, and Christmas gifts to children who had nothing. It looked like volunteering to work with Habitat for Humanity, buying gifts for Angel Tree, and donating time and money to many nonprofits. Doing things to help make the world better and to help people that were unable to do for themselves. That concept was imbedded in me by watching my parents live their lives that way.

To have devoted so much to humanity and to the pursuit of justice, I was devastated to watch my case being ignored. Evidence was spoiled or failed to be collected, things I can only attribute to a lack of commitment from those whose job it was to pursue justice for me. It wasn't just the lack of pursuit that bothered me. It was the apparent disinterest.

I had requested photos, asked for my shirt and necklace to be picked up as evidence, and researched a weapons expert to match the knife blade to the marks in my car. I begged for someone to interview the man who called my office stating he noticed Morrison hanging around the back door of my building. All of this was ignored. Completely ignored.

I called the Kentucky State Police Post asking for someone to investigate my case.

Nothing happened.

I called the Commonwealth's Attorney Office asking for someone to interview me so I didn't have to write more than one witness statement.

Nothing happened.

I called the Attorney General's Office asking for a different prosecutor.

Nothing happened.

My life was on the line, and it appeared no one was doing what the public relied on a public servant to do. I was told the prosecutor's office was busy with murder trials and would get to mine later. Unfortunately, evidence expires. It must be collected in a timely manner and preserved properly, or the jury will never see it. A decent defense attorney could easily kick out everything if it was not collected properly. I finally lost my patience.

I called the prosecutor's office and got a recording, not unusual. I shouted into the answering machine that if someone didn't start paying attention to my case, there would be another murder case for them to deal with. That one did get me a return call. To placate me, they set up a meeting with an assistant prosecutor but one who had nothing to do with my case.

I tried protecting myself by working within the legal system, but that didn't work. I tried protecting myself by using the media, but that didn't work either. Nothing worked.

I was done. I had to take care of things myself.

CHAPTER 13

THE STAIRWELL

Chance favors the prepared mind.

—Louis Pasteur

I got back to the gym. Every day I worked out, getting stronger, knowing I was ready to beat Morrison in a physical confrontation if I had to. Eventually, I discovered Krav Maga, a practical and intuitive self-defense system without all the complications of other classes I'd taken, and loved it. These boosted my confidence, though my mindset and my gun would always be my primary sources of security.

But I also had to consider the cocaine found in Morrison's system when he kidnapped me. Combined with his natural adrenaline, it made him almost unstoppable. He just kept coming. I experienced the adrenaline phenomenon myself one day in a self-defense class when I was "attacked" from behind, with a bag thrown over my head, and had to fight my way out. I beat the attacker mercilessly and refused to let him tap out. He tried three times, but my adrenaline was pumping so hard, I didn't stop. He tried to collapse, but I picked him up and kept going. I ended up breaking a toe but didn't notice it for hours due to adrenaline blocking the pain.

How would I manage Morrison if he came back jacked-up on drugs? I hoped I would respond the same way I did in class that day, but the way my body reacted to him in the courtroom told me I had a lot of training to do to be ready.

One day, a friend of mine and bailiff in the Courthouse, Deputy Jim Traylor, stopped me after a court appearance. Jim was a certified sniper trainer and worked with law enforcement agencies all over the United States.

"How are you doing, dear?" he said as he leaned in close.

"I'm here but not sure I'm okay. Trying to stay safe but never feeling that way. I can't even shoot, my hands shake so violently. And I know I'll have to use my gun when he comes back for me."

Jim stepped in closer and said, "I'll tell you what we will do. I'll take you to the range and help you feel safe again."

We started training that week.

A few weeks later, my dad called "How is your practice at the range?"

"It's unbelievable how bad I am. I'm lucky to hit the target."

"I've been concerned about your relying on a handgun. When your hands are shaking, your aim will be unreliable. And if he is on drugs, he may not slow down even if you do hit him. I'd like you to consider a pump-action shotgun for your home. You wouldn't have to be as precise or as close."

I liked the idea of not having to be close to him. I'd read that if a perp gets into within twenty-one feet, he can get to you with a knife before you can draw your gun and shoot. My house was so small that his presence in any room would put him within twelve feet of me.

Buying a shotgun. My life was now made up of strange new sources of comfort—my new normal.

I loved that my dad kept asking if he could take me to the range, but I didn't want him to see the tears that poured down my face while I fired my gun. I also didn't want him to know that my practice had changed. I had asked Jim for some very specific training.

It was like any other spring day. From my desk in my second-story office, the beautiful blue sky drew my eyes outward. I saw the Justice Building, parking lot, Sheriff's Office, and . . . inmates?

A group of inmates from another county, led by a sheriff's deputy, filed into the Courthouse. I stared at the prisoners through the window, and then something caught in my mind. I pushed back from my desk and headed straight out the door.

I knew exactly what I needed to do.

I told Judy I'd be back, crossed the parking lot, and made my way to the Circuit Clerk's office to check on the charges I had filed against Morrison in Scott County the Monday after the incident. There was no date yet on the docket, so I had time before he would be transferred here for his arraignment.

As I left the building, I checked the doors the deputies brought inmates through. They required a swipe card, so I couldn't open them. I could, however, access the back stairs, blocked from the general public and typically used to move inmates to the courtroom.

One of the deputies who transported prisoners is a friend. I went to find him. We had discussed my case many times, and he knew I was training at the range to try to feel safe. I caught up with him as he walked across the parking lot from the Courthouse to the Sheriff's Office.

I greeted him and asked, "Can you tell me how it works when you transport prisoners from another county?"

It came out more intense than I would have liked.

"What specifically do you want to know?" he asked without curiosity.

"Which set of steps would you use to get them to the courtroom?"

After a pause he responded, "Which set of steps would you like me to use?"

Uh-oh. He knows what I'm thinking. "The back steps?" I said, but it came out more like a question. I couldn't believe what I was saying.

"Okay."

"What would you do if you saw me waiting in the stairwell?"

After a longer pause, "I'm sure I wouldn't see a thing." As he dropped his head and walked away, I caught a glimpse of something in his eyes, maybe pity.

I had a plan. I'd wait for Morrison in the stairwell. With my gun.

I was no longer the prey—I was the hunter. I felt strong. And I liked it. I was tired of being afraid.

It may have appeared from the outside that I was coping as well as someone could. I responded with strength and determination, researching my case, pushing the prosecutor, taking self-defense classes, making my home a fortress, getting my license to carry a deadly weapon, and keeping a gun with me at all times. A look at my inner workings would reveal I was terrified—faking my way through life. That level of fear was what drove me to create a logic-driven form of self-preservation, what I called "proactive self-protection," ensuring my safety would not be left to chance. Chance favors only the prepared mind.

Proactive self-protection is when you refuse to sit by and watch someone stalk, hunt, or plan to cause you grievous bodily harm. Instead, you don't wait until you are victimized; you take action when the threat is present. Self-defense means you are already vulnerable, reacting to some act of violence. To protect myself, I needed to be proactive, not reactive. Logically this made sense, but I couldn't figure out where to draw the line. Certainly, as a lawyer, I couldn't condone it—it was not a recognizable, affirmative defense in court. But as a former victim, I was a big fan. Once I came up with the concept, I embraced it wholeheartedly and slept better at night. It felt like the fog that enveloped me started to lift. I didn't have to wait every day the rest of my life wondering when he was coming back to do unspeakable things to me and hope I'd survive. I was going to get to him first.

Despite the newfound hope of coming up with a plan, my soul still felt charred black, never to be whole again. Morrison had marred me internally. It festered until a disturbing bond formed between perpetrator and victim, something evil that tethered our souls together and linked his future to mine. Oddly, someone who previously meant nothing to me, a client I would not recognize in a crowd, transitioned from immaterial to indissoluble. The experience created a suffocating and vile connection to that menace. The very presence of it made me feel dirty, like I'd been dragged down to a pit by a bottom feeder, drowning me. This oppressive darkness hung over me like the Sword of Damocles. It was as if I were dead already. It was going to be me or him—but we both couldn't survive this. This plan was freedom.

One thing I was sure of—as ignorant as Morrison was, he wouldn't bring a knife. Not next time. Which of us survived depended on who remained calm, had the best aim, and pulled the trigger faster and longer.

Jim and I practiced at the range with all types of scenarios. He had me use my left hand, my right hand; pull the gun off a bench, from my side, from a car door;

and change clips with lightning speed. We practiced with my eyes shut, with him pushing me physically, and with him getting in my personal space making aggressive moves and verbal threats. At first I couldn't see the target as tears flooded my eyes. After a few weeks, I was shooting tight center clusters. Confident. Ready.

I went to the gun range often and practiced shooting, seeing Morrison's face on each target. I imagined all types of scenarios: his coming at me with a gun, his breaking into my house, and his waiting for me outside my office, inside my office, or in a parking lot. Morrison would have to know I was ready for him this time. I was determined to be better, faster, and more precise with my gun than he would be. I ran drills in my home, counting how many seconds it would take for someone to bust down my door and get to my bed. I then practiced until I got up, grabbed my gun, and had it ready to shoot in less time than it took for the imaginary assailant to get to my bed.

To train my mind I worked with experts who studied trauma and the brain and attended a full week of counselor training for a process called EMDR, Eye Movement Desensitization and Reprocessing. It's used to reprogram the biomechanics of the brain and reduce the side effects after injury from trauma. For me, the trauma manifested itself as the adrenaline rush that caused shaking and which consumed me at times. I wanted to know I could manage it—a huge consideration in my ability to hit a target, a moving target no less.

My confidence grew along with my skills. I knew I would not react the same way the next time Morrison came for me, and I knew there would be a next time. But no amount of therapy or safety measures was effective in getting the fear of Morrison out of my head. The only thing I knew with confidence was that waiting for him to return and hope I'd survive the second time was no longer an option. I had to be proactive.

I didn't see it as killing a man. It seemed no different than avoiding any other certain form of death. If while driving, a car wreck occurred in front of me, I would break in an attempt to maneuver around the imminent danger created by a pileup of vehicles. My actions would be primarily driven by instinct. The same instinct for self-preservation fueled my proactive self-protection.

I didn't just decide one day to plan a murder. The idea came to me over time, one tiny seed planted hundreds of times a day with the mismanaged criminal case, the fear I lived with, the waiting for it to happen again. It developed so subtly that when I realized what I'd been thinking about, the decision seemed practical, necessary, and completely logical.

In the Old Testament I'd read of Moses witnessing an Egyptian beating an Israelite, and the injustice of it made Moses so angry he beat the Egyptian to death. Yet God later referred to Moses as his friend—he even struck Moses's sister with leprosy when she spoke ill of him. Then there was David who killed Uriah in order to hide his adultery with Uriah's wife. Yet God later referred to David as a man after His own heart.

These men, patriarchs of the Christian and Jewish religions, committed many acts of great faith. I'd read their stories since I was a child, but I was seeing them in a new and twisted light, one that fueled my own burgeoning ideas.

To me, what I planned was justifiable both morally and spiritually. I was a wolf, circling my prey and waiting for access. I just needed to get to him.

CHAPTER 14

FREEDOM

To forgive is to set a prisoner free and discover that the prisoner is you.

—Lewis B. Smedes

AUGUST 2006

After 120 days made up of hundreds of thoughts each day about my personal safety, living in a prison of my own while waiting for him to return, I had an unusual experience.

It was a Monday morning, and I was taking my time getting ready for work. I didn't have to be in court that day, so I decided to read my Bible in bed and indulge in quiet time to think about things. I still felt empty and black inside even though my new plan gave me a glimmer of hope that I wouldn't have to live this way forever.

Feeling like a wolf ushered in a sense of power but at the same time drained me. I thought my sense of security would return, but it didn't. While praying, I had a strong impression that I should attend the Faces of Christ retreat, an intense spiritual retreat where attendees disconnect from the world from a Thursday to a Sunday. But I'd been to that retreat in the past and had even volunteered to help. They always sold out of tickets long before the event, and the next one was scheduled for the following Thursday. Organizers needed to know well in advance who was coming because they ask people who know the attendees to contribute information to make the weekend more meaningful.

I told myself all the reasons why I shouldn't contact the leader of the retreat. Who goes twice? It's not like my life was falling apart.

The impression morphed into a feeling, a persistent feeling that irritated me. So I called Lea who runs the program.

When I asked about the prospect of attending, this was, of course, her answer: "What great timing, Sharon, we just had a cancellation."

Ugh. Even doing the absolute minimum, this retreat would still take a lot of effort. It required attendees to think about their lives, and I was already doing that nonstop. I really didn't have the strength to examine myself more. But with the strange, persistent feeling and the odd timing of the cancellation, I thought there could be a reason I needed to reflect on my life, to stop reacting out of fear and start acting out of my will. I couldn't imagine why God would think I needed something like that.

If you are laughing or rolling your eyes in disbelief, I promise I had that exact thought. Yes, I was planning to murder someone, but it was proactive self-protection and placed me with the likes of David and Moses, so what kind of issue could God have with that?

That Thursday, I headed to southern Indiana to a beautiful lodge surrounded by woods and a giant lake. I walked into the lobby wondering what was in store for me since I had experienced such an intense pull to go there.

As we made our way through the program, I was convinced God had brought me here to consider a better balance between my work and personal life. And nothing more.

The time away from devices, television, reporters calling my house, and people asking me about the incident was peaceful. I spent a lot time thinking, praying, and considering my future. It never crossed my mind that my plan for Morrison was why God wanted my full attention. I believed God created and loved Morrison as much as He loved me. I didn't think He liked him as much—I was sure of it—but my plan to shoot Morrison while cuffed and in custody in the stairwell still seemed like a clever and logical plan.

On Saturday night we gathered in a quiet room with soft music and heard a presentation about God's great love for us. Then we were left with time alone to meditate and pray. It was a particularly moving event, but again, all my thoughts and prayers were about my future, areas of my life I needed to change to be a better daughter, partner, and friend.

After spending time in deep thought, I walked to a designated area to kneel and pray. We were asked to write about areas of our lives we were willing to turn over to God, not to ignore them but to petition God for help and acknowledge that these things were beyond our control. As I started writing, my hand seemed to have a mind of its own. I watched as the pencil scratched out LARRY MORRISON—FORGIVENESS—RELEASE. I paused, confused by what I wrote. Why was I thinking about Morrison? A prayer started forming on paper. I had forgiven him the night of the incident, so what was this about forgiveness? I watched, quieted my mind, and saw a beautiful prayer fill the page. I prayed it and openly wept.

I thought the black, scorched part of me that consumed me, eating me alive from the inside out, had been because of him. That my time in the car with Morrison had "rubbed off" some of the evil attached to him that ate away at me.

A stream of losses ran through my head. I could no longer go to the grocery store without a gun and an escape plan, sleep at night, enjoy a walk in my neighborhood, drive with the windows down, visit a friend, walk out my door without checking my postage-stamp-sized front yard. Hundreds of moments that took place repeatedly every day. With each moment, my rage toward Morrison grew. And that black vine grew too, wrapping around my organs and choking the life out of me until I was a hollow shell mirroring other people because I forgot how to live life.

The emptiness I'd felt, the hardened rage, the almost consuming need to liberate the feral Morrison was gone. Literally gone. I had thought getting rid of Morrison was the only way to get my soul back, to find myself again, to live again. But I didn't realize that every moment I thought about it, dwelled on it, planned for it, was destroying me. Morrison hadn't stolen my joy—I'd given it away.

I knelt there in shock. Shock that the intense drive to hunt him down was gone, shock that I wasn't filled with rage at the thought of him, shock that my perspective had changed on all the things I had seen as a loss, things I now saw I'd chosen to do to stay safe. Not to see his death as my only way out but rather my response, my perspective, as my way out. This change brought me up out of the pit of my own making. Letting go of him, releasing him, forgiving him had nothing to do with Morrison and everything to do with me. My resentment was destroying me, and now I was free. Truly free.

I didn't expect this turning point. I didn't think I needed it. I didn't want it. I had enjoyed feeling like a predator, a wolf, a warrior. And I was going to stay in that mode. It would just look very different now.

Since I wasn't going to kill Morrison, I had to find a way to stay out of his crosshairs if he was released, a way to live life without his getting to me. Early on, I planned to go to Russia. Within the first few weeks, I put my passport, documents for a Russian visa, and $30,000 cash in a safety deposit box. My mom agreed to manage my financial affairs, including renting out my house, if I decided to flee. I told my family and friends and Kim and Judy at the office that if they didn't hear from me for a day or two, I was likely headed to Russia and would contact them later. I arranged for another attorney to take over my practice. I could live a long time in Russia with $30,000.00 cash. I had friends who would help me find housing, I could work for a while teaching law and wait it out. Wait for the trial to come and pray for a life sentence.

Why Russia? I lived there for three years as a missionary. I had incredible adventures with friends I love and adore to this day. Yuri, Marina, Kostya, Elena, and Yana. Slava Tarasov and his family. I lived in St. Petersburg and later Chelyabinsk, close to the Ural Mountains. Morrison would never find me there.

When I decided running wasn't going to work for me, I had to come up with a different plan. The plan to get to him first. After seeing the flaws in that logic, I had to find a way to live my life and stay safe. Exercising, practicing with my gun, and developing a personal safety mindset would have to work.

Let me be clear, if Morrison were released, I would defend myself using everything I had. What is different is now I am not going to hunt him down or ambush him in a stairwell. I would pray he died in prison. But if he ever got out, I would be waiting. And I'd be ready.

CHAPTER 15

TRIAL WEAR

Dress shabbily and they remember the dress; dress impeccably and they remember the woman.

—Coco Chanel

The trial date I had been living and dying for was moved eight times, eventually landing on April 18–24, 2007, a year after my abduction. Each change in the date was a roller coaster of emotion, frustration, anger, and fear. It meant adjusting how long I had to hold my breath to wait for my life to start again.

My entire life rested on this one event. I divided my life into two parts, before trial and after. I would think about dating again, I might take a walk outside or ride my bike, I could go to the grocery without a loaded gun in my purse, and I would sleep at night . . . all after the trial. Life was hanging in the balance knowing my future, post-trial, could be unrecognizable. Juries do strange things. I had to be prepared for a not guilty verdict. Each trial postponement drained my breath, my optimism, and my waning hope.

So I desperately clung to what I could control. I never stopped pushing, begging, and pleading with the prosecutor's office, but I switched my focus to my time on the stand. How would I get the jury to feel the need to protect me, to be more concerned with my future than with Morrison's? I didn't want them to focus on what a life sentence would take away from him but rather what anything less than a life sentence for him would take away from me.

This prosecutor's office dives into a case right before it starts—not my modus operandi—but I could grow comfortable with their process *if* evidence was gathered and preserved the way the law requires. But it wasn't. Most was outdated, spoiled, and inadmissible. Knowing there would be a paucity of physical evidence at trial, the only thing I could do was endear myself to the jury and hope that was enough.

As a trial attorney, I know juries are often persuaded by the personalities, appearance, and demeanor of the attorneys. Take my first jury trial. Opposing counsel had been practicing law longer than I'd been alive, yet I won. When I stood to approach the jury for my opening and closing arguments, I had to lean on the jury box because my pantyhose were sliding down my waist toward my knees, yet I won. I was sweating profusely and spoke to the jury with long pauses between each point, distracted by trying to keep my hose from dropping to my ankles, yet I won.

The next day, my friend Anna called to ask if I represented a client in a trial the previous day. Her co-worker was the jury foreperson and had told her what an effective attorney I'd been. The jury loved how I walked right up to the jury bench, spoke slowly, and paused between statements to give them time to think. When I told Anna the real reason behind my actions, we both laughed until we cried. The lesson: you can't predict what a jury will like or what a jury will do.

Still, no matter how you do it, the goal of any lawyer is to win the hearts of the jury. If they like you, they will trust you, and if they like and trust you, it goes a long way toward your client. For my part, this definitely meant appropriate eye contact with and appreciation for the jury, just not to the point of appearing phony. Juries smell phony a mile away. Also, as the victim and not the attorney, it was not in my best interest to appear strong, confident, or powerful. I hated the word *victim*, but I needed to show myself as that to this jury—starting with my wardrobe. My appearance was one of the few aspects of the trial I could control, and I intended to take full advantage. It felt horribly vulnerable and powerless to place my future in the hands of twelve strangers, but I had to present myself to them as a victim so they would embrace my story.

Trial wear may seem trifling, but it is not. In the time it takes me to walk the well—the space in front of the judge's bench to the witness stand—the jury will decide if they like me, if they trust me, and if they want to protect me. I'd known this for years from reading countless articles in trial lawyer publications. Jury research ordinarily excited me as I prepared for trial, but that was as an attorney. Now, it was more critical. For me, it was life or death. I needed this jury to like me more than I ever needed anything.

Jurors understandably get confused by the volume of disparate information presented in a court. They are forced to make snap decisions to manage the amount of information that comes at them during trial. Their initial judgment about me must be positive so everything else they hear from me reinforces their positive perception.

Of course, I researched what to wear, and every jury expert I interviewed added another angle to consider. I learned certain colors evoke certain emotions, and some clothing cuts equate to vulnerability as opposed to power. Loose clothing shows vulnerability, but experts advised to avoid baggy, as that appears sloppy. Soft solid-colored tops and sweater sets would demur my breasts, and a simple skirt—a little too big and below the knee—would cover my legs. No jewelry, light natural makeup, light-pink nail polish, and hair pulled back. I didn't want a curl bouncing around my face to distract the jury during my testimony.

After research, I invited several friends, including Steve, to my trial-wear show. As I modeled different outfits, poor Steve found himself surrounded by ladies offering their opinions. We had music, food, drinks, and laughs as they considered how I appeared trustworthy but not like a powerful attorney. Not a prairie muffin but not sexy either, my clothing flattering yet neutral. The jury had to like what I wore but forget it the moment I started talking. They had to see every expression and feel what I had felt that day—not remember the cute shirt I was wearing.

For testifying, we decided on a plain gray pencil skirt and a cornflower blue sweater set, one size too big. Being in the same courtroom with Morrison was going to be hard enough. I needed confidence about my appearance since I'd be shaking inside. I would be forced to relive the most harrowing experience of my life with TV cameras rolling, Morrison watching, and the pain-filled faces of family and friends looking on as they heard the horrific details for the first time. I'd be faced with a jury of strangers deciding my future and cross-examined by an attorney paid to free the man who wanted to come back and kill me. So a detail as small as skirt color or shoe style may *seem* inconsequential, but any advantage was crucial. With my life on the line and only a few hours to present my story, my feelings, and my personality to twelve strangers, every single detail mattered. To me.

After getting comfortable with my look for the jury, the next question was how to best paint a compelling story for the jury. What words would lead them to a guilty verdict and life sentence? Speaking in present tense, painting them a picture of what my future would look like if they didn't convict, and asking them to protect me all required preparation. I worked with Carol Lozier, a trauma counselor, practicing to control my emotions and body. My body would shake while in court and I knew it would be worse on the stand. I was concerned the adrenaline rush I felt every time I got near Morrison would prevent me from getting my story across to the jury. I almost didn't.

CHAPTER 16

THE PLEA OFFER

Never have a battle of wits with an unarmed person.

—MARK TWAIN

Just before the trial and after ten months of making a lot of noise about the failure to collect and preserve evidence, I had a surprise visitor at work.

Judy buzzed my office saying, "Sharon, a Detective Murrell is here to see you."

What was he doing here?

Murrell was the detective who interviewed Morrison the night of the incident. I had listened to the recording for the prosecutor, making notes for him on what was true and false. I assumed this visit was the result of my furious yet futile attempts to get someone to investigate, locate witnesses, and take customary measures to prepare a case for trial.

I assumed wrong.

"I'm Detective Murrell, nice to meet you."

"Are you here to collect my shirt, necklace, and car?" I asked, ever hopeful.

"Not today."

Of course, not today.

Detective Murrell told me about his interview with Morrison the night of the incident.

When he finished sharing the details I said, "Thank you for your work that night. I listened to the recording, and I could tell you were trying to get him to make some admissions. I appreciate that."

We then started talking about specific people in Georgetown—if I had met this person or knew that person. Detective Murrell listed off several names but none familiar.

"I don't know any of these people but let me check my computer to see if I've represented them or if they were an opposing client or witness I had in a case."

He waited while I did a thorough search on my office server.

"None of those names come up, not even as a consultation or expert witness. Let me check my computer to see if I have any of their contact information." That search also produced nothing.

Who were these people? I had no record of any of them.

Then Detective Murrell told me Morrison alleged I was a dangerous drug dealer who could have him killed if I wanted to. He didn't ask me a question, but just left it hanging out there as if he wanted a response. So I gave him one.

"If that were true, I assure you he would have been dead a long time ago."

We returned to checking my computer as he give me additional names. Same result. Nothing. I was exasperated.

Clearly he wasn't concerned about collecting evidence, so why was he here?

Then it hit me.

He was interrogating me. And he was doing it across my desk.

I'd provided countless sources of evidence for this investigation which had all been ignored, and he sits across my desk interrogating me? This is his first move?

In an effort to contain the rumbling thunder inside of me, I made an excuse to leave my office. I grabbed my cell phone and walked to my file room while dialing Steve's number. Thankfully, Steve always answered his phone unless he was in court. He knew a call from me likely meant my mind was swirling around the legal issues not being addressed. He would often answer the phone with "Are you swirling?" and remained professional and confident, objective yet caring. He was a trusted friend and looked out for me. I knew he would protect and help keep me safe. Whispering, I told him what was happening.

He reeled me back, for a moment. "It's okay, Sharon. They need to investigate you to confirm Morrison's claims aren't true. You have nothing to hide. Just go back in and answer his questions." Steve. Always reasonable.

I understood the jury needed to hear Detective Murrell testify he investigated Morrison's claims and none of them were true. But I couldn't ignore the fact that the only part of my case being worked—two months before trial—was interrogating me.

When I hung up the phone I was going to follow Steve's advice: walk in and respond to all questions in a professional and detached manner. Fortunately, or unfortunately, that is not at all what happened.

I returned to my office and apologized for the delay, telling the Detective we could resume the interview. "I've looked everywhere. I have no idea who these people are or how I am supposed to know them. Can you give me some point of reference?"

Detective Murrell explained that Morrison claimed he bought drugs from me and that he had watched me perform sex acts with these named men and women as "entertainment" at late-night parties. He alleged I was the major drug supplier for the surrounding counties and so connected and powerful that that he, Morrison, was actually afraid of me.

At this point, the prosecutors had now invested more time investigating me than they had the lifelong felon, Morrison. Detective Murrell then went through the rest of the list of names of people I allegedly either had sex with or sold drugs to. I felt my chest getting tight with anger, frustration, and humiliation at having to answer these questions. I tried to remain calm as he was the only person who had shown any interest in my case to date. But it wasn't working.

"Detective Murrell, I am a Christian. I have a lot of flaws, but having sex with people for entertainment at drug parties isn't one of them."

Then he asked if I had accepted drugs from clients for payment for services.

That's it, I am done.

All the rage, frustration, and fear of my future continually at risk due to their inattention came out. Tolerating the discussion of my sex life, or detailing my faith-based choice for a lack thereof, was enough. Alleging I accepted drugs for payment and was a bisexual drug lord? Too much.

I turned my back to him to get something out of my credenza.

It was a newspaper clipping of a letter to the editor titled "Student owes much to her Muse." A client wrote of how she was only in fifth grade when she came to my office to "retain" me. I took her case pro bono and worked for years to remove her from an abusive home and place her in a safe and loving home with her grandmother. She wrote that I saved her life and she wanted to be an attorney like Sharon Muse, one who fought for kids.

I slammed down the clipping and stood up abruptly, leaned over the large executive desk, and banged my fist while shouting, "I am a fucking Sunday school teacher! I am cleaner than your mother. You show up at my office, ten months after the incident, not having investigated any of the leads I gave you, and you want to interrogate me? The arresting state trooper stops by as a result of my countless calls to him only to tell me he has not had time to investigate my case and won't collect my evidence but that he received an award for writing citations for speeding."

I came up for air, then, "Do you have any idea who I am or what I stand for? I do more pro bono work than all the attorneys in this town combined. I have worked tirelessly to help children, I spent years overseas working in orphanages, volunteered legal services to nonprofits. I have traveled to Russia, Bulgaria, and Ethiopia to meet with government officials, orphanage directors, and local faith-based institutions, trying to improve the lives of the children who never get adopted. I have worked with programs for the homeless and countless nonprofits.

"You can search my home, my office, my car. I'll give you releases for medical records. You can see doctor notes and all my prescriptions ever written. I'll give you access to every bank account, every credit card, every penny. I am cleaner than you are, so don't you dare walk in here asking me if I'm a drug-dealer who has clients pay in drugs. Ask anyone who knows me, and they will tell you what I am about!"

My voice rose. "Why not investigate the felon who kidnapped me, the one who was out of prison for six days before he showed up at my office with a knife and a pre-planned route to kidnap and murder me and ensure my body was never found? Why not take a look at what he was reading while in prison? Did he check out maps of Bourbon County? Who sent him mail or visited him? Who helped him, and how did he know about that abandoned property? You haven't collected the shirt I had on or the necklace I was wearing with the knife marks in it. My car still hasn't been taken to the crime lab. You haven't matched the knife to the gouges in my car.

Do you have my drug tests from the hospital? Do you have the cell phone records from Jeff? Have you still not interviewed the witnesses? Have you found his bag? What about the wad of cash?"

Now my filter was completely gone, "Is there something you are waiting for? Please tell me!" My rage-induced diatribe left me with a heaving chest and tears in my eyes.

I stood frozen, still leaning forward, palms down with fingers splayed across the desk, as if ready to jump over it.

He sat motionless.

Detective Murrell explained his hands were tied somewhat because of the prosecutor's office, promised to help move the case forward, and left me his business card and cell phone number.

Murrell seemed genuine and sincere. Maybe for the first time, I'd found someone who cared. Still, this new flicker of hope did not give me confidence that my floundering case would end with a jury verdict in my favor.

How could a jury convict without evidence?

Steve called in early March, asking to come speak with me about the trial scheduled for next month. "We need to think through the charges and what possible sentences Morrison may get."

We sat on my back porch and walked through each charge. Kidnapping ten to twenty years, sexual abuse five years, resisting arrest less than one year in jail.

"Steve, he could easily end up serving ten years and get out." My voice trembled.

"That is true, Sharon. But he is charged with persistent felony offender [PFO]. Once they find him guilty at the trial and we move into sentencing phase, the prosecutor will walk through Morrison's criminal history with the jury. The judge would instruct the jury to find him guilty of PFO if he has prior felony convictions, which he does. Kidnapping will go from ten to twenty to twenty to life, sexual assault will move up to ten years, but the resisting arrest will stay the same as the maximum for a misdemeanor."

"So if they convict him of kidnapping, he could get a life sentence?" Hope returned as I saw Morrison's sentence inextricably intertwined with my life.

"Yes, but remember that a life sentence in your case still means he is up for parole in twenty years. The parole board doesn't have to release him, but they can."

We continued to talk for quite some time. He was trying to help keep my expectations realistic, to prepare me for all the possibilities. Especially in light of the lack of contact with the prosecutor's office.

We decided that a twenty-year sentence would be something I could live with. At least I could live for twenty years and figure it out from there.

Finally, I met with the prosecutor's office. Not the lengthy trial-prep meeting I'd hoped for but I had to take what I could get. They gave me copies of recorded interviews of two men who shared cells with Morrison during his incarceration. The men knew details of our working relationship that had not been made public, lending an air of truth to what they said. They also fabricated absurd stories that sounded like something Morrison would claim, stories I would categorically deny. Complete fiction. The prosecutor asked me to listen to them and decipher what was true and what was not. It sounded easy, but these guys were professional snitches. They had become good at overhearing bits and pieces and weaving it into a novella of fact—as if they had been present during the events of which they spoke. Why? So they could parlay it in to some relief from their current sentence by playing nice for the prosecution. I didn't want to muddy the waters with jailhouse snitches, who are inherently untrustworthy, when I had total strangers and a preacher to back me up. Nevertheless, I did my homework and did it with gusto. I didn't want to discourage the prosecution from pursuing my case. I'd help in any way.

Steve came over, and we sat on the basement floor, playing the recordings and taking frantic notes. They wove ridiculous tales with bits and pieces that rang true. Listening to recordings of snitches sitting around talking about how "Morrison said he was going to really fuck her up" before he killed me was incomprehensible, painful, and frightening. Did these guys know before it happened? Could they not have given me some warning?

When Steve and I finished, the accurate list was very short and the fabricated list was long. Long and ludicrous.

Ten days before the trial I started hearing from investigators about evidence. *Now* they wanted my car taken to the crime lab. They said I'd have to drive it myself, so I asked a friend to drive it. By then, I couldn't stand riding in it. We got to the crime lab only to be told the damage was done too long ago and they couldn't determine anything that would hold up in court. This was the same crime lab I called shortly after the incident asking if they could match the marks in my dashboard to the knife recovered. They could, but it didn't matter twelve months later. Evidence spoils.

I was going to lose this trial.

Where was the rolled up wad of cash? The knife? The bag he had with him?

I was going to lose this trial.

Was anyone doing anything to preserve evidence to show the jury?

I was going to lose this trial.

FRIDAY, APRIL 13, 2007

The trial was scheduled to start Wednesday, April 18. I had been asked to meet Gordie, the prosecutor, at the Courthouse in Scott County the Friday before. I thought he would discuss his trial strategy, give me a list of questions he was going to ask on the stand, and do some trial prep. I should have given up trying to speculate. Every time I thought one thing was going to happen, I got hit with something else I would have never imagined.

Gordie was very laid back, almost like he was hanging out at Starbucks with a friend. His demeanor threw me.

He asked if I would accept a five year plea. "Five years? Including the year he has already served, I suppose?"

He asked again if I would agree to the offer. No conversation. Just waiting for me to respond.

"No! That means he'd get out soon and I'll be dead." I knew I didn't have any say in how this case moved forward but I did know if I stood in court and told Judge Johnson that I thought their offer was too weak he wouldn't accept it. Thank God for Judge Johnson.

We sat silent for a long beat before Gordie told me about a new development that happened just before I arrived.

He explained that Morrison wrote a letter to his attorney detailing what happened in the car. He asked a cellmate to sign it as a witness. The witness read the letter and contacted the jailer, asking him to get in touch with the prosecutor's office.

"You have it? Can I see it?"

He slid me a copy.

He waited while I read it. It felt like Christmas morning. If the jury read this, it would mean a guaranteed conviction. He admitted to not getting out of the car, holding me down, and pulling out his knife. Kidnapping—game over. With the PFO charges, he'd be looking at twenty to life. This was like manna from heaven.

"I can't wait for the jury to read this!"

"They can't."

We spent the next few minutes holding a lively debate on the admissibility of this letter. Gordie said it was inadmissible at trial because it was protected by attorney-client privilege; I argued the signature of the witness would pierce any attorney-client privilege. I was right, and I knew I was right. This was basic law school stuff. But as my dad would say, "You can't have a battle of wits with an unarmed man," or in this case, one that wouldn't be bothered to participate. This baffled me. Gordie had to know this. He is smart.

I got a copy of the letter, and our meeting ended. No trial prep whatsoever.

I called my friend Amy to help and headed straight to Kinko's. She met me there. I bought a four by five-foot foam core board with a section of the letter blown up: "She said you've got to get. . . . out of my car . . . I grabbed her arm and she pulled away . . . I was very mad . . . I pulled a knife out and pulled it up." I wanted this big enough that the jury could read it from across the room. I wanted them to be able to look at it over and over until they adjourned to deliberate. I then ordered twenty copies on eight and a half by eleven-inch paper to give each juror plus some extra.

"Did you notice how everyone in there was uncomfortable once they read what was written on the board?" Amy asked as we climbed into the truck I borrowed because the exhibit was too big for my car.

"No, I was so excited about it, I didn't pay attention."

Good. Maybe the jury would find it disturbing too.

SUNDAY, APRIL 15

I went to church looking for assurances that God saw me and was watching over me. I wasn't sure what I was looking for but I was expecting God to show up. I sat stunned and listened with tears flowing down my face as Pastor Dave Stone delivered his sermon entitled "Facing the Giant of Fear." Comforting and encouraging, it gave me more hope than I'd had since April 7, 2006, fifty-four weeks ago. In a church of eighteen thousand, it seemed as if the message were written just for me. Dave spoke about Gideon, a surprising warrior in the Old Testament who conquered his foes, foes that outnumbered him more than four hundred to one, all because he trusted God to fight his battles for him. I realized the same God who fought for Gideon could surely fight for me. My church friends decided to call me "Little Giddy" in honor of my new perspective.

On Sunday night, Steve came and asked to take a walk, something apparently on his mind. Despite my kidnapping trial, I understood that my friends and family all had their own lives and problems to face, and I appreciated the time they shared with me. Steve and I walked and walked—and walked. Sunday, then again on Monday and Tuesday. I wasn't too talkative, but he shared all kinds of stories with me. Not trials or legal work. Personal stories, fun times in college, previous jobs, and the adventures he had with a convertible when he was younger. As we were walking Tuesday night, I said, "You're trying to distract me, aren't you? That's what these long walks are about."

MONDAY, APRIL 16

I emailed Gordie the memorandum of law I worked on all weekend. Steve helped me, and I provided Kentucky Rules of Evidence with loads of supporting case law to admit the handwritten letter as evidence, establishing it was not privileged. Since Morrison detailed what happened and admitted to having the knife, this was my smoking gun. I drove to the prosecutor's office and took the giant exhibits I made with the jury handouts. As I left, I said, "I hope to see these in court Wednesday."

No response.

I spent the rest of Monday in my home, thinking through my testimony and visiting with friends. Some lovely ladies from church called to let me know they had coolers of homemade food and drinks they would bring to the courthouse daily during the trial. They had heard me say I was going to have to stay in the courthouse during lunch so I wouldn't run into the jury members, and someone decided to provide me and my family with fresh fruit and salads as opposed to the vending machine fare all week. Thank God for such great friends; they showed up and walked through this with me every day.

TUESDAY, APRIL 17

As Wednesday neared, I reminded my family that I didn't want them to come. I didn't want them to see me on the stand, to hear what was said, to go through the unfiltered version they had never heard. And there was no way I was letting my dad in the same room with Morrison.

I spoke with Steve and confirmed our meeting time. He was going to drive me to the courthouse, so we could talk on the way, and my friends would follow. Everything was ready.

Amy spent the night with me that Tuesday. I paced and went over my testimony, trying to anticipate how the defense would cross-examine me. When I have a trial, I prep my clients. They know exactly what I am going to ask them. I type up the questions, we go through it in my office, and I send them a copy. It helps them feel secure and know what is coming. An attorney should know exactly what a client is going to say during direct examination. No surprises. I also put clients through a rigorous cross, so they aren't being cross-examined for the first time in front of a jury. No one had done this with me. I had no idea what to expect on direct and could only speculate about cross. It made me feel insecure and more frightened.

I couldn't calm my mind or body. Amy had told me for weeks that she was praying there wouldn't be a trial. I appreciated her positive attitude. But I already had my game face on, and I laughed right in hers at such an unlikely hope.

"Your childlike faith is precious, and I appreciate it. But they just asked me to accept a five-year plea. Morrison is certainly not going to stand up and plead guilty and accept a twenty-year sentence."

Too bad she just didn't understand how the legal system works. Too bad she didn't know what I knew. The case was a mess, and I'd not been prepped at all. I'd be lucky to get a guilty verdict.

The pacing and practice continued until a group of friends arrived with mounds of food. They filled my kitchen with breakfast and dinners for the week of the trial. They sensed my anxiety and asked to pray with me. We sat in a circle with each of them praying, which calmed me and made me feel like I wasn't fighting this alone. They left, and I actually slept a bit. Not much, but I slept.

WEDNESDAY, APRIL 18

The panic was waiting for me when I woke up. Amy was in my only bathroom. I feared she'd make us late. I stood in the hallway saying, "Okay, you shower first. No, wait, I need to go first. But you take longer so you go first. Wait . . . I have to be on the stand, I should go first."

As I spoke, Amy ping-ponged back and forth in my tiny hallway. Walking into the bathroom, then walking out. Back in, back out. She never spoke. Just did what I said. I literally could not make the decision. Finally, we somehow got ready and met up with Steve.

While we drove, Steve and I discussed the trial schedule. Part of me wanted to be there for every minute of it, but I would be sequestered until called to testify sometime after lunch. Despite my recent Gideon-ish confidence of victory, the practical lawyer in me knew the case wasn't worked. I should lose, but I now had a feeling I wouldn't.

Concerns about the jury weighed heavily on my mind. Would they blame me for "letting" him in the car as the lady on the grand jury did? I was talking to Steve about this when my phone rang. I didn't recognize the number but something nudged me to answer.

"This is Sharon." I said in a clipped tone, discouraging a lengthy call.

It was Trooper Arnett. He told me Larry Morrison plead guilty to all charges for a twenty year recommendation from the prosecutor. He called to get my approval because Judge Johnson would not accept the plea without my consent.

"Twenty years?"

It was the minimum sentence for a guy with a proven violent history.

Was anyone going to talk to me about the offer? Why was it made? What did they think we could get at trial? I'm not getting any help with this decision.

Steve was now half driving, half trying to hear the other end of my conversation. He knew me well enough to know I was about to blow. All I could imagine was Morrison walking out of prison in twenty years and killing me. "No, I don't agree to twenty years! I want a life sentence or a trial. Call me back when life is on the table."

For the second time since I met him, I slammed the phone down in Trooper Arnett's ear.

CHAPTER 17

THAT'S JUST WHAT WE DO

Laws are like cobwebs, which may catch small flies, but let wasps and hornets break through.

—JONATHAN SWIFT

"Sharon, remember what we talked about on your back porch?" Steve began slowly, his soothing voice belied the white of his face. "Remember we were talking about juries, how difficult they can be, how they often make decisions that make no sense? Didn't we decide that if they came to you with twenty years, you would accept it as opposed to the risk of a trial?"

"Things were different then," came my quick reply. That conversation was calm, with a rational me, not the Gideon-like warrior I had become. I could face any odds because God was going in front of me. "No, I want a trial and a life sentence. Twenty years just means a twenty-year countdown until Morrison gets out to come back for me."

After a long talk, I agreed with Steve. I trusted his judgment better than mine right now. My head was spinning. Twenty years was better than a gamble, and maybe this was the Gideon version. I didn't have to do anything, just accept the plea. If I'd had any idea how strong the testimony was from the other witnesses, I'm not sure Steve nor I would have agreed to twenty years. Absent communication from the prosecutor, I would take what I could get.

"Call them back, Sharon. This judge will not go against your wishes, so you have to approve it."

I called Arnett and agreed to the plea.

I sat quietly stunned at what just happened as Steve reassured me this was great news.

Still thirty minutes out on the ninety-minute ride to the courthouse, Steve sped up leaving my caravan of friends behind. He wanted me in front of Judge Johnson posthaste. Steve parked, and we practically ran to the building. My caravan was streaming in as we crossed the street. I gave them a brief rundown and told them to come in as fast as they could. The trial was over.

We made our way to the courtroom to find it empty. No judge, no Morrison. A bailiff approached to usher us to a conference room where witnesses wait during trial and where the jury deliberates. We filled the space in the room as my friends filed in behind me.

Everyone was quiet.

Gordie, Trooper Arnett, and Detective Murrell were seated at the conference table waiting for me. Gordie informed us the Judge Johnson did not want to wait for me to arrive and moved forward with Morrison's guilty plea. I'm thankful. No need to give him the time to change his mind.

Arnett said he recorded the guilty plea. His lack of training had certainly caused me great pain up until now, but I appreciated that he made the effort to document the plea for me. Through the static, we could hear the judge walk Morrison through a lengthy colloquy. The judge asked if Morrison was on any medication, and if so, did this mediation in any way interfere with his ability to make decisions? He asked if Morrison's attorney advised him during this decision, and the judge repeated several times that the sentence would be up to the judge and not limited to the twenty years the prosecutor recommended.

"Thank God," someone whispered as we all listened.

Morrison was going to prison for twenty years. He had already served one for this crime so he would be out in nineteen. Judge Johnson set the date for his formal sentencing in September. This was what I heard on the tape. It played in a room where, but for the voices on the recorder, you could hear a pin drop. Everyone stood frozen, hanging on every word.

Once the recorder stopped, Steve asked a few questions, but I stood numb, unable to find words.

"Thank you, Mr. Shaw. We appreciate everything you've done," Steve said, then looked at me—the intent of his expression clear.

I didn't feel grateful to Mr. Shaw. This plea came from the work of God, not Gordie. If up to the prosecutor, Morrison would likely be walking out a free man after a not-guilty verdict.

"Yes, thank you," I said, following Steve's silent instructions. Everyone in the room but Gordie knew I didn't mean it.

I looked around for the miniature billboard exhibits I had made at Kinko's. I saw the trial folders but no exhibits. Of course not. Unprepared even with my doing the work. Another reason to be thankful for the plea.

Gordie leaned back, raised both arms, locked his fingers behind his head and said, "That's just what we do."

Unbelievable. The hubris.

I heard my friend Marti sigh. I knew that sigh. It was one of frustration and disbelief.

My friends still occasionally joke, "That's just what we do," when something works out well that we had no hand in.

I thanked Detective Murrell, and I meant it. He was the only one who made me feel like my case mattered enough for him to do the work and prosecute the case. I appreciated him. He was the bright spot in an overwhelmingly disappointing performance by the Trooper and the prosecutor.

We all walked out of the courthouse, quiet in our own thoughts. Most were still in shock, except Amy. You'll recall Amy had prayed there wouldn't be a trial, at which I had laughed. I had doubted her understanding of the legal system. Clearly, it was *I* who didn't understand *her* faith. As a lifelong Christian, I was humbled.

Steve suggested we all meet for lunch to talk. I don't remember where we went. I remember a round table and a large picture window. I remember my friends peppering Steve with questions. I remember wrestling with my own thoughts. Should I feel relieved? I was glad not to endure a trial. I was glad to escape the possibility of losing. I was glad I didn't have to relive my worst moments for the TV cameras. But after the years flew by, then what? I would still be hunted, just by a hunter delayed for a few years. Not sure how to feel about that.

* * *

While Steve had been breaking the sound barrier to get me to the courthouse, Morrison stood in front of Judge Johnson and entered a guilty plea. His decision came after the jury was seated and immediately prior to opening statements. Maybe he didn't like the look of the jury, or maybe the fear of a potential life sentence spooked him. For some reason, Morrison, who just five days before had discussed five years, was now willing to plea to twenty.

Morrison's attorney and the prosecutor met the judge at the bench to discuss the plea. Then they took their meeting to the grand jury room to discuss the agreement further outside the presence of the jury. The guilty plea the judge took from Morrison stated in part:

> **Judge Johnson to Morrison:** Again, you're entering here today is what's called a blind plea, which basically means the Court will accept a recommendation from the Commonwealth, but it does not mean the Court will follow that.

Judge Johnson started that statement with "again" because this guilty plea, when transcribed, was twenty-eight pages. A twenty-eight-page colloquy that included repeated questions about Morrison's understanding, stating that the Court was not obligated to follow the Commonwealth's sentencing recommendations and inquiring as to any medications or possible side effects that would affect his decision. These two items were covered no less than eight times. Otherwise, the discussion involved a litany of questions confirming Morrison's belief that his attorney, Ms. Bellew, had represented him to the best of her ability professionally and ethically. It covered the discussions between Morrison and his attorney the week prior to the agreement. The pages detailed specific instructions that Morrison review the Presentence Investigation Report to ensure the information was accurate.

> **Judge Johnson to Morrison:** In this particular case, the report is probably more important than most other cases I deal with because it's not just a matter of accepting an agreement from the Commonwealth.

It's a matter of making a final decision in this case
as to what the actual sentence will be. So it's very
important that you make sure I understand specifically and accurately the information in this case and
about your history.

Morrison crossed the Rubicon by throwing himself at the mercy of the court, and Judge Johnson let him know that. Morrison didn't plead guilty out of some sudden sense of integrity or responsibility for his actions. He was hoping for leniency from Judge Johnson in exchange for agreeing to the path of least resistance. When faced with an impaneled jury, many defendants determine they may want to gamble with the judge instead. They make last-minute pleas like a Hail Mary in football. Sometimes it pays off, sometimes it doesn't.

Since bail was out of the equation between now and the sentencing in September, I knew he couldn't get to me. I started trying to live again. I traded in my white Honda crime-scene-car and bought a black Toyota my friends named Black Beauty. I continued taking steps to live like before the incident, not yet realizing I would never live that way again.

I started to adjust to what I hoped was my new life, and that life included one of my passions—travel. I planned to travel to Greece with a separate trip to Turkey later that year. Within a few days of the plea, my dad sent me; my mom; my sister Lisa, and her daughter, Cali, on a cruise. My trial was over, Cali had graduated high school, and it was Mother's Day. There was much to celebrate.

We played on beaches, swam in crystal-clear waters, and ate delicious food. One day I noticed something felt strange. Unusual. It took me a minute to realize I felt safe. For the first time in more than a year. It was so foreign that it literally startled me. But it was exciting. At long last, I started seeing glimpses of myself again.

Over the next few days, I grew excited about my new version of normal. I envisioned no more putting life on hold, waiting for court rulings. Once again I would be able to sleep, take walks beyond my front yard, work on Fridays after 5:00 p.m., and even drive with my windows down. A whole new world awaited, and I was anxious to put the past year behind me.

Tragically, the lovely vision of the future was interrupted by a phone call from the present—a call from the victims' advocate with the prosecutor's office. As she updated me, her words drained the hope and sense of safety I had just started to enjoy. My niece Cali reflected my fear on her face, and I could feel myself hollow out. The numbness was back.

MAY 1, 2007

While I was on my trip Morrison got busy and filed two handwritten motions, one to set aside his guilty plea and the second to fire his attorney and have a new one appointed. Somehow it took him thirteen days to realize he had entered a guilty plea, but now he wanted to withdraw it. His handwritten motion was hard for me to read—hard for all the legitimate, maddening reasons anyone could imagine and also frustrating due to his assault on the English language. He had a lifetime of prior felony convictions, and he now failed to understand the system? His motion incredibly read, in part, as follows:

```
My attorney Melisa Bellew had me enter a guilty plea
to all said charges. it would let Sharon Muse know I
was truly sorry. My plea could get me 20 year sen-
tence an it would be probated providing I never com-
mit simaler charges. An reason im Filing motion to
withdraw my Guilty Plea I witdraw my plea because I
was on Strong medication an I Dont remember pleading
Guilty.
```

He actually said he thought his twenty-year plea would be twenty years on probation, not actually serving time unless he kidnapped someone again. The motion went on to argue that his attorney told him that upon his plea, he would rightfully be released from jail and his record expunged. She forced him to take the plea while under the influence of his "Strong medication," which prevented him from making good decisions, he opined. He promised a complaint to the Kentucky Bar Association against his unprofessional attorney and said he remained "in shock" that he had entered into such an agreement or that Ms. Bellew as his counsel would allow him to.

Why would a public defender allow their client to plead guilty? He pontificated.

Let me explain why.

Morrison was a PFO. Since he'd already committed more than two felonies, his sentencing was enhanced to the next felony level, so for Morrison, that made the kidnapping alone a Class A Felony with a sentence range from a twenty years to life. If he were to get a life sentence he would serve twenty years before being parole eligible. If he were to take a twenty year plea, (which was a weak offer from the prosecutor as it was the minimum on only one charge) he would be parole eligible after serving four years. He would then get credit for one year. So, he would essentially be able to be released in three years. Twenty years doesn't mean twenty years. Not even close. This was his best-case scenario if found guilty, and it logically followed that Attorney Bellew would recommend it. Unfortunately for me, the prosecutor's office never discussed this with me. Bellew could not predict how unprepared the prosecution was. The strength of other witnesses may have pulled the case through, but my testimony would have been a mess. I was not prepared. Even with the prosecution's failures, Morrison would still have been gambling with his future. Despite lacking a firm grasp on English composition, Morrison was street smart . . . smart enough to know the option for parole in three years was better than a solid chance at life.

Such logic escaped Morrison, however. According to him, he had been mistreated and abused. He was the victim.

CHAPTER 18

GREAT IS THY FAITHFULNESS

If you are going to be a good and faithful judge, you have to resign your-self to the fact that you're not always going to like the conclusions you reach. If you like them all the time, you're probably doing something wrong.

—ANTONIN SCALIA

The months that followed were some of the most painful and exhausting of my life. Having been so close to returning to a normal life after the guilty plea, I found myself ill prepared to be involuntarily thrown back to a life I barely survived the first time. I closely followed the case online and appeared every time my case was on the docket making the three-hour round-trip drive. I had to keep tabs on what Morrison was up to. Every time he brought an issue to the court's attention—and he did quite a lot—a motion was filed and a time set for the judge to hear it. Each party would argue their side, and if the judge decided he needed to hear additional testimony, he would set a date for a hearing—like a mini-trial without a jury.

That's what I showed up to watch. Over and over. I was tired of being in the courtroom—shaking, crying, and humiliated—watching the other attorneys watch me. And the cavernous emptiness I felt afterward.

Since Morrison filed for a new attorney and wanted to withdraw his guilty plea, the judge needed to hear testimony on the conversations Morrison had with his counsel and on what he did and didn't understand. I got so sick of being there—shaking, crying, and humiliated—and watching the other attorneys watch me. And the cavernous emptiness I felt afterward.

MAY 5, 2007

Just days following the start of my new life on the peaceful cruise, I returned to court where Morrison argued he didn't know what he was doing when he plead guilty, he was impaired by medication, and his attorney coerced him into it. Judge Johnson appointed a new attorney, Brian Canupp, to replace Ms. Bellew and set the motion to withdraw the plea for hearing on May 14.

MAY 14, 2007

The Court heard arguments on Morrison's motion to withdraw his guilty plea. Neither the prosecution nor the defense called Bellew to testify at this hearing. The judge admonished both sides as Bellew's interactions with Morrison were crucial to his arguments. The judge quickly granted Morrison's request for new counsel, but the motion to withdraw his guilty plea would require evidence to support or attack his alleged incapacity to understand the plea. As a result, Judge Johnson ordered Morrison to undergo competency and psychiatric evaluations.

JUNE–AUGUST 2007

There were a variety of motions heard in June and July. The most significant hearing—the competency hearing—was scheduled for August 29. I'd been waiting for this day. If Morrison was found incompetent or unable to stand trial, everything would change. Steve and I sat focused, trying to listen through the court audio system, but my heart pounding in my ears made it hard to hear. The attorneys and Morrison stood before the judge as experts testified over the phone. Steve reassured me Morrison would be found competent while I shook, cried, and prayed my way through it.

After lengthy back and forth arguments from both sides, Judge Johnson thoughtfully considered what he heard. He found Morrison to be competent, the plea was not withdrawn, and the Pre-Sentencing Investigation (PSI) was ordered. The sentencing process moved forward.

SEPTEMBER 11, 2007

Morrison filed his second request for new counsel. Yes, he was now dissatisfied with Brian Canupp and wanted him removed. What was more, his motion railed about a lack of confidence in Canupp and that he wanted to have faith in his counsel the way he did in his first attorney, Ms. Bellew, the very same one he had removed for allegedly strong-arming him into a deal. Then he referenced the deal Bellew "forced" him to take as "pure suicide." He "begged" the Court for a second new attorney in four months so he could "Prayerfully regain 100% with adjustments to medication." Judge Johnson saw through this lack of logic and gave Morrison the option to keep his current counsel or represent himself.

The best part of his motion read as follows:

```
Mr Morrison wAnts to Let tHe Court NotE for tHe
RecorD He only wants to take care of His meDical
cares an prove to tHe plaintiff [he meant me] tHat He
is tRuLy Sorry For His Actions tHAt CauseD ALL of
tHis MeSS. .... An ASKS For tHe pLAintiFF "Sharon
Muses ForGiveness.
```

In most cases this would have been deemed an admission of guilt of some bad act. Why? Because it was. Was it ever shown to the jury? No.

The wheels of justice are often slowed by a defendant with legitimate concerns or rights to assert, but to be slowed by Morrison's stream-of-consciousness motions was neither acceptable nor tolerable. It looked as though he got high, scribbled random thoughts, and called it a motion and then forced the rest of us to respond as if it were legitimate.

SEPTEMBER 12, 2007

Defense Counsel Canupp filed a motion to withdraw, arguing that:

```
The relationship between Counsel and his Client have
reached the point where [Canupp] does not believe
```

```
communication . . . is adequate pursuant to rules of
Professional Responsibility.
```

This was clever. Basically Canupp described his relationship with Morrison as so contentious that Canupp would be violating the rules of ethics that govern attorneys if he continued to represent Morrison. In a way, Canupp boxed in Judge Johnson with an argument that would force the judge to allow Canupp to withdraw. Canupp supported the motion with case law opining that a defendant's right to counsel might be violated if he was not allowed to obtain new counsel. Remember, Canupp was representing a violent felon for trying to murder his previous attorney whom he reportedly liked. Morrison apparently didn't like Canupp, so I didn't blame him for wanting to get out of the case.

SEPTEMBER 13, 2007

Judge Johnson ruled Morrison had no grounds to file a motion for a new counsel, and he held Canupp's motion in abeyance, stating that it appeared to be an attempt to delay the process.

SEPTEMBER 21, 2007
SENTENCING DAY

After a long and painful journey, Morrison would stand in front of the judge today. So would I. Finally I'd have an idea of what my future might look like, a future that had been on indefinite hold. I'd lost so many things over the past year to this case, even my ability to be a mom. I have always struggled with fertility issues so I had planned to adopt by the age of thirty-five. The incident happened before I could finalize an adoption. I had spoken with an international adoption agency to adopt as a single person, but the status of my court case created an unsafe home environment under the agency guidelines which made me ineligible. A devastating, life-changing loss. Another in the string of blows brought by Morrison, but I understood their reasoning.

The caravan reassembled once again. We drove to Bourbon County and took our seats together in the courtroom.

I walked toward the bench while my friend Marti stood as a buffer to block my line of sight to Morrison. Darin barricaded me from the news cameras. Lori stood directly behind me for physical support, more friends piled up beside Lori, and my mom and former brother-in-law, David, sat near the front of the gallery. Steve stood to my right, locked arm in arm with me, and Amy stood to my left, ready with written bullet points when I had to speak. As I spoke, she would follow down the list with her finger so I didn't have to rely on my memory during such a crucial moment.

Standing there, even with friends taking up half the courtroom, I opened my mouth but couldn't speak. I dropped my head to gather my thoughts. Amy pointed to the paper to help, but all I could see were tears flooding my eyes. I started to speak, and the judge leaned in to hear.

Steve whispered, "The judge can't hear you. He has to hear you."

"I'm sorry," I whispered as I wept. Everyone waited, and the room was still. Even the clerks and bailiffs who typically kept themselves busy all stopped and stared. No papers shuffling, no one coming in and going out. Everyone waited to hear what the lawyer who had been kidnapped had to say. I tried again to speak, but there was no sound. Lori whispered, "You can do this," and I tried again. Eventually sound joined my words. The judge had already read my victim impact statement, including more than forty letters from friends and family, to help him understand the impact this crime had on my life.

I tried to paint a vivid picture of what it looked like to live through the crime, to try to survive after, and then try to regain some kind of normalcy. "You are the only one who can help me. The moment he gets out of jail, my life will end. He only waited six days before he came to kill me. If it were up to him, I wouldn't be standing here today. My mom would be speaking on my behalf, and this would be a murder trial. We both have to serve sentences. You have the responsibility to decide who you are going to sentence to life. Me or Morrison. Any sentence for Morrison less than life is a death sentence for me. Please give me my life. Let me live without the fear of being hunted and killed."

Judge Johnson was compelled by my statements. He could feel my passion, pain, and fear. I could see it in his eyes. Morrison spoke through his attorney. It was brief and unworthy of repeating here.

The judge recessed to review documents and consider his ruling. While we waited, Steve repeatedly assured me Judge Johnson was going to sentence Morrison to life. I had hope but not his confidence.

Judge Johnson returned to the bench. I sat on the front row with my mom at my side and surrounded by friends. Judge Johnson listed the documents he reviewed, taking into consideration the statements of both the victim and defendant through his attorney. Then he went on to say Morrison was one of the most dangerous people to have passed through his courtroom. Only waiting six days from his release from prison to commit this series of felonies against the victim showed that twenty years would not be long enough. Morrison would serve a life sentence.

Life. I couldn't believe it. Judge Johnson sentenced him to so much more than the prosecutor offered. I hadn't allowed myself to hope for something so amazing. I sat numb listening to the gasps and cheers around me. He heard me. Judge Johnson heard me when the prosecutors didn't. He righted this wrong. He kept me safe. I can't speak for Judge Johnson but I imagine this was one of the times that he liked the conclusion he came to.

Do you know how Judge Johnson got to be my judge? The clerks randomly assign cases as they come in. I thank God Judge Johnson was given my case. Him being my judge made all the difference. He gave me my life back.

After bailiffs removed Morrison from the courtroom, I made my way to Morrison's attorney Brian Canupp and shook his hand. "Thank you for doing a good job. I appreciate and respect your work."

My friends and I celebrated in the hall. Tears flowed freely from everyone. Even the bailiffs teared up. From there, we went to the abandoned farm where Morrison had taken me. We all piled up in the driveway and took a photo together . . . a sort of graduation.

This wasn't the first time I had returned to the scene. I decided to make the same drive prior to trial so I would be better prepared to answer questions. My car had a six-CD changer, and I kept it filled with a disparate range of music: Christian praise, rap, classical, pop. As I approached the last turn in retracing my drive, Larnelle Harris start singing "Great Is Thy Faithfulness," one of my favorite hymns.

I particularly liked the old lyrics, which brought thoughts of the generations before me who listened to these same words and leaned on them for comfort. For situations I can't imagine, direr than mine, people have clung to these truths that God is faithful. When we don't see him, he is faithful; when we don't understand, he is faithful; and even when we are mad at him, he is faithful.

I pulled up to the place where I was going to be raped, beaten, stabbed, and left behind a barn to die. To feel each blow and each stab of the blade, to feel the blood run down my chest and hear myself struggle to breathe, my lungs burning as I took my last breath—to know I was dying—this was what I would have experienced. This was the place Morrison planned to bring me while in prison—those years I ran around carefree while someone planned my murder. This was the place where God knew Morrison would try to destroy me. But God showed up and snatched me from the fowler's snare. He rescued me. This became not a place of death but a place of life, not a place for me to fear but a battleground where I was victorious. I would claim this not as the place I almost died but the place where God stepped in and gave me back my life.

I got out of my car, blasted my old-school hymn, and sang at the top of my lungs. Tears pouring, arms stretched out, and face tilted toward the sun. Feeling the rays dance across my face, I stood there and reclaimed my ground. I was no victim, and this was not a crime scene anymore.

This was the place, surrounded by loved ones and with Morrison in prison for life, where the rest of *my* life began.

PART THREE
THE TRIAL

CHAPTER 19

THE JUICE ISN'T WORTH THE SQUEEZE

Adversity is a school in which few men wish to be educated.

—A letter from John Randolph
to Thomas Jefferson (1779)

AUGUST 28, 2009

"This is Sharon," I answered with my usual greeting, half paying attention to the phone, focused on the curve in the road ahead of me.

"This is Bonnie with the Attorney General's Office." The office responsible for the appeal of my case.

I caught my breath. I knew the next words out of her mouth would have a profound effect on the rest of my life. I was right.

"I'm calling to tell you the Kentucky Supreme Court has reversed and remanded Judge Johnson's ruling. They held that Morrison is either to get a new trial or a twenty-year sentence."

After reviewing Morrison's many appellate issues, the Kentucky Supreme Court had concluded the trial court was correct in determining that Morrison was competent, that his guilty plea was made voluntarily, and that he was not rendered ineffective assistance of counsel, by Bellew, at the time of the plea. But they also found that the trial court should have allowed Morrison to withdraw his guilty plea when the Court sentenced him to more than twenty years. This was a split decision. If one person had voted differently, the next four years of my life would have been very different.

Life was no longer an option. Not for him. Or for me.

During the months following my kidnapping, my friends came up with a running joke: "At least I'm not Sharon." No matter how bad life got, you could always feel better if you paused to consider mine. So that became my gift to the world, to make everyone else feel better about their lives for reasons too numerous, obvious, and odious to mention. We laughed and joked about T-shirts and bumper stickers with our new motto.

We also joked about what characters would play us in a movie. We debated which actress would play our respective roles. Charlize Theron, Julia Roberts, or Jennifer Lawrence. Who wouldn't want to be portrayed by them in a movie? These delightful distractions helped me through as we mapped out scenes and picked the actors to portray everyone involved.

I'd fall back on these memories during the hardest parts of my case. Like now. I was shell-shocked by this latest news. I flashed back to a recent conversation with my friend Debbie Carper when I said, "With all I've learned about myself and how my relationship with God has grown, I would do it all over again if that was the only way for me to become who I am now."

"God," I wailed, "that was figurative, not literal. I didn't mean I actually wanted to do this again!" I had to pull over as the tears came with such force they blinded me. I pressed my head back against my seat and stared out my sunroof. This couldn't be happening again.

As I heard the words coming out of Bonnie's mouth, my hand went limp, and I dropped the phone. I knew she could hear the sobs and groans that erupted from me. Immediately, I tried to comfort myself by thinking about how much better prepared I was to be a witness this time. I knew we would win, not like last time.

Despite the deafening sound of blood rushing through my ears, I continued to think about possible benefits for me. Since we were starting from ground zero, then we should *really* start at ground zero. I was going to push the prosecutor to file attempted murder and attempted rape charges. I know, I am relentless, but this is my life, my future, and I'd like to live it without looking over my shoulder in a couple of years.

Then "At least I'm not Sharon" popped into my head followed by bits from funny conversations about our future movie. Maybe this was the beginning of our sequel? Humor helped me deal with the stress, and the tears slowed down. I called my friend Stephanie, whom I was about to meet for lunch, and shared the news. She said we would discuss a plan while we ate. She knew me well. A plan always made me feel better.

The first step in the plan was to confirm Gordie was willing to pursue the case. He didn't have to, and if he didn't, I had no recourse. I called to confirm and then suggested he add attempted murder and attempted rape to the charges.

He responded by telling me he couldn't add any charges or change the original ones as that would be seen as malicious prosecution.

It was fair to charge Morrison with attempted rape and attempted murder and give him the opportunity to defend it. He earned it and deserved to be accountable for it. Each charge meant more time behind bars if he was found guilty. That was my end goal—a guilty verdict and as much time as possible for Morrison, so I didn't have to keep showing up and begging the parole board to keep him in prison.

I politely disagreed with the prosecutor, arguing that when a case is remanded, it starts over for both the defense and prosecution. This was a rare occasion in criminal law where it wasn't weighted heavily in favor of the defendant. I was pushing for us to take advantage of it. Gordie held firm in his position, so I drafted another memorandum to provide the case law supporting my position. I wanted to go into this trial locked and loaded. Let Morrison defend every charge he earned.

The road to the second trial was littered with debris from the defendant utilizing the many, many rights he had while I watched and waited with no input in the case that shaped my future. It was expected, even admirable, for the defense to avail themselves of all remedies the law allowed, but it was different to exploit the system with needless delays and nonsensical motions.

The new defense team of two attorneys filed a flurry of motions which led to multiple hearings. Each motion meant more waiting, more uncertainty, more fear of Morrison's possible acquittal. More everything.

My life returned to the rut and routine of enduring repeated court appearances and the draining aftereffect for me. Shaking, tears, no sleep, numb. I walked around hollow, pretending to live a normal life. Back in and out of court with its hearings, delays, and continuances and the three-hour drive to sit in a courtroom only feet away from the man who tried to kill me depleted what little reserves I had. But I wanted Judge Johnson to see my face every single court date.

Some of the defense motions made sense, some felt like a waste of court resources, and some actually made me laugh and feel a tiny bit sorry for them.

MARCH 10, 2010

Morrison added a third attorney to his court-appointed, tax-funded team, Mr. Scott West. He immediately tried to remove Judge Johnson from the case, citing the judge's statements during the sentencing that he believed Morrison to be a dangerous person with the ability to hurt people and that he was "in fact, a danger to society."

Thankfully, Judge Johnson overruled this motion. The guilt of the defendant would be determined by a panel of twelve jurors, not the judge, although judges determine the sentence. Every time a case returns from a higher court it goes back to the original judge. That is how the process works. But it was a clear signal that this guy was going to file every motion he could, reasonable or not.

I referred to Morrison's team of three lawyers as the dream team. Mr. West, Mr. Hart, and a female who never spoke in court, so I didn't catch her name, but she was always present. Eventually, I created individual nicknames for them. Was that snarky? Yes. Unprofessional? Definitely. Could it be helped? Of course. But I needed some form of relief to entertain my mind during hearings. Humor is what I used. My creative names were funny, but good manners won't allow me to share them as they were, well, unflattering. I'm sure they were all good people, but I didn't like how they practiced law and played with my life. I was also irritated that Morrison had three attorneys, and the Commonwealth showed up with one. All the lawyers were being paid by the same tax base, so I expected a more balanced distribution of funds.

A pleasant surprise came when I found out that Morrison wasn't the only one with a team of attorneys. Keith Eardley, an Assistant Commonwealth's Attorney had been working with Gordie as co-counsel. I just hadn't met him, seen him, or talked to him yet. Apparently I had a team too.

The one source of hope I had in this case was Judge Johnson. He had already made it very clear that he was not going to accept a plea deal in this case—unless it was a life sentence. This meant the prosecutors couldn't force me into a plea deal again. They had to take the case to trial. Everyone involved understood that. So I reached out to Keith and asked him to meet with me. He agreed. Apparently, his case file did not give a good picture of the facts. He directed a sheriff's deputy to drive us along the route Morrison had forced me to drive during our meeting. I explained everything as we drove. I appreciated this. I hoped it would help my case but later came to regret it.

Until then, I had been primarily focused on evidence either not collected or lost: the TV interview, the confession letter Morrison wrote, the evidence of the violent fight in my car that the crime lab ruled out as having been processed too late, the shirt I was wearing that at some point had been lost, Morrison's missing bag with the roll of cash, cocaine, tape, rope, and most significantly, the knife—the knife he'd shoved into my throat, the one we'd fought over whose tip broke off leaving deep gouges in my car. None of this would be seen by the jury.

MAY 28, 2010

The dream team filed a notice of intent to introduce evidence of mental illness or insanity claiming Morrison wasn't responsible for his actions. This motion terrified me.

I sat in my usual position behind the prosecutor's table straining to hear the conversation between the judge and the attorneys. As always, I watched the judge for any indication—the slight movement of his head, squinting of his eyes, or tightening his lips—to help me predict how he was going to rule. Thankfully, this motion to introduce mental illness was entirely unsupported and judiciously overruled.

*   *   *

My courtroom attendance was a source of humiliation since many people recognized me as a practicing attorney, yet I sat there silent, occasionally with tears pouring down my face. It would start with a pit in my stomach that intensified with the words *Commonwealth versus Larry Morrison*. With that, the squatty, mullet-haired felon would be escorted into the courtroom with deputies flanking him. Each time he appeared—orange jumpsuit on, hands cuffed, legs shackled—he'd scan the room for me. Each time, *every time*, I'd lock eyes from the moment he crossed the courtroom threshold to the moment he turned his back to me. I engaged him in silent combat, my eyes expressing my thoughts: *I beat you in the car, I'll beat you in court, and if you are dumb enough to come back, I'll beat you again.* Once he sat down with his defense team, I'd melt. In the worst of times, the entire bench could feel the tremors passing down the wooden pew; in the best, I sat pale and numb.

Morrison's third set of attorneys appeared to be checking off a Trial Practice 101 list of motions, warranted or not, to create as much opportunity for appealable error as possible. You may argue this is the precise job of a defense attorney, but there is a difference between zealous representation and wasting time and resources with ridiculous motions. In my mind, lawyers are charged with a higher level of duty, morality, truth, and justice. This team's apparent Plan B approach to the case—to overload the system with needless and baseless motions and to get their client off at any cost—offended my sense of justice. And safety.

KRE 404 cited portions:
KRE 404 Character evidence and evidence of other crimes
Character evidence generally. Evidence of a person's character or a trait of character is not admissible for the purpose of proving action in conformity therewith on a particular occasion, except:

Other crimes, wrongs, or acts. Evidence of other crimes, wrongs, or acts is not admissible to prove the

character of a person in order to show action in conformity therewith. It may, however, be admissible:

If offered for some other purpose, such as proof of
motive, opportunity, intent, preparation, plan, knowledge, identity, or absence of mistake or accident.

You may think 404(b) sounds like a random grouping of numbers and letters, but I saw it as the cornerstone of my case. The law doesn't allow testimony about a defendant's prior criminal record during the guilt phase of a trial. The idea is that it would be overly prejudicial for the defendant and a jury may convict based on the defendant having committed crimes in the past. To ensure that doesn't happen any mention of a prior crime must meet the elements of 404(b). On the day of the hearing, the 404(b) felt bigger than the upcoming trial itself. Morrison's team was arguing to keep me from explaining to the jury that I had represented Morrison in a previous criminal charge. If they kept this out the crime makes even less sense.

Motive is not a required element to prove in a crime, but without it, a jury wouldn't understand why he obsessed about me, longed to hurt me, control me, rape me, and kill me. I don't understand why he did what he did, and I knew a jury wouldn't either. If a jury did not know what connected Morrison to me, they would have too many questions. *Why her? How does he know her? Why would he intend to hurt her?* When juries have significant unanswered questions, they typically do not send defendants to prison for the rest of their natural lives. The unanswered "why her" question might create doubt, reasonable doubt.

No one should be convicted based exclusively on past behavior, but the past crimes in this case were the only connection he had to me, and without that information, a jury would be confused. Juries work in the dark, absent the light of truth, only knowing what the law allows to be filtered down to them. But they have to hear a story that makes sense to them, the answer to *Why did this happen?*

If the defense won this motion, how did they plan to explain how Morrison knew me? Would they tell the jury we were just old friends? Apparently yes, but you'll get the details on that later.

On the day of the 404(b) hearing, Steve and I sat in our usual place behind the prosecutor's table.

The defense had also filed a motion to change venue, meaning they wanted the trial moved to a different county because they believed Morrison couldn't get a fair trial in Bourbon County because of all the media coverage. West's sole basis for his motion to change venue was that he had two witnesses that had seen so much media exposure about this case that an unbiased jury would be impossible to find in Bourbon County. Although I was stressed about the 404(b) motion, the venue motion didn't concern me at all. The Honorable Robert G. Johnson, Chief Judge, presided over the case from start to finish. Having him on the bench gave me confidence. As long as Judge Johnson was presiding, we could have the trial in my garage, and I wouldn't mind. The change of venue motion should be perfunctory and uneventful, so I expected to be bored while I listened. I was wrong.

The bailiff called the court to order, and West made his motion for change of venue.

JUDGE JOHNSON: Okay.

MR. WEST: And, Your Honor, I would like to contact a Ms. Lorna Vessel and have her take the stand.

BAILIFF: Do you want separation of the witnesses?

MR. WEST: I'm sorry?

BAILIFF: Do you all want the separation of the witnesses?

MR. WEST: I don't care. I'm not making that motion.

I waited for Gordie to make the motion the bailiff suggested. He didn't. It was a standard rule to separate witnesses so they couldn't hear the testimony of the other witnesses or hear the questions asked by opposing counsel. Clearly it happens all the time, or the bailiff wouldn't have asked if they wanted it. This motion was one of the first you learn about in law school, and as a general rule, you employ in every hearing or trial—always separate the witnesses. Of course, Morrison's lawyers wouldn't make that motion—it would help their defense witnesses by knowing what they were going to be asked. As it turned out, they needed all the help they could get.

When Lorna Vessel took the stand, West started by establishing that she didn't know him. He went on to ask questions based on the sworn statement she signed and submitted to the court that she didn't think Morrison could get a fair trial. Unfortunately, none of the answers she gave in court were consistent with the document she signed.

When West finished Gordie explored her lack of knowledge of the case further. She said she was not only unfamiliar with the case and hadn't seen any media coverage of it but didn't know the defendant's prior criminal history and wasn't even sure of his name. Yet she claimed he probably wouldn't be able to get a fair trial. Why? Because if he *did* have any prior history, it would affect his ability to get unbiased treatment. Gordie pinned her down by asking if that would apply to anybody, not just this defendant, and she agreed.

And this was a local resident who'd seen so much coverage of the trial, she wouldn't be able to hand down an impartial verdict? That was one down, one to go.

West then called Elizabeth Beeler, who had just witnessed Lorna Vessel's testimony, to the stand. Her testimony paralleled the first except she said she didn't really know why she was there except it had something to do with not having a fair trial.

The written documents West filed with the court were completely different that the ladies' testimony. I felt sorry for them. I'd been listening with my mouth gaping open, like a fish mounted above a mantel. I was stupefied, frozen with disbelief. Despite my sympathy for the witnesses I enjoyed my time in court for the first time. I shrank down in my seat with my hand over my mouth to contain my laughter. Steve and I couldn't believe what we were witnessing. It was a train wreck. Bless his heart.

I had been praying that God would confuse the defense team and cause them to create problems for each other. During hearings, I had drilled holes in the back of their heads with my eyes and prayed over them. Or maybe it was more like curses? I was not sure God really worked this way, but I did know many Old Testament stories where God confused the enemies of the Israelites so they turned on themselves, and the Israelites had a victory without lifting a finger. Although I was not an Israelite trying to enter the promised land, I was waging my own kind of war. Whatever it took. Other than hunting Morrison down—I'd given that up for good.

West had to backpedal to save his witnesses from committing perjury, but it was impossible to save himself from looking ill prepared and sloppy. As embarrassed as West clearly was, I couldn't help but wonder if Morrison noticed the mistakes, obsessed over them, and tucked them away as fodder to blame his attorneys if he was convicted.

I was no longer laughing.

JUDGE'S RULING

JUDGE: Well, having heard the testimony, having previously read the motion for change of venue, KRS 452.210 does require significant—or *some* evidence indicating that he couldn't get a fair trial based upon general population's ideas and also the media coverage. I'm going to overrule the defendant's motion for change of venue. Next motion.

MR. WEST: Your Honor, the next motion would be the Commonwealth's motion, 404b evidence.

MR. SHAW: That's correct, Your Honor. As far as the Commonwealth's 404b motion, quite frankly, I don't think I've ever seen a situation where 404b evidence we intend to introduce fits a rule any better than in this situation. The Commonwealth's proof is going to be that Mr. Morrison, while he was in prison and once he got out, established a plan to lure our victim into a situation where he could basically seek revenge on her, and that this was motivated and originated from her prior representation of him. That is their only connection. It couldn't be more formfitting to the rule than the evidence we're intended to seek.

MR. WEST: Your Honor, we respectfully disagree. The fact that it shows that he was arrested and went to jail is very prejudicial, so I think any probative value that this immaterial fact would have is substantially outweighed by the danger of undue prejudice. It doesn't look like anything but good work on the part of Ms. Muse and certainly not any work that was material for him to have bad feelings.

JUDGE: Are we going to hear testimony at this point?

MR. WEST: Your Honor, I would like to call Mr. Morrison for the limited purpose of asking about that prior representation and just to confirm the facts that I've told the Court.

Morrison was about to speak, to manipulate the details and put his coached spin on what happened. I knew what I was about to hear would enrage me, and I had a flash of myself diving over the bar, grabbing Morrison's head, and smashing it into the defense table. The image left as quickly as it came.

JUDGE: Mr. Morrison, you can actually testify from where you're sitting there.

During his direct examination, Mr. West walked Morrison through a well-rehearsed dialogue of the basic information—his wife retained me, I did a good job, we all parted friends.

CROSS-EXAMINATION OF LARRY MORRISON
[BY COMMONWEALTH'S ATTORNEY, MR. SHAW]

Q: How much money did you all pay Ms. Muse?

A: You know, I'm not really sure, Mr. Shaw.

Q: And you don't have any idea what the fee here—what it amounted to be?

A: No. My wife had got her, and she got me out of jail, but I'm not sure the amount that was paid.

Q: Do you recall telling other people what the amount was?

A: No.

Q: Would you deny that you told other people what the amount was?

A: Yeah.

Q: Would you deny that you ever talked to anybody else about Ms. Muse's representation of you?

A: Let's see. I—I can't say that for sure because my wife knew. My grandmother knew. I think my aunt and close family knew.

Q: How about after you were arrested? Would you deny you talked to anybody about her representing you?

A: Yeah. I never said any—but I don't remember telling anybody.

Q: Do you remember telling anybody you weren't happy with her representation?

A: No, not at all. The lady was good to me. She got me out of jail. That's why I'm having trouble to understand why she is afraid of me.

Without thinking, I leaned forward off my seat and blurted out, "Maybe because you stuck a knife in my throat and tried to kill me?!" Long, silent pause as I waited to be reprimanded by the judge.

Steve firmly put his hand on my arm and pulled me back down. He left it there to keep me in my seat. Thankfully, Gordie continued his questioning.

Q: So earlier when I asked you if you've ever talked to anybody about her representing you, you said no.

A: Mm-hmm.

Q: But it sounds like you have talked to other people maybe about why she stopped representing you?

A: It might have been my wife or my grandmother.

Q: Have you ever told anybody that she charged you $600?

A: Unless it was my attorney. He'd be the only one that—

Q: Did you say anything about her not representing you when you kidnapped her or when you were with her?

A: No. I ain't said nothing to nobody about her not doing me right or none of that. No.

Q: Did you ever ask her about any kind of back surgery?

A: Not that I can recall. I don't even have nothing against Ms. Muse. She got me out of jail, and I'm grateful for what's she done for me. That's what

I'm having such a hard time understanding. I
know I was—

MR. WEST [INTERRUPTING]: Mr. Morrison, wait for him
to ask a question and you can answer.

He *was* answering, but Morrison was about to make an admission so West
interrupted.

A: I just don't have nothing—

MR. WEST: Wait for him to ask you a question. You
just—let's just . . .

West interrupts again here, I'm dying for Morrison to just blurt it out. Blurt out an
admission of guilt.

Q: Do you recall any conversations with any cellmates about the representation?

A: No.

Q: Do you remember writing anything down about the
representation?

A: No knowledge.

Q: And you've never written or said anything about
not approving of her prior representation?

A: No. She didn't do nothing but be good to me.
Just being honest, I mean.

Q: Right. But while you're being honest, you deny
that you've ever written or said anything about
her?

A: Other than my family or my attorneys.

Q: Well, I mean, did you tell your family or your
attorneys that you weren't happy with her
representation?

A: No.

Q: So you never ever said that. Is that right?

A: Well, she's been—like I said, she's been good to me and I have nothing against Ms. Muse.

Q: You recognize you're under oath right now?

A: Yes.

MR. SHAW: No more questions, Your Honor.

Gordie did exactly what you want to do on a cross. He knew his facts and pressed Morrison into a corner. He systematically walked Morrison through the statements made in the letter he wrote to his attorney and conversations with his cellmates when he discussed how much he paid me, a fictional back surgery, and his satisfaction with my work. He forced Morrison to lie—repeatedly. Unless Gordie entered the letter into evidence, the judge and jury would never know Morrison was lying. Gordie frustrated me the way he managed or mismanaged my case, lost evidence, made significant procedural errors, and failed to enter the letter as evidence, but I couldn't deny there were times he was good in the courtroom.

JUDGE: Okay. Do you all want to finish arguments regarding this particular issue?

MR. WEST: I believe that motive not being material— we would just ask, Your Honor, that you not allow in the 404b evidence. Thank you.

JUDGE: Mr. Shaw.

MR. SHAW: Thank you, Your Honor. This is a situation evidently perfectly foreseen by the drafters of the rule that we've been using for years now, that it is explicitly intended for these types of situations. But the fact was there *was* a crime and a motive for it. This rule squarely made it permissible for the Commonwealth to introduce that evidence when it fit the rule, and it did here.

JUDGE: Pursuant to KRE 404b, I'm going to order that these specific crimes that the victim represented the defendant on are able to be given to the jury.

Mr. West then requested limiting instructions for the jury to admonish them to consider my testimony about representing Morrison only as it related to how he knew me and possible motive. That's perfect. The more you warn the jury not to give weight to certain testimony, the more they will wonder why.

JUNE 2010

The defense team filed motions to exclude certain evidence, like the letter Morrison had written to his attorney as well as the statements to his cellmates about my representation of him and his plans for me behind that barn. Everything Gordie questioned Morrison about on cross-examination.

Ultimately, I was pleased that the statements to Morrison's cellmates were not brought in. We had a clean case and didn't need to muddy it up with jailhouse snitches. They are inherently unreliable. Nobody likes a snitch. Or as inmates say, "Snitches get stiches and end up in ditches."

The letter Morrison wrote and the video of the interview with local news reporter Leigh Searcy were admissible under the rules of evidence, yet the jury never saw them. I still don't know why.

DECEMBER 20, 2010

Over the Christmas holiday, my family gathered at my home to visit and support me since the trial date was only six weeks away. One night, my brother, Rick, asked about my trial prep, and I updated him on the court's rulings before heading to bed. I joked that maybe he should represent me since he had been such a successful advocate as a child when representing himself against me after stealing inventory from my dining room store. Rick and I have always been close. Best friends and constant companions as children, frequent contact and playing long distance pranks while we were in college several states apart, and daily conversations as adults. He is my brother, best friend, and protector. Having him near me always made me feel safe. He is smart, talented, and could solve any problem. Yet we both knew he was powerless to fix this.

Hours later, in the middle of the night, I sat straight up in my bed, as high, tinny notes shattered the still air—it was my voice, screaming myself awake. My brother burst into my room to help me, thinking something had happened. My screams were loud, guttural, and real. I collapsed, drenched in sweat.

In the morning, Rick asked if I remembered what happened. I couldn't remember screaming, but the evidence was there in my scratchy throat. The closer I got to the trial date, the more fear crept back into my life, day and night.

As we approached the trial I considered what my life would look life if Morrison was acquitted. I had to—juries were unpredictable. I researched protection dogs, specifically female German Shepherds with special training. I learned how quickly the dogs could clear a house and return to me, that they would circle around me growling and showing a "bitch grin" if they perceived a threat. These dogs were a dream. But they came with a hefty price tag, and I would have to treat them as working dogs, not pets. I couldn't imagine not being able to cuddle my dog—isn't that what dogs are for? Nevertheless, I contacted trainers and decided if my trial didn't go well, I would get a dog within a week.

JANUARY 2011

I geared up again for more last-minute motions. The defendant moved the court to exclude a confidential informant (CI) as a witness. Prosecution had used a CI to approach Morrison to engage him in a drug deal while in jail. Morrison bit. I wanted the jury to know Morrison had not been rehabilitated and found Jesus as he'd claimed in the first sentencing.

Additional CIs claimed to know information about Morrison's plans for me, but they also created some wild facts that were unsupported. CIs were low-hanging fruit that even the most inexperienced attorney could discredit on the stand. Imagine the questions: "So how long have you been a CI for the prosecution? When did you decide to target Morrison? Were you acting as an agent of the prosecution? What did the Commonwealth promise you in return for your testimony today?" The juice wasn't worth the squeeze on this one.

Heading into this trial was completely different from the first one. I'd read more, researched more, and spoken with more experts of all types. I was not as scared. I was a wolf. I was ready. I dared that defense team to try to attack my credibility.

Without any guidance from the prosecutors I prepared myself as much as any person can prepare themselves for the performance of a lifetime. That is what being on the stand is—a performance. To share my story in such a way that twelve strangers feel comfortable recommending Morrison lose the rest of his life to prison despite having a professionally trained team of interrogators attack my story at every point. I had a squeaky-clean record and had been able to avoid a lot of the issues other victims sadly get beaten up over. Defense attorneys notoriously pounced on victims with questions about what were victims wearing, their history with the defendant, or if they were drinking or on drugs. Some well-intentioned jurors may rely on answers to questions like these to determine the victim had some culpability. Even though they shouldn't. The prosecutor's job with me was easy. I'd demanded a drug screen. *Nobody* did *that*.

My mind was sharp, and I was confident that no matter what happened, I was going to be okay. I was scared, even terrified. I had no idea what my life might look like after the trial, but I knew I was going to survive.

FEBRUARY 20, 2011

My brother Rick called. He was driving from North Carolina to be there for the trial, which started the next morning. He asked how I was doing.

"I am great. God is going to show up and kick ass, Rick. He is going to kick some ass in that courtroom!"

Pause. Silence. Then, "Yes, he is Sharon. Yes, he is!"

I come from a family where you don't use profanity. My parents told us anyone could do it. They also encouraged us to be mindful and creative in the ways we expressed ourselves. I'm sure that's why I've never liked the sound of those words. So when I said that to my brother, it took us both by surprise.

Rick and I made plans to meet the next morning with my sister, mom, and the rest of my friends and family. Times like this made my dad's absence even more painful—he was such a source of strength for me. His unexpected passing in 2009 was felt every day. Today just more than usual.

My friend Beth spent the night with me. While getting ready the next morning, I blared music in my room, singing at the top of my lungs as a song came on K-LOVE, my favorite music station. The lyrics were about God roaring like a lion, and without realizing what I was doing, I roared like a lion. I promise. I jumped around, adrenaline pumping, like a prize-fighter getting ready for a match. It reminded me of when I saw Laila Ali in a boxing match. She came out of the dressing room with a look of such intensity and focus that she intimidated everyone in the arena. She was focused and ready. I was, too.

No delays or continuances today, I thought. *I've waited for this for five years, and this is going to be my week.*

We drove the ninety minutes to Bourbon County and walked into the courthouse. Steve wasn't with me for this trial. He had a family emergency. I couldn't have survived the first trial without Steve, and I would have loved to have him here but things were different now. I was different. My friends stuck with me and I met my family in the hall. We headed toward the jury room where I'd be sequestered throughout the trial.

As I walked past the courtroom door, I saw Jeff Ballard on the stand being questioned. It hit me. We were finally doing this. I'd shown up here so many times, once for a trial and many times for hearings when things were moved, passed, or changed. It was finally happening.

The end had begun.

I had asked my supporters to be in the courtroom so they could share details from the trial after the verdict—otherwise, I wouldn't know. As everyone started to file out, Rachel asked Amy to leave with her and I said, "No, Amy stays here." She'd been through so much with me, and I needed her to help me stay calm before

I walked out. As they left, everyone encouraged me with looks and words but not with hugs. I didn't want to hug anyone for fear I'd melt into them and not stop sobbing.

My brother understood what I was doing and approached me with the intensity of Muhammad Ali. He grabbed my shoulders and squeezed hard as if he was holding me up. His eyes drilled into mine, and red faced, he said, "Sharon, God is going to show up today and kick ass."

"Yeah, he is going to kick ass!"

We all but chest-bumped and high-fived. Like a prize-fighter stepping into the ring, I was full of adrenaline, fearless, and ready to crush this.

That lasted about a minute.

CHAPTER 20

TRIAL PART I—THE JURY'S DILEMMA

POLICE INTERVIEW OF LARRY MORRISON

DATE: April 7, 2006

BOURBON COUNTY JAIL

[QUESTIONING BY DETECTIVE MURRELL]

> **Q:** Okay. Where did you ask her to give you a ride to?
>
> **A:** [Meemaw's].
>
> **Q:** About what time you think she picked you up today?
>
> **A:** I'm going to say—I don't know—4:30, maybe 5:00 or something like that, I guess.
>
> **Q:** Okay. And what happened then?
>
> **A:** Well, [we] went for a ride.

Juries want answers and without them they waver. It is the jury's dilemma. So trial attorneys become storytellers. We weave the facts that support our case into a narrative that answers the biggest question for the jury: Why did this happen? In opening, you cast a vision with the jury—creating a theme. With each witness you pull out facts to fill in gaps in the story. On cross-examination you score a few points and get out. And in closing, you argue why your theme works and opposing counsel's does not. Solve the jury's dilemma and get your verdict.

During the course of the trial I sat sequestered in a back room with the other witnesses. So the transcripts you read are taken straight from the trial. It isn't my perspective—I wasn't there—but the narrative is all mine.

When I first read the transcripts, I was grateful I had not been in the courtroom. Remembering how I leaned forward and barked at Morrison during the 404(b) motion, I'm not sure I would have contained myself during trial. Even as I reviewed transcripts to write this, I mumbled nasty things through gritted teeth.

Often, an event so anticipated, so longed for, seems anticlimatic in its arrival. Not so here. This trial not only delivered the significance and impact it would have on the rest of my life, it determined how long my life might be.

Judge Johnson presided over the trial. We moved to voir dire, where each side selected the jury and then presented *their* respective version of the facts during opening statements.

As you read through the testimony, consider the lesson I learned from my brother in fourth grade. The whole truth is often conspicuously absent in a courtroom. You will read through highlights of the opening, witness testimony, and closing arguments. I challenge you to decide if you would find Morrison guilty or not guilty. Innocence is not for a jury to decide. All a jury may determine is if the evidence presented in the isolation of a courtroom establishes beyond a reasonable doubt that the defendant committed the crime.

"You can't un-ring a bell," is an expression used in the law to mean that once a jury hears something they can't un-hear it. It takes great self-awareness to prevent something you should not have heard from influencing your decision. As a juror, you have no idea Morrison stood in front of the judge in 2007 and pleaded guilty to every charge. A juror would not know everything you've read, only what was presented in the courtroom. You'll have to check your reasoning to determine if your decision was derived from only the evidence presented.

No one said being a juror was easy.

JUDGE: The Commonwealth may proceed.

OPENING STATEMENT

[BY COMMONWEALTH'S ATTORNEY, Mr. Gordie Shaw]

Ladies and Gentlemen, we are here at the opening statement. This is where we give the roadmap. It's nothing like closing argument. In fact, argument's not even proper at this point. So we'll simply be laying out how the Commonwealth intends to prove its case and some of the things you'll be hearing and the basic outline of the case to you. Some of the proof that the Commonwealth will put forward is going to come from the testimony of Jeff Ballard. Mr. Ballard was a close friend at the time of Sharon Muse. And Ms. Muse is our victim in this case where, as the judge has read to you, there's allegations in the indictment of kidnapping, sexual abuse in the first degree, and resisting arrest.

Gordie distinguished the purpose of opening statements and closing arguments for the jury. Attorneys can't argue in their openings. They simply give a statement of the facts in a way that supports their theme. The facts they know are going to be presented during the trial. In closing, they argue their case, weaving in the facts that were presented in testimony to their theme for the case, answering the questions they know the jury has, and closing the deal. Each side has a theme. At the end of deliberation you want the jury to accept yours.

He went on to explain that law enforcement officers would testify, they would hear a recorded interview with Morrison from the night of the incident along with my 911 call, and they would hear from witnesses that came upon the scene. He thanked the jury and sat down. The defense rose to begin their opening.

OPENING STATEMENT

[BY ATTORNEY FOR THE DEFENSE, MR. WEST]

Ladies and gentlemen of the jury. Larry, I'll call him Larry instead of Mr. Morrison. I've come to know him as Larry. He has had demons in his life. At some point, he lost his wife and he doesn't have a—he stays some with his—his meemaw, Eva Johnson, an elderly lady. And at some point, he gets in his mind he needs a lawyer. He makes a call or two. And at some point, I think he actually connects with Ms. Muse's secretary, not hiding who he is, he doesn't get up with her at that point. But at some point, because Ms. Muse's office is walking distance of where's he's staying and he has no other means, he sees her and he's got these papers in hand and he'd been drinking. And you're going to hear that he had cocaine in his system. Like I said, a lot of demons.

He's looking to Ms. Muse as probably the—one of the few friendly voices he's ever heard—[to] help [him]. Not intent on kidnapping, not intent on terrorizing her, but very intent on trying to get her ear. He said, "Will you give me a ride?" She says yes. They get in the car. And at some point, Ms. Muse must have realized that well, this isn't the straight trip down to his meemaw's that I thought this was. You know, we're out of Georgetown. We're on the road. At some point she says he's got a gun, she's in a full-blown panic. He's trying to keep her from getting out of the car.

And what this trial is about, in large part, is what happened between those scant seconds when the phone went dead and she did get out of the car, what was said, what was thought was said, what was the state of mind, what was going on. That's really what this trial is going to be about. But we think when you hear all of the evidence, you'll find that he never intended to kidnap anybody. He panicked in a situation with the cocaine-alcohol mix. That doesn't excuse anything. But it gives you a context for this person who's basically looking out for someone—this is really the only person he can think of he can get to. But he intended no sex abuse. When you hear these differing views of evidence, we want you to think about not just what was said but the physical evidence in the case. We want you to look at the whole of the evidence.

In reality, the absence of evidence is not evidence of absence, but to a jury it is. Naturally, West focuses on the lack of physical evidence. If we operated in truth, there would be a plethora of physical evidence: the knife, marks in car, injuries to my body, the cash with the cocaine in the middle, the green duffle bag, the notes from his phone calls to my office where he wouldn't leave his name, my shirt, my necklace, my drug tests, the letter Morrison wrote to his attorney, the TV news interview where he admitted what he did, et cetera. If these things were not collected, preserved, and admitted the jury will never know they exist.

From Mr. West's opening, I'm guessing very little physical evidence will be introduced. He knows what is coming, I don't. From what I know of the lack of law enforcement working my case, I expect a weak display of evidence. And the way he speaks from Morrison's point of view means he must call Morrison to testify. His statement has to be a prediction of what the jury will hear. He can't testify for Morrison, only tell us what Morrison will say during testimony at trial.

DIRECT EXAMINATION OF JEFF BALLARD

[BY COMMONWEALTH'S ATTORNEY, MR. GORDIE SHAW]

JUDGE: Go ahead and call your first witness.

MR. SHAW: Jeff Ballard.

Gordie walks through Jeff's history as a pastor and our relationship. He asks Jeff about taking notes while on the phone with me and his reaction to learning Morrison had recently been released from prison.

Q: What was that like, hearing her ask that question ["*Out of . . . prison?*"]?

A: I can't describe it. I was mortified. I—if there was any doubt before, there was no longer any doubt that she called me because she was afraid, that there was a man in her car, that she was suspicious about his intentions. She was asking him questions that he didn't have many answers for. And then whether she was just remembering it in that moment, when she said prison, I was terrified because the implication was clear that she was in the car with an ex-convict that was making her very uneasy.

She kept saying, "Where are we going?" And I could hear him give directions, you know, turn left here; go through that intersection. And she would ask, "Didn't you say this was just down the street; where are we going?" And so at that point, he speaks up clearly really for the first time. And he says, "What is that in your hand over there? Is that some sort of tape recorder," he said. And Sharon said, "No, this is just my cell phone." And he said, "Well, is it on?" And she said, "Yes, in fact, it is," and said, "My friend, Jeff, is on the other end of the line." And so for a few moments she put the phone to her ear and we could talk for the first time. And I said, "Hey, what's going on? Do I need to call the police?" And she said, "I'm not sure yet, but please stay on the line. I need you on the line with me." And I said, "Sharon, you know I'm not very familiar with Georgetown." I said, "Any road sign you see, try to say it out loud. Any landmark you drive past that you can say out loud, please, please do that, so I'm taking notes here. I'm writing this down. You've got help me find you." And so at that point, the phone was taken from her.

Any time they came to an intersection, she would try to find something helpful that she could say out loud. "Are we out by the airport now? What is that over there, a lumberyard?" And so I'm just writing down airport, question mark, lumberyard. She sees a road, and I hear her say to this man, "Is this the road back to Georgetown; I need to get back home; is this the road?" She didn't know—she didn't know where she was. She was getting turned around out there and so—

Q: Let me ask you.
A: Yes.

Q: During this conversation, for the first one you hear that you listen to, was there ever any change in tone between the two of them or—

A: Sharon's tone changed drastically in the conversation starting off with what you might just describe as suspicion like—like any clever woman who knows when a guy is feeding her a line. By the end of their time in the car, she's screaming and she's horrified.

Q: Well, let's go with the phone call ended abruptly while you were talking to defendant. Did you call back? Did they call you back? What happened?

A: Yes. As soon as the line went dead when the defendant and I were talking, I was trying to reconnect the line.

Q: What do you hear at that point?

A: Sharon sees a building ahead, clearly confused, but she says, trying to help me, what is that up there, Larry? And by this time, she's calling him by name. What is that up there, Larry? Is that a store? And he says, "Hey, this is it; turn right here." And so presumably, she does. And a few more moments of silence, and he said, "This driveway right here; this is the one. This is the driveway; pull in here." And so you hear the car slow. You hear it come to idle. And this is where Sharon decides that she's had enough, and so in a very stern voice, she says, "Larry, that gate is closed. That place back there looks deserted. I am not driving down that road. I am turning my car around, and I want you to get out now."

Q: Did you hear him give her any commands either before or after?

A: No. No. At that point, I heard nothing from him except as soon as she said, "get out of my car now," there was instant commotion in the car. I mean, like wrestling sounds, grunting. I don't know to describe it but obvious commotion and activity in the car. And then the next thing I hear is Sharon's screams, and she says, "Jeff, he's got a gun; call the police." And then the line went dead.

Q: Did you ever hear him ask her to drive up toward a barn?

A: Yes.

Q: What—what did you—

A: What am I going to tell the police? She's in a white Honda. She thinks she's in Bourbon County.

Q: What did you do after the line went dead?

A: Called the police.

Q: And were you able to describe for them in any detail?

A: Those notes was all I had with me, you know. She's with a man apparently named Larry. Apparently, he recently got out of jail. Apparently, they're in Bourbon County. They might be out by an airport somewhere. How this can be helpful to them? It was obvious the police needed to be called, but I felt totally helpless to be able to direct them there.

From West's opening and his remarks about the "scant seconds" between when the phone died and I called 911, it was clear that he was trying to establish I was so panicked that my testimony couldn't be trusted. He was painting the picture that what I said was based on what I feared may have happened, not what actually happened. In his version, I was the last friendly face Morrison saw before he went to prison—even though the last time he saw my face was November 2001 and he didn't go to prison until two years later in October 2003 after eight additional arrests with thirteen charges. Morrison picked up six years on one charge alone, but served only two and a half. Six days later, he showed up at my office. No friendly faces in two years? That would have been nice to point out to the jury. According to West, Morrison was just riding around with his old buddy Sharon, listening to music, maybe stopping to get a burger at Wendy's—until Sharon panicked.

But Jeff is smart, much smarter than the average person, and I knew he would not have his words twisted on the stand. I'm thankful he was one of my star witnesses at trial. He laid a foundation that would make it hard for West to attack my testimony—not that he didn't try.

CROSS-EXAMINATION OF JEFF BALLARD

[BY ATTORNEY FOR THE DEFENSE, MR. WEST]

Q: Okay. And is she [Sharon] able to pretty much keep it together at this point in terms of the tone of her voice? Was she in a full-blown panic at this point?

A: That's difficult to answer. She's an amazingly strong woman. And the fact that she had the presence of mind to hit a button on her phone to dial me so I could hear what was going on showed me that she was very concerned, frightened, but I wouldn't say "panicked" because a panicked person wouldn't think that clearly, so it's difficult to have one answer to that.

Q: During this time that she was communicating with you during these twenty to twenty-two minutes, I don't see where you recorded anything where she said words to the effect of "You're touching my neck" or "Why are you touching my neck?" Did she?

A: Not to my recollection, but if I may, the notes that I was taking while we were on the phone were primarily for the purpose of how am I going to help the police find her, not for the purpose of how frightened is she or is she being touched. My concern at that point was she's not sure where she's going; I have no earthly idea where they're going. I was trying to pay attention to those landmarks or street signs.

Q: Okay. Were you able to determine on your end of the line if the car was already stopped at that point? [when in the driveway to the farm]

A: The car was not stopped right up until that moment because Sharon told him plainly, "I'm turning around, and I want you out of my car now." So she had every intention of driving off. So—so no, sir, the car was not off. But then, it was nothing but commotion in the car after that and it would be very difficult to tell whether a key had been turned off or not amidst the screaming and the commotion.

REDIRECT EXAMINATION OF JEFF BALLARD

[BY COMMONWEALTH'S ATTORNEY, MR. GORDIE SHAW]

Q: And was there ever a point when you're hearing these voices, hearing her voice asking, "Where are we going?" where you could detect fear?

A: Absolutely. She—again, I felt from the very beginning that the reason that she called me—the reason that she wanted me to hear that this is a man recently out of prison, that this is a man who may have been drinking, that this is a man telling her stories and changing his story during the ride about are we going to my meemaw's house, are we going to my aunt's house, and is it down the street, or is it way out in Bourbon County? The entire process right up until the very end, I felt like she—she knew she had a reason to be afraid of this man and this situation, but she was incredibly composed, that she was—she was not going to let him see her fear, that she was not—she was not going to be anybody's easy victim.

Q: Was the level of fear you heard in her voice when it—the car first started and you got that first call, did it differ from the fear you heard in her voice as the calls progressed?

A: Yes. Again, early on, her tone sounded like what I would just describe as suspicious. The story's not adding up. You're not really believable. Maybe you've been drinking. Early on, it was a suspicious tone. By the end—I mean, she's—she's pointedly saying is this the road back to Georgetown; I need to get back home. And—and then by the very end just refusing to follow any more instructions from him, demanding that he get out of the car, and then—and then screaming.

Q: How would you characterize her statement when she said "I need to get back home," if you can?

A: Almost pleading, you know, like "please."

MR. SHAW: No more questions, Your Honor.

This was amazing. How many times will the jury hear Jeff say Morrison was just out of prison? The defense fought so hard to keep me from saying it, yet Jeff repeats it over and over. I love it.

RE-CROSS-EXAMINATION OF JEFF BALLARD

[BY ATTORNEY FOR THE DEFENSE, MR. WEST]

Q: And the only time that she ever yells out, "Jeff, call the police" is the final two seconds of these twenty to twenty-two minutes of phone calls?

A: Yes, sir. Now, obviously, if I had two phones right there, you can call the police with one line and be talking on the other, but I didn't have that. And so she had to choose then whether "Jeff, I need you to stay on the line with me," or "Jeff, I need you to call the police," and she chose stay on the line with me. And if I may, I believe the reason for that is that if I called the police earlier, I have no idea where they ended up. I have no idea what he's done to her.

Q: Again, until the last two seconds when she was in a panic and she says, "Jeff, call the police"?

A: The last two seconds when—what sounded like a fight began and when he produced a weapon, that's when she knew there's nothing else to wait to listen for. It's time to call the police.

Q: And did you know where she was at that time?

A: I had no clue.

Q: Did you have any idea from what you heard Ms. Muse say on the phone whether she knew where she was at that time?

A: She indicated more than once that she was confused; she was disoriented. She kept asking him, "Where are we? Are we out by the airport? Where are we going? Is that the road back to Georgetown?" I believe with all my heart that she did not know where she was. It was with some degree of certainty that she knew she was in Bourbon County and that's about it.

I was so proud of Jeff. He crushed it. But it shocked me to learn he described me as composed. In my mind I was a wreck. He had asked me if he should call the police, and I chose to keep him on the phone with me. Jeff understood why, but any defense attorney would use that as proof of my lack of fear. Why wouldn't I want him to call the police? Because they can't do anything for me if they can't find me. It shows a sense of my mental clarity I didn't feel like I had at the time. I was aware enough not to rush and have him call the police but instead, thought through the logic of it. Jeff had nothing that would help law enforcement. At least he was taking notes and helping me. I would do it all the same again if in a similar situation.

DIRECT EXAMINATION OF CHRIS ARNETT

[BY COMMONWEALTH'S ATTORNEY, MR. GORDIE SHAW]

JUDGE: Commonwealth call their next witness.

MR. SHAW: Chris Arnett.

Q: Would you please state your name for the record?
A: Christopher David Arnett.

Q: And it's obvious how you're employed, but I'll—I'll ask anyway.
A: Kentucky State Police as a trooper.

Q: I think—can you go ahead and describe her [Sharon's] appearance and emotional state?
A: She was crying, very upset that she let something like that happen to her.

Q: And did you take any further actions there at the scene?
A: I just interviewed her, took pictures of the car and her.

"Upset that she let something like that happen to her"? Really? I am going to give Trooper Arnett the benefit of the doubt and hope that wasn't his professional opinion. Maybe he is repeating what I said. But since so many other details were off in this testimony, I doubt he would recall a quote from me five years prior, and I don't know that I said it at the scene. As for the photos he testifies of taking, the only photos of my car, and the ones of my body at the hospital entered into evidence were taken by my direction. In my open records request of his file years later, I saw no photos. But this was the same man who discouraged me from getting the drug screen at the hospital. I'm not sure what I expected from him on the stand.

Why? Why all the mistakes? I have no answer to these enigmatic observations. Never will. But mistakes continue. And not just from law enforcement.

DIRECT EXAMINATION BY MR. SHAW CONTINUES

Q: I'm going to show you a certified copy of Georgetown Community Hospital records marked as Exhibit 20, and it may take you a second, but I'm

going to ask you to see if there's a toxicology
report in there that refers to illegal drugs
such as cocaine or barbiturates or marijuana in
there.

A: This is negative.

Q: Okay. And what was the date of that test?

A: It was on—it was on 4-7 of 2006.

Q: Very good.

MR. SHAW: Your Honor, if there's no objection, the
Commonwealth would move to introduce Item 20.

JUDGE: Any objection?

MR. WEST: No objection.

The rules of evidence don't allow using a police officer to enter a hospital toxicology report into evidence. You've read about my fixation with collection, preservation, and admissibility of evidence. This was about admissibility. To enter a scientific lab report, you must have someone from the lab that administered it answer questions regarding the validity of the testing. This is very basic. Yet Shaw didn't do it, and West didn't object. Why do I care? Because mistakes like these may be tantamount to a reversal on appeal. I've already experienced one and I don't want another. Pay attention to this issue—we will definitely see this again.

DIRECT EXAMINATION BY MR. SHAW CONTINUES

Q: Did you collect any items of evidence from the
scene that day on Russell Cave?

A: The knife.

Q: Anything else?

A: Not that I recall.

Q: Do you recall any discussions or seeing a duffle
bag?

A: I remember seeing a green duffle bag.

Q: Do you know who that belonged to or what happened to it?

A: They said it was Larry Morrison's, but I don't
know—I don't know what happened to it.

Q: Okay. That wasn't collected as part of it
evidence?

A: No.

Q: Did you inspect Ms. Muse's vehicle that day at
the scene?

A: Yes. I took pictures of it also.

Q: And did you find any contraband inside the car?

A: No.

He looked in my car at the hospital, not at the crime scene. No photos were in his
file. I have no idea what he is talking about.

Q: Do you know what the condition of the knife was?
Was it in good shape?

A: I believe it was bent on the end of it [the tip].

Q: Can you describe whether or not as far as his
degree of sobriety whether he [Morrison] was
sober or drunk, in between? Do you recall anything like that?

A: He seemed fine to me.

Q: Did you sense any type of influence?

A: I could smell odor of alcohol, but it really
wasn't that strong. I could just smell it in the
car.

Q: Did he understand the questions you posed to
him?

A: Yes.

Q: Okay. Did you recover any other evidence as far as this case is concerned?

A: No. I did not.

Trooper Arnett and I agree that Morrison sounded fine and the odor of alcohol was not noticeable until confined to the car. That seems to be our only shared recollection.

MR. SHAW: No more questions, Your Honor.

JUDGE: Okay. Mr. West?

CROSS-EXAMINATION OF CHRIS ARNETT

[BY ATTORNEY FOR THE DEFENSE, MR. WEST]

Q: Trooper, were you the officer in charge of this investigation?

A: Yes.

Q: You were? Is that why you collected the knife as evidence?

A: Yes, sir.

Q: And you saw the duffle bag, but you did not collect it?

A: I don't know what happened to the duffle bag.

Q: Okay. But you know you did not collect it, right?

A: Right. I saw the duffle bag.

Q: I'm sorry?

A: I saw the duffle bag, but I didn't collect it.

Q: You said you found no money?

A: No.

Q: You didn't find a wad of bills with a rubber band around it with something stuck in the middle of it?

A: No.

Q: Okay. Now, I want to ask you something. You said that you've been a trooper for twenty-five years? Did I hear that right?

A: Five years.

Q: I'm sorry. Five years. Okay. So how long had you been a trooper at this time?

A: Four months.

Q: Are you the one that collected the necklace that is now into evidence?

A: No.

Q: Okay. Do you know who did collect the evidence— the necklace which is now into evidence?

A: I can't tell you for sure. It's probably Detective Murrell.

Q: And what happened to Ms. Muse's vehicle? How did it leave the scene?

A: Excuse me? I'm sorry?

Q: How did it leave the scene?

A: I believe she drove it.

The jury has just been told I drove myself to the hospital. Odd for Arnett to state that since he had me pulled out of the ambulance to identify Morrison.

CHAPTER 21

TRIAL PART II—WHO WAS IN CHARGE?

JUDGE JOHNSON: Next witness, please.

MR. SHAW: Sergeant Murrell would be next, Your
Honor.

DIRECT EXAMINATION OF JEREMY MURRELL
[BY COMMONWEALTH'S ATTORNEY, MR. GORDIE SHAW]

Q: Sergeant, would you please state your name for
   the record?

A: Jeremy Edward Murrell.

Q: And how are you employed?

A: I am currently the Detective Sergeant of the
   Kentucky State Police, Post 6 at Dry Ridge.

After some time walking Murrell through his work history and involvement in this case, Shaw then moved to play the recording of Detective Murrell interviewing Morrison in jail the night of the kidnapping. Murrell's job was to put Morrison at ease and convince him that Murrell shared Morrison's questionable morals and his non-existent character and that he was there to help. They could talk about sex, drugs, and anything Morrison wanted. Murrell tried to get a confession, but Morrison knew better. Murrell did get Morrison to talk himself into a corner with a story that I was able to easily disprove.

POLICE INTERVIEW OF LARRY MORRISION
DATE: April 7, 2006
BOURBON COUNTY JAIL
[QUESTIONING BY DETECTIVE MURRELL]

MORRISON: So what's—what's been brought against me?

Q: Well, I'm going to explain that to you, okay?
We'll look at your citation here.
Do you know Sharon Muse?

A: Yes. I do.

Q: Okay. How do you know her?

A: Knowed her for a long, long time. Mm-hmm. She give me a ride.

Q: All right. Well, we—

A: I ain't going to tell on her. You know, I don't want to get her in trouble.
All right. We went for a ride and we discussing over a probate thing that's over a lot of money. That's what it boils down to. It's over [money].

Q: How much money you talking about?

A: Way up—I mean, over $250,000.

Q: $250,000? Okay. That's a lot of money. That's a quarter of a million.
Okay. Were you trying to get Sharon to represent you in that?

A: Yeah. I was going to get her to do that. Maybe it's—I was a little too forward with her, you know, and—

Q: Let me ask you this. What do you mean by "forward," okay? You tell me—

A: Well, I was drinking. Maybe I was just saying, "Hey, I need you to take care of this. I need you to help me," and she wanted me to get out. She made a big scene, though. She jumped out—she jumped out of the car and made a big scene. She made a big scene. I said "whoa," you know, and I told her—

Q: So she told you—

A: I told the witnesses—I said, "Look, whoa, wait a minute. She's just panicking." I walked over three-quarters of a mile down the highway and was shot at and I crossed the fence. That's where they found me at. Well, when you got a girl, you know, sitting here going through this and that and, you know, they made the *Dukes of Hazzard* scene or something so . . .

Q: *Dukes of Hazzard*, huh?

A: Boy, I've been beat and abused. I'm telling you.

Q: Okay. Well, let's go back to this, anything else happen tonight you need to tell me about or—?

A: No. I don't want to, you know, put her on the spot, you know, give her no more—I know she's powerful.

Q: Well, hang on. Hang on.

A: You know, she's got some power, and I wouldn't put her in a predicament. Really, I wouldn't.

Q: Now, you're telling me that you don't want to hang her out on anything.

A: Yeah.

Q: But here you sit with a B felony and looking at a Persistent Felony Offender, okay? So we're—I need the truth from you, Larry, okay? You've done some time before. How long did you do?

A: I killed a five-year sentence.

Q: So you did all five?

A: I did a real hard five.

No. He did a real hard twenty-nine months. Can he not do math or is he just confused?

Q: We need to start over with your story because right now, you're leaving a lot out, okay?

A: You want me to tell about her cocaine history and what she did and what we was doing out in the country?

Q: If that's the truth—

A: It is. I'll take a lie detector test.

Q: You need to tell me about it, okay?

A: She had quite a bit of cocaine.

Q: I don't want you to make up stuff to make you look good though, okay?

A: I'm telling you. I'm not making stuff up.

Q: She had some cocaine with her? All right, Larry. This part's important, okay?

A: This shit's burying me what I'm telling you, really.

Q: Well, how's it going to bury you? Sharon Muse is a big-time coke dealer? She sell coke?

A: You talk about some powerful stuff really. I probably could get killed for what I know, really. Seriously.

Q: Well, don't jerk my chain, man. I've heard a bunch of people say that.

A: I ain't playing. I ain't. This is serious. I'm telling you something that's huge.

Q: I can definitely hook you up with the right people, okay. Have them in here tomorrow. They'll talk to you, all right?

A: She pushed me, you know, really, I mean—And she said "Are you getting high still?" "Sharon, I've been clean for a long time." She said I—well, "I know you've been drinking a lot, Larry. Let's do some coke." I said, "Sharon, look." I said, "whatever, I mean, yeah, let's do it." I'll never forget. It was a Mickey Mouse thing that was rolled up and we snorted two lines apiece.

Q: Her cocaine? Where'd she get it? Out of her purse?

A: Little vial that she had. Yes. Well, she had more than that.

Q: Where'd she pour the cocaine out onto?

A: A little—like a little mirror—like a little square one like that—a cosmetic mirror.

Q: She poured it onto a cosmetic mirror. What'd she use to—what'd she use to divide up the lines?

A: Yeah. I don't know if it had Whitaker Bank on it. It had something on it. I couldn't tell what it was.

Q: Okay. Where were you when you did this? Were you way out in Bourbon County or . . . ?

A: Yeah. We was in a driveway.

Q: Okay. Was it the same driveway that you—she got out of and made the scene at or—

A: Yeah.

Q: Okay. What brought on the—what brought on her making the scene? What happened there?

A: Somebody that she was talking with on the phone. I don't know who it was, but she made a big deal. "Larry, I thought we was going to your grandma's." I don't know who she was talking to on the telephone. Told me to get out. I mean, she made a—like I said, look where I'm at right now, over all this shit.

Q: She just told you—

A: To get out. And I—you know, when you do that shit, it—I said, "Whoa, Sharon." I grabbed her. I said, "whoa, wait a minute now."

Q: You grabbed her shirt?

A: I did grab her shirt. She just made a fucking huge scene.

Q: What did you do when you grabbed—you grabbed her shirt?

A: She got out and said "whoa." Calm down, man. She flagged somebody down right here in the road. Here we're in this little driveway.

Q: You pull a knife out and hold it to her throat?

A: No. I did not.

Q: But you gave a knife to one of the witnesses.

A: I did. It was right there in the seat, but it was never pulled.

Q: Was it yours?

A: It was mine. That was my play knife. Yeah. I said "whoa." I pulled it off of my belt, and I said here it is.

Q: Here's where you're hurting me, okay? You just told me just a second ago you pulled it out between the seats. So it was on your belt.

A: I said here, whoa. Then I just sit there I took it off my belt. I sit there. I said here, here. Whoa, uh-uh, there.

Q: Did you ever tell her to pull up behind the barn?

A: No.

Q: Okay. She tells us you held that knife to her throat, told her to pull around that barn, and she was going to have sex with you. You ever had sex with her before?

A: No.

Q: So that thought never crossed your mind?

A: No.

Q: Okay. Not even after being a little high on a little coke? Come on, man. She's a pretty girl.

A: Pretty girl. I mean, she went through her little thing, though, and didn't. I mean, I'm being honest with you.

Q: Well, here's the problem, man. Here's the problem, Larry. She's got bruises on her, dude.

A: Bruises?

Q: She's bruised up pretty good and it's new stuff, okay? I was trying to help you, man.

A: If she's got bruises, that didn't happen with me, so . . .

Q: It's on the right side of her body which would be the one that—the side that's closest to you, okay. So if you grabbed her like you're saying, you know, it's kind of consistent with where you would grab her. I just don't think she would bruise herself, all right?

A: So they were right on her arm then?

Q: Yes, sir.

A: I'm tell you, I grabbed her on her arms.

Q: Okay.

A: If she got a bruise, then I'm guilty of that.

Q: So maybe you just didn't know how hard you grabbed her? You might have been high on coke a little bit. That might have been—

A: Yes, sir.

Q: Okay. So maybe you just told her to drive?

A: Drive, just drive.

Q: You remember maybe you just said, "hey, turn, take this road" or "turn this road"? Could you have done that?

A: It's possible. Anything's possible.

Q: Okay. So you're just driving and listening to music, right?

A: Yeah.

Q: So you was doing coke on the way while you was driving?

A: Yes.

Q: Okay.

A: Maybe she'll have somebody kill me, but whatever. I mean, I'm a little further out there.

Q: Oh, come on, now.

A: Because I know how much power she's got with people. I just don't like—you know, my grandmother's out there, and I can't put her in nothing bad. If she wants—

Q: So are you going to tell me that—well, man, if you don't want to put yourself in, do a hard twenty. Tell me that you held the knife to her throat. Tell me that you wanted—to have sex with her back behind the barn and—

A: I can't do that.

Q: But you did—you did grab her?

A: Yes. I did.

Q: Okay. Did you tell her to pull back behind the barn? Be honest with me.

A: In the driveway, yes.

Q: Then you did some more coke there?

A: Yeah.

Q: Well, you told me you asked her to pull behind the barn, but she just stopped at the end of the driveway.

A: I don't know nothing about no barn.

Q: Okay. So your story's changed on me, man.

A: It's changed?

Q: That's number three, okay? At that point, you grab her by the shirt?

A: Yeah.

Q: And say, "Whoa, Sharon, calm down." Okay. Let me ask you this, man. You've been clean—

A: Long time.

Q: —for five years. How could she talk you into snorting coke that quick? Was you hoping to get a little piece off of her? Don't lie to me, man.

A: I wasn't really thinking about no pussy, man, but just having a good time with her, I mean, for real.

Q: Okay. All right, man. Well, why would she say—

A: I don't know how—

Q: —that you pulled a knife on her?

A: I would want to kidnap her, though. I don't understand none of that.

Q: Well, I mean, you know—

A: I told that officer—I said can I file a counter-suit [charge Sharon with kidnapping] against her now?

Q: What would you want—

A: It happened to me. I mean, it's her vehicle.

When Morrison asked that night if he could charge me with kidnapping, since it was my car, he was serious. The detective asked if he thought I texted on my phone, but Morrison didn't know—he hadn't been out of prison long enough to know

what texting was. So if his interview was hard to understand, it's because he has
trouble keeping up with the lies. And likes to say "Whoa" a lot.

CROSS-EXAMINATION OF DETECTIVE JEREMY MURRELL
[BY ATTORNEY FOR THE DEFENSE, MR. WEST]

JUDGE: Okay. Go ahead.

Q: Detective Murrell, The first thing I want to ask
you about, and Mr. Shaw hit on just previously,
was about the knife. You submitted that knife
because—against tool marks that were found in
the car?

A: Yes, sir.

Q: Okay. But you did not send the knife in for DNA
testing, did you?

A: No, sir. I did not.

Q: Of course, Kentucky does have a DNA lab?

A: Yes, sir. They do.

Q: In fact, [don't] they have several of them?

A: I think several of the regional labs can do DNA.
Yes.

Q: And it only takes a very small amount of DNA for
them to do testing, doesn't it?

A: I believe it's safe to say yes to that question.
I don't know the exact amount they need of DNA
to find it.

Q: But certainly the people at the lab would know
how much they needed—

A: Yes, sir.

Q: —and whether they could collect it off of a—a knife, for instance?

A: Yes, sir.

Q: And you also submitted into evidence this necklace, didn't you?

A: That appears to be the necklace that I collected from Ms. Muse's office and her blouse and took to the Commonwealth Attorney's office. Yes, sir.

Q: Okay. And there's a chip off of it?

A: I—I never personally examined the necklace, sir.

Q: Okay. You didn't submit this to the lab to see if they could see if the knife could have done this chip?

A: No, sir. I did not.

Q: Okay. This seems to be like some kind of hard plastic, or do you know what that is?

A: No, sir. I do not know what that is.

It is a semi-precious stone. No resemblance to plastic.

Q: Okay. Do you have any idea how much force it would take to make a chip like that?

A: No, sir. I do not.

Q: Okay. Who was responsible for taking photographs of any injury that Ms. Muse had?

A: I believe Trooper Arnett did that.

No, Georgetown Police did it. Arnett didn't take one photo that I've found.

Q: Who was the officer in charge of this investigation?

A: It was Trooper Chris Arnett's investigation, sir.

Q: Okay. Who was in charge of collecting the evidence?

A: That would be Trooper Chris Arnett.

Q: Do you know what happened to the green duffle bag?

A: The only knowledge I have of the green duffle bag is in reading Trooper Arnett's investigative narrative. I've never seen nor heard of it.

Q: You don't know that it was collected?

A: I have no idea if it was collected or not.

Q: Okay. Well, we do know that Mr. Morrison didn't take it with him when he went to the jail, right?

A: I know—I don't know what all was in his jail property, but again, the only time I've seen the green duffle bag mentioned was in his case report narrative. I've not seen it.

Q: What about a wad of bills circled by a rubber band with something in it? Did you see anything like that, a big wad of bills?

A: No, sir. Again, I responded only to the detention center on that evening—

Q: You don't know if an ambulance was called to the scene, do you?

A: No, not for certain. I do not know.

Q: And you don't know how Ms. Muse's car left the scene?

A: I don't know the answer to that either. No, sir.

Q: Who would I need to ask to know the answer to that?

A: I assume you'd have to ask Trooper Arnett.

West spends time pointing out the things I've worn Gordie out about since standing at the crime scene: properly collecting and assessing the physical evidence. Despite not being the officer in charge, Murrell collected more evidence than Arnett. Murrell took my necklace and shirt to the Commonwealth's Attorney office, although my shirt was never seen again. He also arranged for my car to be taken to the crime lab—a year after the kidnapping, but at least he did it. Two things prevented the knife from being matched: one—almost a year had passed and two—the end of the knife was broken off, or so I was told by Arnett.

Arnett got that wrong, too. Or did he? He testified the knife had bent, even though he was the one to tell me it broke and asked to search my car for the tip. I wouldn't know if it was broken or bent since I never saw the knife again. Neither did the jury. I had been told the crime lab lost it. In my open records request, I found where Arnett sent an order to the crime lab to destroy the knife during the appeal in 2007. I can't begin to even guess why this would happen. As for the wad of money wrapped around cocaine? I bet it is in the green duffle. Wherever that is.

CHAPTER 22

TRIAL PART III—THE FIVE-YEAR WAIT

I sat down the hall, sequestered in the witness room, and waited to testify. As other witnesses were called and released, the room got less crowded. Finally, Dolly, the bailiff called my name. I stood and walked down the hall straight for the courtroom.

At the door, I caught the judge's eye, and when my right foot crossed the threshold, I saw the jury turn to look at me. The trial was suddenly real. I moved backward, as if a gale-force wind had swept through the courtroom and forced me into the hall against my will. I stopped, frozen, when my back collided with the wall and turned only my head toward the bailiff standing by the door. With eyes wide and tear filled, I shook my head no. She looked stunned.

"I can't do it," I whispered, barely audible.

"You have to go in," she said, uncertainty in her voice.

We waited. The judge leaned over the bench, head tilted and brows furrowed first in confusion, then in concern.

"Will you walk in with me?" I asked the bailiff.

Despite the incredulity on her face, she nodded. I turned my body to face the open doorway, and I took one step, then another.

Entering the courtroom that day took every ounce of my willpower. I was terrified, scared the jury wouldn't help me, and humiliated that the feral beast who did this reveled in the display of devastation he brought to my life. I'd visualized this moment many times trying to prepare myself, and that mental preparation finally kicked in. I imagined I was surrounded by ten-foot-tall angels with flaming swords—my personal Pretorian Guard ready to slice Morrison in half if he made a move toward me.

COMMONWEALTH OF KENTUCKY

v.

LARRY MORRISON

DIRECT EXAMINATION OF SHARON MUSE

PROSECUTION: Commonwealth calls Sharon Muse.

JUDGE: If you'll raise your right hand, please. Do you solemnly swear or affirm to tell the truth, the whole truth, and nothing but the truth, so help you God?

I opened my mouth to speak, and the words died in my throat. I'm not sure I was breathing. I had my right hand in the air and paused in the witness stand facing the judge as he swore me in. My hand visibly shook, my eyes filled with tears, and I could not find my voice. Every pair of eyes in the courtroom focused on me. Morrison was staring, and I had no doubt he wanted me to feel his eyes boring through me. His attorneys were holding their breath, waiting to see what type of witness I would be. The TV cameras were pointed directly at me. Somehow, I fumbled through the swearing in and sat down.

Then I found the face of my precious friend, Tom, a pastor with a huge heart for God and for people. He had brought his anointing oil that morning and anointed anything and everything that wasn't bolted down—the table where the jury was going to deliberate, the witness stand where I was going to sit, and me. No doubt the cotton handkerchief Tom had the bailiff hand me had been prayed over, too. Tom sat in the back of the courtroom nodding his head at me. What a comfort to see his smile and the passionate nod signaling to me that he was confident that God, my protector, was in the room. The God of the Old Testament was showing up and taking names like he did for Gideon, kicking ass, if you will. Tom's encouragement brought me back to focus on God which helped me endure what was ahead of me.

I could hardly hear my own voice and was sure the jury couldn't either. My hands were hidden behind a wooden partition running along the front of the witness stand. I twisted and untwisted the handkerchief ad nauseam, my knuckles white with strain. It was a balancing act to maintain a show of strength in front of Morrison while being vulnerable before the jury. As a trial lawyer, I was very comfortable in a courtroom, but this was my first time on the stand. I was literally fighting for my life. I would finally be able to tell my story. Unfortunately, I had to do it a few feet away from the man who kidnapped me and attempted to rape and murder me, knowing that if he had the opportunity, he would return to finish what he started.

The prosecutor entered my 911 call as evidence and started the recording.

I was unable to look at the jury. I knew what we were about to hear. I sucked in stale air, trying not to cry, and held it until my lungs roared and tears flooded my eyes. As the call started to play, I looked at my mom, wanting to comfort her, to let her know I was okay despite what she was about to hear. Details I had kept from her on purpose. Sounds no mother needs to hear from her child. I remained still, quietly weeping.

> **CALLER:** There's a woman here. She ran into the road with her shirt down. She was screaming . . .

It hurt me to watch my family and friends listen to my recorded cries fill the courtroom. Eventually I dropped my head into my hands, unable to hold it up on my own and unwilling to make eye contact with my supporters. I let out a long, ragged breath, as tears streamed down my face. I just wanted the recording to end.

From the jury box, someone coughed. I glanced up to see an older gentleman leaning forward, listening closely to every word. One woman dabbed at tears while another, I was shocked to see, sat impassive—showing no sign of which way she might be leaning other than boredom. Then she nodded off. I couldn't believe what I was seeing. My life hung in the balance, and she was napping. How could I get her attention? She had to hear this.

A third young woman smiled at me as if to cheer me on, and the lawyer part of me kicked in. I studied every juror, noted every move, every expression, trying to read their thoughts. *Did they trust me? Did they like me? Would they help me?*

I saw sorrow on most of their faces. The jurors felt my raw pain. I needed them to empathize with me, to protect me.

I needed them to convict Morrison to stop him from coming back to finish what he started.

While the 911 call was being played, Mr. West stood up, objected, and called for an argument outside the presence of the jury. In the middle of the most moving part of my time on the stand. Judge Johnson allowed the jury to take a break during this time, and I was taken to the grand jury room to wait. Eventually a bailiff brought me back to the courtroom and put me back on the stand. Judge Johnson overruled Mr. West's objections and we moved forward. This was excruciating and could have been avoided if Keith and Gordie had filed a pre-trial motion. The one good thing about this was the jury informed the judge that they still couldn't hear me. Judge Johnson politely requested I speak up, reminding me how important it was for the jury to hear me.

Throughout direct examination, I refused to glance at Morrison. I leaned out of my chair to avoid eye contact with him as the prosecutor questioning me, Keith Eardley, asked me to view the exhibits set up near the defense table. I didn't know how I would respond if we locked eyes. Part of me feared I would melt down, and the other part feared I'd leap over the railing that separated us and beat his head against the defense table. During previous court hearings, I'd caught myself thinking about doing just that.

I was frustrated with Keith as every time I was at a crucial place in my testimony, where the jury was leaning in and engaging with me, he would interrupt to ask me a question unrelated to what we were talking about or to point to something on the map. Each time I lost the jury and had to get them back with me, feeling the event, in the moment. Then another question about the map. I think he was so tied to a script he couldn't tell the questions were hurting, not helping. If only he had prepped me this could have been so much smoother.

As the prosecutor walked me through my testimony, he asked me multiple times to speak up. The judge asked me to speak up. The jury asked me to speak up. But my body language changed dramatically when we transitioned from questions intended to allow the jury to get to know me to questions about the incident. When defense counsel stood up to cross-examine me, I transformed from weepy to warrior. I sat up taller and squared off my shoulders. My anger at the defense counsel's blatant disregard for truth outweighed the fear that had kept me trembling, and I found my voice. It came back strong. Maybe too strong.

I tried to stay calm, think first, answer briefly, and not over-analyze the questions. I also tried to use my 80/20 rule that I preach to clients. Think about your answer and say 20 percent of what you think you should say. Unfortunately, I wasn't able to follow my own advice. The rules of criminal procedure didn't allow the prosecutor to know any details of Morrison's defense prior to the trial. This meant I had to listen carefully to figure out what West was trying to prove. He wouldn't spell it out for me; that would be in his closing. But if I could determine where he wanted to go, I could make sure he didn't take me there. I didn't want him quoting me to the jury to support his case. This was hard to do since I wasn't allowed in the courtroom other than while testifying, so I had to figure this out as the questions came flying at me. I would never advise a client to do this.

COMMONWEALTH OF KENTUCKY

v.

LARRY MORRISON

DATE: February 21, 2011

CROSS-EXAMINATION OF SHARON MUSE

[BY ATTORNEY FOR THE DEFENSE, MR. WEST]

Q: Ms. Muse, you've seen me before, haven't you?

A: Yes.

Q: You know I represent Mr. Morrison?

A: Yes

Q: Okay. Now, you've given several statements in this case. Have you not?

A: Yes, sir.

Q: And is the first one the oral statement that you gave at the hospital that night?

A: I would think so. I—I'm going to say yes.

Q: Okay. And then sometime later, do recall this statement?

A: Can I see it?

Q: Absolutely.

A: Yes, sir.

Q: Okay. Do you remember when you did *this* statement?

A: No. I don't.

Q: And so that I don't put a word in your mouth here, this purports to be a general summary of what happened that night?

A: Yes.

Q: All right. So that makes me think that this third statement—do you recognize this third statement?

A: Yes.

Q: That's a more detailed statement, correct?

A: Well, it's got more details, but it's still a general summary.

I know what he wants to get from me now.

Q: Okay.

A: It would obviously be impossible to write down everything that took place.

Q: Do you know if you wrote this one after the previous one I just showed you or before?

A: I don't know.

Q: Okay. And therefore, could this one also have been a couple of weeks to a month afterwards?

A: I don't know when I was asked to do it. I don't know what the terms were. Do you want a long one, short one? This one's general. This one's very general. This one, a few more details. I have no idea.

Q: Okay. When I ask you a question from one of them, I'll try to make sure that you know which one. I'm going to call this one the short one.

A: Okay.

Q: Okay. Now, when you were interviewed that night, you didn't mention anything about him putting his hand between your legs, did you?

A: There was a lot of things I didn't mention that night. My mom and dad were in the room.

Q: Okay. But I'm talking about that one specific thing now.

A: Well, is that all you want to know or do you want to know other things I left out?

Q: No. We're going to go—we'll—we'll talk about that as time goes on.

A: Okay.

Q: But for now, I want to know about that specific statement. Today, you said that he had his hands between your legs. That night, you didn't mention that, correct?

A: I don't know if I did or not. I'd have to look at the statement. Is it not in any of my statements?

Yes, it is. And I know it is.

Q: Well, we'll get there, but I—I'm wanting to ask you first if it is in the interview [first statement taken in hospital room].

A: I don't mind to defer to you if you've read that and say that it's not in there.

Because I know what is coming.

Q: It's not in there. But you do mention it in the short statement.

A: Yes.

Q: And I want to show you where it—you say, "He also put his hand on my leg."

A: Mm-hmm.

Q: Okay. So he—in this statement you say he put his hand on your leg.

A: Well, he touched my leg more than once so if I'm supposed to say that's the time he touched the top of my thigh; that's the time he touched my inner thigh near my genitalia; that's the time he—

Q: Oh, did you say—did—did he touch your genitalia?

A: Well, his hand was—do you want me to show you where he touched me? [witness rises from chair to demonstrate]

Q: No, just—Well, I mean, did his hand—let me put it the way that you—you said it. Did his hand touch your genitalia?

A: Part of his hand did. He was at the very top of my inner thigh and part of his hand was on my inner thigh, part of it was—

Q: Okay. You realize in none of your three statements do you ever say that he touched your genitalia?

A: I realize I've never given a complete, detailed statement.

I did this on purpose.

Q: Okay.

A: Nobody asked me to.

Q: No one asked you to give a complete, detailed statement?

A: I was asked to do general statements. Are you asking what the attorneys asked me to do?

Q: Anybody in this investigation.

A: Well, nobody else asked me to write anything down.

Q: All right.

A: I'm not—I'm not trying to be difficult. I'm just a little confused. I'm not sure what you're asking me.

I am sure, but I wanted to get him off this genitalia thing. He was too excited about it.

Q: No. You've answered that part of the question. Let me ask you about him touching your neck, okay?

A: Okay.

Q: Now, that happened before you talked to Jeff on the phone. Did it not?

A: I don't know.

Q: Okay. Can I refresh?

A: Sure.

MR. EARDLEY: Long statement?

MR. WEST: Long statement.

Q: "He grabbed me by the back of the neck, squeezed it, and then ran his fingers down my back—"

A: Mm-hmm.

Q: "—just a few inches."

A: Mm-hmm.

Q: Right?

A: Mm-hmm.

Q: Then you say, "He noticed the cell phone and kept asking if it was a tape recorder—"

A: Mm-hmm.

Q: "—and asked if it was recording him. I said no, it was my cell phone."

A: Mm-hmm.

Q: Then down here is, "I gave him the phone because I wanted him to know there was a man on the phone."

A: Mm-hmm.

Q: "He started talking to Jeff."

A: Mm-hmm.

Q: So this all happened before he was talking to Jeff?

A: That's not chronological. I don't see where it says that. And he grabbed the back of my neck

more than once. Are you talking about the time,
the creepy [moment when he said,] "ooh, it's nice
to be in this car with you?"

Q: Well, I never see it in any statement more than
once. Are you saying that it happened multiple
times and you talked about a different time each
time you gave a statement?

A: I gave a general statement each time I did it
[wrote a statement]. I didn't know I was supposed
to do a play-by-play of "first we did this, then
we turned left, then we went here," because
that's not how my brain works. Nobody said, "How
many times did he touch you? make sure you say
that." Nobody said, "Exactly where did he touch
you? make sure you put that in there."

Q: Well, you're an attorney, right?
A: I'm not in this case.

Q: I understand, but you—you are one by profession.
A: It's a little bit difficult to represent yourself
[I lean in to the mic] when you've been
kidnapped.

Well, so much for the demure woman the jury could barely hear on direct examination. It seemed I was ready to go to war with this guy.

Several things made me angry. The most significant one was that if Gordie hadn't told me to write three different statements, we wouldn't be having this conversation in front of the jury. I purposefully wrote in a vague manner and stated at the bottom that they were general statements. What is most frustrating is that if Gordie had called me to his office and asked me to tell him my story while he wrote it down, the defense would have never seen that. Of course I would have to provide a statement, but only one. Gordie's written version would be protected from discovery as work product. My statement was evidence that defense reviewed and tore apart for months or years prior to my testimony. Three requests for statements? I'd never seen such a thing.

And Keith, was he paying attention while I was on the stand or just stuck to a script? Why didn't he engage? Why did he stop my questions every time I was on a roll with the jury? Why didn't he clean up the fake message to the jury that I drove my car to the hospital? That would have been easy since it was written in the medical records I referenced from the witness stand.

Another point of frustration was West. The clever but contemptible perversion of the facts and real effects of trauma made me thank God for Jeff, the Gibsons, and my drug screen. Without them, what would the jury think?

He tried to manipulate the jury by twisting the truth and creating his own facts well enough to elicit a not guilty verdict. Truth was irrelevant. His client was guilty, and he knew it. He couldn't ask the jury not to believe me at all. I was too good a witness and he couldn't blatantly attack me without running the risk of alienating the jury.

I knew I should just listen and answer West's questions, but the lawyer in me found it impossible to do that. I could hardly contain myself on the stand. Apparently, I *didn't* contain myself.

> **Q:** Understood, but you're—you are an attorney?
> **A:** Yes, I am.
> **Q:** Okay. And you know that when you give statements, that it's a possibility that it's going to come out in court as to what you said [in your statements] and when?
> **A:** Sure, and everything in there is true, in all of them.
> **Q:** So, if one statement says that he touched your neck before you talked to Jeff and the other one *seems to indicate* afterwards.

I lean up and with a firm voice, ask . . . .

A: *Seems* to indicate?

Q: Yes.

A: Or does it *say* it?

Q: Well—

A: Because what you just read off the long statement doesn't say I called Jeff after this. You
said he touched my neck. I had a phone. He asked
what it was. He talked to Jeff. It doesn't say
this was first. That was second.

Q: Well, that's right. I'm just reading it in the
order that you wrote it.

A: Right, which—

Q: Are you—are you saying that this happened—this
could have happened after the statement about
talking to Jeff instead of before?

A: I'm saying I can't tell you at three minutes and
twenty seconds into it, he touched me here and
then I called Jeff. I can't say that and be
honest.

Q: Well, I understand that.

A: I think you're misinterpreting that [statements]
if you believe it to be detailed, all-inclusive,
[and in] chronological order and that nothing
happened during [the kidnapping] that wasn't
specifically detailed in those general summary
statements.

Q: So you're saying that his hand was between your
legs at that time and that's where your phone
was?

A: We discussed this earlier [hinting to my attorney to object to asked and answered]. He would lean over and put his hand on the top [of my leg]. Maybe he'd put it on the inside. It was a very chaotic, bizarre situation, but that's how I would guess he realized it [the phone] was there, if I had to guess. Which I'm not comfortable doing.

The words came out before I could filter them. On a list of mistakes to make while being crossed, I made most of them, speaking too quickly and arguing with opposing counsel. I would not recommend someone respond on cross-examination the way I did. But I wouldn't change any of it.

Q: At some point during your direct, I thought you said that you didn't want him to hit you again so I'm asking if—if he had hit you.

A: Well, he punched me all over my whole body. It was neck, face, shoulder,—I mean, the medical records speak for themselves.

Q: And that's another detail that's not in either of your—any of your statements that he punched you all over, right?

Check.

A: Well, I didn't think it had to be. They pulled me out in an ambulance.

Checkmate.

MR. WEST: No further questions.

"No further questions." No sweeter words had been spoken in a long time. He thought he cornered me with his last question, but my response hung in the air giving the jury time to absorb it. Even while on the stand, I felt like I proved him wrong, showing the jury he was not to be trusted. It felt like a victory, but what I didn't know at the time was the last word the jury heard from Arnett was that I drove myself to the hospital. Implication—Sharon was so traumatized, she created a fictional scenario where she rode in an ambulance. Her testimony can't be trusted.

The verdict would determine if it was a victory or not.

CHAPTER 23

TRIAL PART IV—THE DOGGONE KNIFE

Time. It seems like a fairly straightforward concept: twenty-four hours in a day, sixty minutes in an hour, sixty seconds in a minute. Not too complicated. Until something happens to make it complicated, like being rear-ended in your car, waiting for a diagnosis, or getting kidnapped. Time is captured and retained differently when the mind is in a highly adrenalized state. Being kidnapped certainly qualifies. What you experience is not being taken in and recorded by your brain in an organized manner like your grandmother's prize recipe or the sports statistics from your favorite team. It is more like experiencing a child's pop-up book. Each time you turn the page, some random bit of information leaps out at you. You don't control it. It controls you. You can't simply sit back and recall what happened from start to finish. It's choppy, starts and stops at its own will. Sometimes there are blanks, sometimes things are out of order, slowed down, or sped up. Like a movie that's gone off the reels and bits of film are flying everywhere and now and then the projector gets a piece of something that shows up on the screen of your mind's eye.

It is frustrating. Trust me. I, more than anyone, wanted to know every detail, what happened when, who said what and in what order. When exactly did he touch me for the first time, when did he get sexual, where was I driving at the time, exactly where did he hit me and how many times? Even during the incident, I had no concept of time or the order of things. Specific moments cemented in my mind, but an overall chronological order was impossible. West knew that, and he used it against me with his questions and unspoken implications. Shouldn't you remember something like that? Certainly you would remember such a violent and destructive experience in your life. You believed your life was in danger, but you can't tell the jury what exactly happened? Five years later, you can't recall if he touched your leg before Jeff called? Seems to me like your testimony isn't credible. Seems to me like it is inconsistent. Seems to me this jury should not believe you and find my client not guilty.

After a brief re-direct by Keith where he failed to mention the medical records that proved I went to the hospital in an ambulance, I was dismissed from testifying. I returned to the jury room and anxiously awaited my friends and family to join me. At first I was frustrated, then livid. I was emotionally drained. I knew before I took the stand West had to do something to defend Morrison—that was his job. I simply couldn't abide the manner in which he chose to do it. Did I push back too hard during cross? Did I alienate the jury? I was desperately hoping the jury would believe me after hearing my testimony, but I kept hearing what I knew West was trying to prove: *Sharon is mistaken. She was scared, panicked. You can't trust her testimony. You must acquit.*

Modern courtrooms have a prosaic and windowless design, maybe to reduce distraction, but the effect is that time doesn't pass in a normal manner. I couldn't check a clock, but it felt that my cross was unduly short. Maybe that was a good thing.

As my group of supporters filed into the jury room, I watched their faces for clues. Their expressions were hard to read.

"How did I do on cross. How did I come across?"

Crickets. Dead air.

I looked at my Aunt Dale, whose face told me something was awry.

No one spoke until Rachel, the ever gentle wordsmith, said, "Well . . . there were times I didn't know who was cross-examining whom."

Carolyn followed up with, "You might have come across as a little aggressive on cross."

Rats. That wasn't the effect I had been going for, but despite all my efforts and preparation, I could not tolerate West's deception.

I hoped the jury still liked me.

*   *   *

I remained sequestered even after I had finished testifying. The rules didn't allow me to be in the courtroom to hear the testimony of other witnesses although the defendant had a constitutional right to be present. Next, David Roe, Codell Gibson, and Vickie Gibson, the people who helped me at the scene of the kidnapping, testified. I had no idea what their testimony would be. If I had known what they had provided the prosecutor in their written statements, I would have been less fearful of a not guilty verdict. Codell and Vickie were amazing. If they'd had an earpiece in and I was coaching them on every answer, they would not have done better. It was five years later, and they were confident, detailed, and consistent. Their testimony would have readily supported additional charges. West couldn't touch them. The testimony from David Roe, whom I knew only as Red Truck, was less clear and helpful, but he still stood with me that day on the road. And I'm grateful. I couldn't thank them enough. I still can't. How exactly do you thank someone who quite literally chose to stand between you and certain death?

DIRECT EXAMINATION OF CODELL GIBSON
[BY COMMONWEALTH'S ATTORNEY, MR. GORDIE SHAW]

JUDGE: Commonwealth, call your next witness.

COMMONWEALTH: The Commonwealth calls Codell Gibson.

Q: Now, Mr. Gibson, I want to go back to April the 7th of 2006. Do you remember that day and what happened?

A: Yes, sir.

Q: Tell us, what had you been doing that day?

A: Me and my wife and three kids had been to Georgetown to get a bite to eat.

Q: So you'd been to Georgetown, and you're coming back?

A: Yes, sir, on the way back home.

Q: Tell us what happened.

A: We was coming north on Russell Cave and we topped a little hill. There's a farm off to the right and there was a white car sitting in the drive—It wasn't in the road, but it was really close. I looked at my wife and I said, "You know, this car is going to pull out in front of me." I'm watching the car, and I'm getting ready to pass the car, and the door swings open, and I seen the lady trying to get out of the car. Her shirt was like if somebody was trying to get out and you're trying to hold it down. And she just looked really, really scared, really red and it looked like she was screaming. She was just really red faced, and she was trying to get out.

Q: And did you know her? Had you ever seen her before?

A: No, sir.

Q: So what did you do?

A: I stopped, of course. I looked at my wife. We both seen what went on—we started backing up, and as I was backing up, I looked over my shoul-der, and I saw her run out in the road in front of a truck—it ended up being my neighbor, David Roe. Then I got out and went back to the woman.

Q: So, Mr. Gibson, what did the woman say?

A: She was real—she was, you know, yelling and screaming. She said that the man had taken her from Georgetown and he had a knife, was going to kill her and she didn't know where she was at.

Codell nailed it. That is exactly what I said. Impressive.

Q: Did she have a phone with her?

A: Yeah. When I came up, she actually handed me the phone and asked me to tell 911 where we were because she wasn't familiar with the area.

Q: Now, what's the man doing during this time?

A: He walked up, and he said she was his girlfriend, didn't know why she was doing this. He actually said, "Sharon, why are you doing this?" Said he didn't have a knife, and then he said, "It's not cool to call 911." And then he looked at us real weird and said, "Don't you know who I am? I'm Larry Morrison." I had no idea who the guy was. I said the police will sort it out.

Q: Now, what was your wife doing during this time?

A: I think when all that happened, my wife took the lady to the back of David Roe's truck to get her away, put as much distance as we could between them.

Q: Okay. Did the man do anything peculiar or anything that caught your attention?

A: Well, he started acting a little nervous. He paced back and forth a little bit. Then he went over to the front passenger side and—that's when I saw he had a knife in his right hand.

Q: But he had said to you before he didn't have a knife?

A: Oh, he denied he had a knife, yeah.

Q: But you saw the knife in his right hand?

A: Oh, yes, sir. I saw it.

Q: So, what did you do?

A: Well, I said, "Hey, I saw the knife." And he denied it. I saw him put it in his pocket, and I told him—I said, "Hey, I saw the knife." He denied it. I got a little nervous, though. You know, I kept—by getting a little louder just to let him know that, you know, hey, I saw the dog-gone knife. So he finally admitted to having it, and he pulled it out of his pocket and he said, "What am I going to do with this? It's a little filet knife," which was, you know, a pretty good-size knife. David had got a metal bar out of the back of his truck because we really didn't know what he was going to do with it.

Q: How did the whole situation come to an end?

A: After the knife thing, we told him to get back— get back over to the car, and he, you know, waited around it seemed like forever. But any-way, he waited, and then he finally says, "Hey, can I leave?" and we told him, "We're not holding you. You're free to leave, just keep away from the lady." And so he gets in the car, and he gets a green backpack out and he starts walking north.

Q: Okay. Mr. Gibson, those are all the questions I have for you. Thank you.

A: Okay.

JUDGE: Cross-examination.

MR. WEST: No questions, Your Honor.

Of course West had no questions. Codell was untouchable.

Like I said, how do you thank someone for standing between you and death? A stranger with three small kids and his wife who had no idea if Morrison had a gun, yet they stopped. I am alive because they stopped.

DIRECT EXAMINATION OF VICKIE GIBSON
[BY COMMONWEALTH'S ATTORNEY, MR. GORDIE SHAW]

COMMONWEALTH: Your Honor, the Commonwealth calls Vickie Gibson.

Q: I'm just going to ask you some questions about April 7th, 2006, the reason why we're all here.

A: Okay.

Q: Do you remember that day?

A: I do.

Q: How's she [Sharon] behaving? Just describe how she was acting for us.

A: Basically hysterical, crying, couldn't understand her at first, so we didn't know really what was going on, and she was crying and screaming and she said that she was an attorney in Georgetown and that an ex-client had kidnapped her at knifepoint and told her he was going to kill her.

The only glitch is the knifepoint kidnapping. That would be easy to infer since I said he kidnapped me and he had a knife.

Q: Okay.

A: She was on the phone with 911 and handed it—the phone—to my husband and said, "I—I don't know where I'm at; will you give directions?"

Q: Did she say anything else about how she got out to the country?

A: Yeah. She said that he had brought her out on a knife and told her which way to go so she said she didn't know where she was at. That's what she said.

Q: What's the man doing?

A: He said, "Sharon, why are you tripping; why are you saying this?" And I guess trying to give the impression that they were out there together.

Q: Did she say anything back to him that you recall?

A: She said, "Don't talk to me. You told me you were going to kill me. You told me you were going to rape me. Don't talk to me."

Q: Okay. Now, if you could, where is the woman during this time? Where is the man during this time?

A: The woman, at this point, is in front of David's truck and behind our truck. The man had been at the car. And a couple of times, he did try to approach [Sharon]. And after my husband got off the phone with 911, he told him to stay back, that he didn't know what was going on and the police could sort it out, but he wanted him to stay away from her. And he asked me to take her to the back of the truck to be away from him.

I'm glad she remembered that he continued to try to get to me even in front of witnesses. The jury needed to know he was determined to hurt me.

Q: Okay. Now, I believe you said the woman said he had a knife?

A: Yes. Yeah. She said he had a knife.

Q: Okay. Do you remember the man saying anything?

A: Yeah. He did ask—he said, "Do you know who I am?" And we—none of us knew him. We said no, and he said, "I'm Larry Morrison."

Q: And—and what happened with the knife, Ms. Gibson?

A: He approached David Roe, and David Roe said, "I don't want you to come close to me," and he kept coming and David said, "I don't want the knife." And he handed it to David so David took it, put it on the hood of his truck, and that's when the lady said, "Don't touch that; that's evidence." So we left it there.

It seems like I'm not too panicked at this point, directing the witness not to touch the evidence. Not as West has argued.

Q: How did the whole situation come to an end?

A: We were behind the truck with the lady. I was. And my husband and David were still at the front of the truck, and I saw [Morrison] start walking down [the road], and he had a green duffle bag at that point.

Q: Tell us what happened when the deputy sheriff arrived.

A: The deputy arrived, and he got out and asked her if this was her boyfriend, and she said no.

MR. WEST: Objection.

Q: Okay. I'm not going to ask you anymore about that.

MR. WEST: Then strike.

Q: Okay. Ms. Gibson, those are all the questions I have for you. Thank you.

JUDGE: Cross-examination?

CROSS-EXAMINATION OF VICKY GIBSON
[BY ATTORNEY FOR THE DEFENSE, MR. WEST]

Q: Ms. Gibson, you have a pretty good recollection of events that day, don't you?

A: Yes, sir.

Q: I want to make sure I'm clear about something. You said that Ms. Muse had identified herself that she was an attorney at Georgetown?

A: Mm-hmm.

Q: That the man in the car was an ex-client?

A: Yes.

Q: That he had kidnapped her?

A: Yes.

Q: Made her drive out in the country?

A: Mm-hmm.

Q: And said he was going to kill her?

A: Yes.

Q: You recall her saying that to you?

A: Yes, sir.

Q: Okay. That's how you remember it?

A: That's how I remember it. Yes.

Q: Okay. Thank you.

The point of cross-examination is to score some points for your client with the jury. You reel the witnesses in, you corner them, and then force them to say something that supports your narrative. I failed to see how the above line of questioning helped his client. It made me wonder what West thought he was accomplishing.

JUDGE: Okay. Ma'am, you're excused.

CHAPTER 24

IS HE SINGLE?

After the prosecution rested, the judge dismissed the jury for lunch. West asked the judge to direct a verdict of not guilty and end the trial.

> **MR. WEST:** Your Honor, at this point, the defendant would move for a directed verdict of not guilty on the grounds that a reasonable jury could not find guilt under the facts. That's not a jury question; it's for the Court. I think that the kidnapping exemption which is codified at K.R.S. 509.050 says that "a person may not be convicted of unlawful imprisonment" or kidnapping "when his interference with the victim's liberty occurs immediately with and incidental to the commission of that [other] offense."

West argued an exception in the kidnapping statute stating if the primary reason for the kidnapping was in furtherance of another crime, then the defendant should be charged only with the other crime. One of many problems with my case was that the prosecution hadn't charged him with any other significant crime, like attempted rape or attempted murder. And they'd put on no evidence for the sexual abuse. Since I got away before Morrison could complete his other crimes, the judge, according to West's argument, should direct the verdict as not guilty and end the trial. Essentially, Morrison would walk.

MR. WEST: Based on all of that, I believe that the kidnapping exemption applies and that charge should be dismissed and not taken back to the jury.

West's duty was to present statutes to the court in the light most favorable to his client. I understood that. But if I had been in the courtroom and heard him make that argument, I would have wanted to make a run for him.

I was thankful Judge Johnson overruled West's motion.

Since the prosecution's case ended, the defense should have started their side of the case. Morrison was too guilty and slow-witted to put on the stand. They had no choice, no other witnesses, and therefore, no case to present. All they could do was attack the prosecution's case. So we moved to closing arguments, but before they could begin, the law required Judge Johnson to find for the record that Morrison was declining to testify of his own free will.

MR. WEST: I have talked with Mr. Morrison. I do not believe he wishes to testify. It is my advice and Mr. Hart's advice that he not testify and that is my advice, and I hope that he follows it.

JUDGE: Are you choosing not to testify in this case?

LARRY MORRISON: Yes, sir.

JUDGE: And is that based upon the advice of your counsel or is that also based upon your decision in this case not to testify?

LARRY MORRISON: The advice of my counsel.

JUDGE: Defense may proceed.

CLOSING ARGUMENT

[BY ATTORNEY FOR THE DEFENSE, MR WEST]

Let me start off by saying that I'm glad that this is a trial on what the evidence shows and that it's a trial on things that the Commonwealth has to prove and that this isn't a referendum on the popularity of my client. Because I'm guessing you're not liking him too much right now. We'll just start off by what you heard in his statement. It was played here in court. You heard some of things that he said in there. And I know that you didn't like some of those things because some of them, quite frankly, were preposterous.

I don't know what it is when someone is accused of something, the first impulse is to tell some lies on—about some of it. Clinton did it when he was accused with the Monica Lewinsky thing. Nixon did when he was accused of Watergate. It seems to go across all walks of life. And when Larry was confronted with some of the accusations made against him, he made some things up. And the biggest one, I think, perhaps the most preposterous is that he did cocaine with Ms. Muse. Nobody here thinks that happened. We know it didn't happen. Ms. Muse had the presence of mind when she was told about it to go have a test, to present the proof. We know Larry had cocaine. We know it was in his system. We know he was high on cocaine.

I'm very thankful today that telling a lie is not a crime that can be prosecuted. But the fact that Larry lied about some things does not remove from the Commonwealth the burden to prove this case beyond a reasonable doubt with the evidence that they have. They have 100 percent of that burden. And in the course of your deliberations, if you think well, there's one more thing I'd like to know, there's one more thing I wish had been said, one more question I wish had been asked, one more piece of evidence I wish had been introduced into evidence, that burden falls squarely and only on the Commonwealth.

Ms. Muse may well have been the last friendly soul that he felt was on his side before he ever went into prison.

Now, did he go there [Sharon's office] with revenge on his mind? Was that a motive? It doesn't really meet with the facts. Ms. Muse didn't do anything that was worthy of any kind of revenge. I submit to you it is more likely that he was going to the last friendly soul that he ever knew. He's out, he doesn't know anybody, but he searches out the last person who showed him kindness before he went into prison.

I have to tell you that I'm real puzzled by some of the evidence that we have heard about what happened in that time.

And let me tell you, I know she was under stress. I know she was terrified, horrified, feeling annoyance. What I'm having trouble is here, five years later, is trying to piece together what has been said from that day forward to what we've heard now because it seems to be changing. I don't think she's telling the truth, but I'm not certain that her fears of what she thought might happen aren't becoming mixed in with memories of what did happen because there's a wide variance between what we have heard here and what has been said along the way.

It was almost physically impossible to keep my mouth shut and sit in my seat while West spoke, but I was acutely aware of my nearness to the jury. If any one of them glanced in my direction, I didn't think they needed to see murderous arrows darting from my eyes. Story changing? I was annoyed? His friendly face routine sounded pathetic and weak, yet it still infuriated me. I hoped Keith made sure the jury knew years passed from when Morrison last saw me to when he went to prison. It would show the jury they couldn't trust West. His arguments were pure fiction.

But I'm not pretending to be objective. It is probably a good thing I was not allowed to be in the courtroom until closing arguments.

He went on to attack me as an attorney, as an attorney I should have done things differently, been able to recall what happened better. Look how much better the witnesses could organize their recollection. Jeff Ballard had notes. I wasn't shocked by this, and it was why I never pulled the court file or made a record where he could see I'd worked my case. He would have used that against me, so I worked it from behind the scenes.

CLOSING CONTINUES

And then I ask her—because remember on direct she said, "He hit me." And I said, "When were you hit?" And she said, "Well, as I was trying to get out, he was hitting me." She used her arm motion—go back to the 911 tape that was played into evidence where the unknown dispatcher said, "Okay. Did he hit you?" And the answer was, "No. He grabbed me."

My spine straightened as rage pounded through my veins. This was deeply subversive and perverted the legitimacy of the effects of trauma on the brain. He used it like junk science to stir reasonable doubt in the minds of the jurors. West grossly misstated the 911 tape. When asked if I needed an ambulance I said, "I . . . don't . . . know . . . " When asked if he hit me I continued describing the fight in the car stating, "He grabbed my shirt and bra . . ." and went on to tell the operator about his pulling the knife. I have the recording and had it transcribed. In West's defense, the transcript the prosecutor showed me did have the answer to the dispatcher's ambulance question as "No." I told Keith Eardley to listen to the tape again. In it, I was sobbing and speaking slowly between breaths and clearly said, "I don't know." I asked him to correct the transcript. He didn't. Now it's being used against me.

CLOSING CONTINUES

In the 911 tape she denied being hit, but now, he was constantly hitting her. So I think she's traumatized, but I think a lot of the details of her memory over what happened have grown over time.

Now, I'm also confused about the ambulance. Ms. Muse talks about an ambulance ride. In her direct examination, she talked about being in an ambulance, but no police officer can remember an ambulance. And the only one that said anything about it, Arnett, thought she drove her own car to Georgetown. That's something that has troubled me in this case because that's a pretty vivid memory to have, being in an ambulance, especially if there's no evidence that you were in one.

This guy is a nightmare. My medical records noted I arrived by ambulance, and as lead defense attorney, West has seen them. He had to agree for them to be admitted as evidence. I even suggested from the stand that Keith refer to my medical records. He never did.

I'm going to lose this case.

CLOSING CONTINUES

Another thing that struck me is the wad of money that Larry had in his pocket that he tried to put in Ms. Muse's pocket that no one is saying was on Larry. It's not in evidence. It wasn't in the car. A wad of bills, rubber band, something in it. That's just odd to me.

I—I know—I don't know about that. Certainly don't
know where he would have gotten it.

I'm sure it came from the same wad of money he used to buy his cocaine that day.
I understood West had a job to do, but did he imagine himself to be a defender of
justice, righting social wrongs, upholding the constitution like Atlas?

CLOSING CONTINUES
There's a lot of details that sometimes are supported
by the evidence and sometimes are not.

He merged fact and fiction until they were indistinguishable. He then returned to
the defense handbook of burden on the Commonwealth, claiming they didn't
meet it, because he had nothing else. Then he finally sat down.
     No sense in trying to hide it any longer. The jury can see I'm furious.
     As Keith walks to the lectern, I pray for him to be passionate, clear, persuasive.

CLOSING ARGUMENT
[BY ASSISTANT COMMONWEALTH'S ATTORNEY, MR. KEITH EARDLEY]

JUDGE: The Commonwealth ready to proceed?

MR. EARDLEY: Yes, sir.

JUDGE: Okay.

MR. EARDLEY: May it please the Court. I'd like to
begin by thanking you on behalf of my office, the
Commonwealth Attorney's office for the 14th Circuit,
for your jury service.

I'd like to start off by just hitting upon a couple
of points that Mr. West mentioned. At the beginning
of his argument, he talked a little bit about lying.

The Presidents lie. Big deal. Larry Morrison lied. Big deal. But think about this, why do people lie? It's really simple. They don't want to get caught. Nixon, Bill Clinton, they didn't want to get caught. They didn't want anybody to find out what they had done.

Larry Morrison lied in a statement repeatedly, especially this business about the cocaine, doing cocaine with Sharon. "Sharon had the cocaine." "Sharon gave me the cocaine." "We snorted lines." "No, we did a gram and a half." Over and over and over in the course of that hour-long statement. Why did he do that? Because he wanted somebody to believe it. He wanted Officer Murrell to believe it. He wanted you to believe it. Fortunately the officer told Sharon, "He says you were doing cocaine." What does Sharon say? "I want a blood test." And we have the results of that blood test. Negative. Negative for cocaine. "A gram and a half of cocaine we did." Over and over and over and over in his statement. Sharon Muse: negative.

Now, let me ask you this. What would have happened had the officer not told Sharon about this allegation of snorting cocaine? What if Sharon had never asked for a blood test and it wasn't before you? What would you think? Maybe they were doing cocaine. That's what Mr. Morrison wanted. What was Mr. Morrison's intent? What was he planning to do April the 7th, 2006? Well, let's look at his actions.

One week out of prison, Mr. Morrison, in his own words, "I'd lost everything," he goes to Sharon's office. Strapped to his leg is a knife. In his system is cocaine. What do you think he was planning to do?

What was his intention of going there? Just to see Sharon? Just to talk? What did he tell Sharon? He said his wife had just died and there was a big estate, a lot of money. His wife had just died. His wife died November 24th, 2002. His wife was dead almost four years. He was there under false pretenses. Why did he ask Sharon for a ride? His reason: he looks up at the sky, sees some dark clouds. "Three blocks to my grandmother's house. Three blocks, that's all I need." That was a lie too. He wanted to go out into the country with her. What was his intention?

And then they get out into the country. They get out to 440 Russell Cave Road by this roundabout route. It takes them about thirty minutes to get out there. And he tells her to drive behind the barn of this old rundown house. What was his intention? What was his plan? What was he wanting to do? It's not very hard to figure out. When a man grabs a woman's chest, puts a knife to her throat and says, "Take off your clothes. This is for the time in prison," what's his intent? "This is for those years in prison." It was revenge, it was payback, and he blamed her. And you know what? He wanted her to know it. He just didn't say, "Hey, take off your clothes." [He said,] "This is for those years in prison." He wanted her to know why he was doing it. "This is for those years in prison." What is "this"? What did he plan to do behind the barn? What do you think?

It was obvious to Sharon. She didn't have a choice. I need to get out of this car right now, no matter what. Somehow she got out of the car, and she ran into the middle of the road, threw her hands up. Remember what she said? "That truck was going to stop, or he was going to hit me." What would have happened had David Roe and Mr. and Mrs. Gibson not pulled up? What do you think Mr. Morrison would have done? What was his plan? Think about that.

He knew exactly what he was doing. I've heard it said that you can't predict how a person's going to react to a traumatic situation. We don't know how we're going to react. And, of course, it was an extremely traumatic experience for Sharon. Should she have let him get into the car? No. But you heard Sharon explain it. "He's talking to me about a case. I do the clicker and the door is unlocked. It's opened. He said three blocks. I don't want to seem rude. I didn't know how to tell him no." I can understand that. I know exactly what Sharon's talking about. It's hard to be rude to people. It's hard to be impolite sometimes. And that's why she let him get in the car.

When she had Jeff on the telephone, should she have told Jeff to call the police? That's really interesting. Remember, the only contact she has is with Jeff. The only person who has any idea of where she is or who she's with is Jeff, and he doesn't know very much. As soon as that phone goes dead, her contact's cut off. Had she said, "Jeff, call the police," what's going to happen? Jeff hangs up the phone. "My girlfriend called me. She's in Bourbon County in a white Honda Accord. I'm not sure where. I'm not sure with whom. I think there might be a problem. Could you go look for her?" What's the 911 operator going to say? How are the police going to respond to that call? And what would Mr. Morrison have done had Sharon said that on the phone to Jeff, "Call the police"? What do you think he would have done? Don't you think Sharon was aware of that? As he's saying things, "Don't disrespect me." Putting his hands on her neck, on her leg, being mean to her. What's going on in Sharon's mind? It might be a good thing she didn't say that. It wouldn't have done her any good. It wouldn't have helped the police find her. Who knows what Mr. Morrison would have done.

Should Sharon have stopped the car earlier and you know, get out? Maybe while they're still in Georgetown. Probably she should have. That's 20/20 hindsight. But as Sharon said it, "As long as I'm driving the car and I'm going where he's telling me to go, for the next minute I'm going to be okay. I know for the next minute I'm going to be okay as long as I do what he says. It's only when I don't do what he says something really bad is going to happen." That's why she didn't stop, and look what happened when she finally did stop.

And she's done the absolute best that she can to cooperate with the police, to cooperate with the Commonwealth Attorney's office, and to tell you what happened. She's given many different statements at different times, summaries of the event. Do the summaries contradict each other? No. They complement each other.

Considering everything we've heard, it's really a wonder that she got away at all. I was working on my closing argument last night and this morning, and the thought foremost in my mind is this man wouldn't know the truth if it was standing in front of him. He's lied so much. But then I thought about it a little bit more, and I said, you know, that's not the best way to characterize Mr. Morrison. He's not just a liar. He's a manipulator. And let's go back and look at the evidence from that perspective.

He's a manipulator, and he will do whatever he needs to do to get what he wants. He'll tell lies, half-truths, he'll flatter, he'll ask for sympathy, he'll slander, he'll intimidate, and he'll use force if he has to. The manipulation, he used on Sharon. The manipulation, he used to get her out to the country so he could [do] this. What did he say to her there at the office? "You're a good attorney." He flattered her. Trust me, every attorney likes to hear that, and it's hard not to like to the person saying it to you. "You're a good attorney." "My wife just died." He's trying to get her sympathy. "Huge estate, lots of money, lots of money in it for you." Well, how's that playing on Sharon, that lie? And of course, "Just three blocks." He's trying to make Sharon think, hey, I'm only going to be in your car for two minutes, and then you can be on your way.

Detective Murrell—manipulation continues. What's Mr. Morrison's intention now? He wants to discredit Sharon. He wants to focus the attention on Sharon, not on him. He says, "Did she tell you about her cocaine history and what she did and what we was doing that day?" She gave him cocaine. "Have you ever bought cocaine from her before?" He says, "Yeah." Make Sharon out to be a cocaine dealer. Why is he doing that? Why do people lie? Because they want people to believe it. Larry Morrison wanted Detective Murrell to believe that Sharon was doing cocaine, some big coke dealer. Take the focus off of him and

put it on her. Oh, wouldn't that be a nice little
story. Local Georgetown attorney dealing cocaine.
That's something to entice the State Police. Murrell
didn't buy into it, not for a second.

And then Mr. Morrison's tone changes. Remember at
the beginning of his interview he was wanting to protect Sharon. What does he say towards the end on page
72? "I didn't kidnap her. I don't understand. I told
that officer I said, 'Can I file a countersuit against
her? She kidnapped me.'"

Mr. Morrison's not only a liar; he's a manipulator.
And this case has shown that he will do whatever he
needs to do to reach his objective or goal. And what
was his goal here?

Each attorney then walked through the jury instructions and slanted them in the
light most favorable to their positions.

CLOSING CONTINUES

Once again, I want to thank you for your time. I'm
going to ask that you consider all of the evidence
that you've heard, and I'm going to ask that you
return verdicts of guilty of kidnapping, guilty of
sexual abuse, first degree, and guilty of resisting
arrest. Thank you.

Keith presented questions to the jury and responded to the attacks against me.
Although he didn't present evidence for any crime other than kidnapping, I did
appreciate his effort.

The jury left with their instructions. Waiting for a group of twelve strangers to
decide if you get to live or die is like drowning while seeing someone in a raft above
you, wondering if they are going to put their arm in the water to save you. Or let
you sink.

I paced the halls, prayed with anyone who would pray with me, played praise songs and sang them out loud, and at one point went into the empty courtroom to wait. My tiny mom followed me in and asked me to sit on her lap. She wanted to make everything better for me as she did when I was a child. Back then, all it took were some soothing words and her rocking chair, and everything was good again.

The jury came back several times with questions for the judge. At one point, the jurors came out and told the judge they didn't think they could come to an agreement. Then they asked if they could agree on guilt but not sentencing, should they go forward? Judge Johnson asked them to deliberate until they had an agreement, yet to do so without violating their convictions.

Why was this hard for them? Were they not going to convict him? I felt like the foreperson was for me, that she empathized with me during my testimony. Her face, her eyes showed compassion. I knew she wanted to help me but I needed all twelve—including the one who fell asleep.

As soon as the jury members were sent back to continue deliberating, I fled to the hallway and spoke with my attorney friend, Carolyn. She and I determined if the jury agreed on guilt but not sentencing Judge Johnson could determine the sentence. Juries only make recommendations. Judges determine the sentence. Part of that felt safe, since I trusted Judge Johnson, but it also exposed me to additional issues for appeal. I could see the appeal in my head challenging the judge's sentence.

I grabbed my friend Debbie Brodfuehrer and said, "What do I do if he's found not guilty. What do I do?"

Debbie's face said it all but I wanted to hear the words. "I don't know, Sharon, I just don't know." She said it softly and lovingly. I appreciated and respected her honesty. At least I wasn't the only one who didn't know.

I returned to the area where the rest of my friends gathered. The waiting was excruciating. They tried to keep my mind distracted with all kinds of conversation including questions about my judge. I was impressed my friends seemed so interested in the legal process until the question came, "Is he single?" I laughed. Judge Johnson was in his early forties—tall, dark-haired, athletically built, and compassionate. I wasn't surprised they found him attractive, just surprised it was at my kidnapping trial.

I went back into the empty courtroom, walked down an aisle, and dropped to my knees. I propped my hands up and put my face on the seat of the bench, silently praying and sobbing. In the middle of my grieving, my deeply wounded self crying out to God, I thought, *Right now your face is where everyone's butts are all day. Do you know the kind of filthy butts that are parked here for criminal court?* Random. In the middle of inexplicable pain, I was distracted by the potential STDs soaked into these wooden benches over the years. But the disgusting prospect of what my face was making contact with didn't faze me. I stayed put and cried out to God to help me live life, no matter what happened. Telling Him I would trust Him to protect me and help me, no matter the verdict. I was going to choose faith, not fear. Not anymore.

The bailiff walked in the courtroom and called court back to session. The verdict was in. Everyone quickly and quietly moved out of the hallway and into the courtroom. I sat on the front row between my mom and Rick.

JUDGE JOHNSON: It's my understanding that the jury has reached a verdict, so we'll bring the jury in.

BAILIFF: Okay. All rise, please. *[Jury enters the courtroom and is seated.]*

JUDGE: Be seated. First of all, have you all elected a foreperson?

FOREPERSON: We have.

JUDGE: Could you hand the verdict form to the bailiff, please. Before I read the verdict, I just want to confirm that this is a unanimous decision of the jury. Is that correct?

FOREPERSON: Yes. It is.

JUDGE: Okay. On Count One on Verdict Form Instruction Number Eight, it says, "We, the jury, find the defendant, Larry Morrison, guilty of

Kidnapping under Instruction Number One." On Count
Two, it says, "We, the jury, find the defendant,
Larry Morrison, not guilty under Count Two of the
indictment." And on Count Three, "We, the jury,
find the defendant, Larry Morrison, not guilty
under Count Three of the indictment."

The courtroom was full of friends and supporters. As the judge walked through the reading of the verdict, we had all held our breath. At the word *guilty* for kidnapping, some sighed with relief, some cheered, some hugged.

I wept.

CHAPTER 25

MALINGERING

FEBRUARY 23, 2011

Everyone returned to court the next day for the sentencing phase when the jury would hear my testimony and any testimony Morrison offered before making their recommendation to the judge. I was grateful for the verdict, but without a long sentence, the guilty verdict was just a piece of paper. Paper wouldn't keep me safe.

As I was walked to the stand, a bench conference was taking place. When I sat down, the judge informed me both parties agreed I could not comment on what West said during his closing argument. What? I'd never heard of anything like this. If West hadn't misled the jury during closing, he would have no need to ask for such instructions. Did he think I was going to tell the jury I wasn't the last friendly face Morrison saw? What was even stranger was that Gordie and Keith agreed "in an abundance of caution."

JUDGE JOHNSON: You may proceed.

DIRECT EXAMINATION OF SHARON MUSE
[BY COMMONWEALTH'S ATTORNEY, MR. GORDIE SHAW]

Q: Good morning, ma'am. We all know you're Sharon Muse. How do you feel today, Sharon?

A: I don't know. I've been waiting for this for five years. I don't know. It's a lot.

Q: Sharon, I'm going to ask you a very general question, and I'd like you to speak from your heart, okay?

A: Okay.

Q: I'd like you to tell the jury how you feel about this case, what's happened, and what should happen.

JUDGE JOHNSON: Ms. Muse, when you're speaking again, if you could just try to speak into that mic as loud as possible.

SHARON MUSE: Okay. I'm sorry. Let me try to get closer to it.

A: Well, first, thank you all so much for—for listening and paying attention and the wisdom you used to sift through all the facts of a very ugly case. I can't tell you how much it means to me that you came back and gave me the first step toward a hope that I can have a normal life again, a peaceful life. It meant everything in the world to me that you found him guilty of kidnapping. Thank you so much.

And I don't know how to honor your time and be respectful and try to briefly share with you what life has been like for five years. I'm overwhelmed, and I don't know how to do that. But I can tell you that my life is nothing like it used to be. Before this happened, I would guess that my life was pretty average. You know, you run into the grocery to buy some milk, you go home, you unload your car, you live your life, you go to bed, you wake up, you worry about paying your bills, you worry about being healthy, you worry about those kind of things. But from the moment that this happened my concern has been: "When is he going to come back to finish what he started? When is he going to get out? When am I going to get that call that says he's out, and when is my life going to end?" Living with this fear, this intense level of fear of having to possibly endure anything like I already endured has been crippling at times.

For years after this happened, it was a full-time job just to function normally. I sought out professional help from trauma therapists just to be able to go to the grocery and not be exhausted. I walk in a strange place, and I'm looking where are the exits, are there any men there that are big that might be able to hurt me? I quickly go get what I need, and I go back home, and I lock the doors. I don't open my windows and enjoy a breeze on a spring day. I am locked down inside my house. I am locked down inside my car. My purse is heavy because I carry a gun with me. I set my home alarm every night before I go to bed, and every time I set that alarm, there is a name and a face that I see. I have no idea why he did this to me. It doesn't—none of it makes sense to me. I beg you to please don't give him the chance to do this to me again, not now, not in ten years, not in twenty. I want to go to sleep without a gun by my bed. I really do. I don't like seeing it there because I know why it's there.

I've had people that have tried to help me and teach me self-defense. Some deputies have tried to teach me how to use a gun and take me to the range. My brother tried to teach me things, and when I show up, my arms shake and tears roll down my face because I'm not there to learn how to be a marksman or how to hunt. I'm there because I think someday I'm going to have to fight for my life again. I got away this time. I got away by God's grace and some miracle. And I don't want to have to endure that again.

I've completely changed my life. I've moved. [I] tried to adopt and I can't adopt because—because they deem me to not have a safe home so I don't—I don't get to be a mom. I don't get to go to bed at night feeling safe. I don't get to walk down the street feeling safe. I have tried really hard to learn to live life despite this, but it is hard to live life when you are terrified because you know there is someone out there that specifically wants to hurt you and hurt you very badly. He planned it, and he tried it, and I know with absolute certainty that if he gets out, he will do it again. He gave me six days last time. He waited six days before he made a plan, strapped on a knife, bought his drugs, and showed up at my office—six days to do this. He's not going to give me any time [next time]. I need you to give me time. You are the only people who can restore what he stole from me and give me the chance to try to live life like you do. I bet you don't run from your car to your house and lock the door right behind you. I bet if it's a pretty spring day, you think, "I'm going to open up my doors and let this breeze come in." Does the hair on the back of your neck stand up when you're in Kroger [grocery] and somebody gets too close to you? Who lives like that?

I am thankful for that guilty verdict because I know you're going to give me some time—some time to live life and I—I just want you to give me my life back because the very second, the very moment his sentence ends is when mine begins. The moment that I get this call telling me he's been released, my life will never be the same again. For the first three years after this, I kept my passport and some cash in a bank box with a visa to a third-world country where I had done some work before, and I knew that I could live for a very long time off very little money. I had mistakenly got a call around Thanksgiving. The notification system messed up. They called and said that he had been released, and I imme-diately got on the computer [to buy airline tickets]. I was ready to leave the country because I—I cannot live with him on the street. I know I keep saying this. Please give me my life back and give me the chance to be a mom and to go to sleep and to live a normal life. I can-not do it without you. Please give him life so I can have mine back.

MR. SHAW: Thank you, Sharon.

The defense had the right to bring forth witnesses at this time, but they could find only one, a paid expert named Dr. Connor. And in the end, the doctor did more for my case than Morrison's.

DIRECT EXAMINATION OF DR. EDWARD CONNER
[BY ATTORNEY FOR THE DEFENSE, MR. HART]

Q: Would you please state your name?

A: My name is Dr. Edward Connor.

Q: And what's your profession? What are your qualifications?

A: I was a participant in a publication on the detection of *malingering*, which is a method where we try to determine if someone is faking a mental illness in order to get a lighter sentence or something of that nature.

Q: Okay. And what was [Morrison's] history?

A: Well, as a child, there really wasn't any mental health treatment administered to him that I could see from the record review. But as an adult, he began to be treated for anxiety and depression. There was a very extensive history of alcohol abuse, alcohol dependency, and also a history of drug abuse and prescription medication abuse.

CROSS-EXAMINATION OF DR. EDWARD CONNER
[BY COMMONWEALTH'S ATTORNEY, MR. GORDIE SHAW]

Q: Did Mr. Morrison allege any sort of physical abuse in his home when he grew up?

A: No. He did not allege any kind of sexual abuse or physical abuse. He denied that there was any history of family violence growing up.

Q: Could it be characterized in lay terms that [Morrison] wasn't being honest or [he was] trying to manipulate the findings or results?

A: I think the use of the term "manipulation" is accurate. In a criminal proceeding such as this, we use the term "malingering." They [defendants] try to manipulate the mental health professional into believing that their symptoms are much worse than what they actually are.

Q: And which section [of the testing] was it that he malingered in?

A: Well, if we look at the test of malingering that was administered to him, he attempted to embellish somewhat in *each* of these categories.

Q: So basically every section you tested in, he tried to manipulate?

A: Yes.

Gordie went further to highlight Morrison's poorly disguised attempts to deceive his own expert witness. When asked, Dr. Conner testified that Morrison didn't remember anything from the day of the kidnapping. Gordie asked Conner if he reviewed the eighty-page interview Murrell had with Morrison on that day. He had not. He then asked Dr. Conner if he knew of his prior felony convictions. He did not. He asked if Dr. Conner knew Morrison had only been out of prison six days prior to showing up at my office with a knife. He did not.

His testimony involved a hypothesis about Morrison not being responsible for his actions due to some impairment of his judgment and memory at the time. When the judge asked if he had any degree of certainty of his hypotheses or anything to support it, Dr. Conner said no. The judge had to exclude it. It was a waste of time and the state's money having this guy here other than his testimony that Morrison tested as an extreme manipulator, otherwise known as a malingerer. Or a liar.

CLOSING ARGUMENT

[BY ATTORNEY FOR THE DEFENSE, MR. HART]

I'd like to thank you for your verdict in this case. Of course, we argued for unlawful imprisonment. That's what we thought the case was. So you found him guilty of kidnapping. We respectively disagree. We'd like to thank you for the—returning not guilty on the sexual abuse charge and the resisting arrest which no one [Keith Eardley] seemed to mention in their closing. I would like to thank you for finding not guilty on that as well.

I don't believe that this is a life sentence case. There is no lifelong injury to Ms. Muse in this case. There is no serious property damage in this case.

Then it hit me. Gordie and Keith failed to address the sexual abuse during trial. I was not asked anything about it while on the stand, so I thought they brought it in through Arnett. I never imagined it was ignored. Now it made sense that the jury didn't convict. I thought they didn't believe me. That wasn't it. They weren't given any evidence at all.

Mr. Hart went on to ask for the minimum because, according to him, I had not been injured or damaged enough to warrant Morrison serving more time. It appeared that I got away too soon. If I had not gotten out and instead let him beat me longer, would he have earned more time? Same with the rape. If I hadn't gotten away until after he penetrated me, then would he be looking at more time? The answer to both is yes.

CLOSING ARGUMENT

[BY ASSISTANT COMMONWEALTH'S ATTORNEY, MR. KEITH EARDLEY]

One thing occurred to me during Dr. Connor's testimony and that was the word "malingering." There's another word that's synonymous with malingering and that's "manipulation." I know you remember what I said yesterday about Mr. Morrison and how he manipulated and tried to manipulate numerous people on April 7th, 2006, to get his way. This just wasn't a one-time occurrence, April 7th, 2006. The pattern of manipulation continues even with Dr. Connor. Mr. Morrison is trying to manipulate his own expert who comes in here to testify for mitigation, to lessen his sentence. He's still playing those games with everybody. This is who he is.

[Morrison] has ten felony convictions. Consider this offense. What did he do? He forced Sharon to drive him out to the country so he could terrorize her. And think about his interview that he gave with Detective Murrell and remember what he did at the end of the interview? He blamed Sharon. He wants to charge her with kidnapping. He took no responsibility whatsoever. And think about why he did it. One week out of prison—one week out of prison when this happened. In his statement, he said "I've lost everything." And to Sharon, he said, "This is for those years in prison."

He blamed her for going to prison, and this was his revenge. Think about that. You think he planned on going back to prison April 7th, 2006? You think he planned on getting caught? With Mr. Morrison, when we look at rehabilitation, the Department of Corrections failed, and they failed badly.

He was not rehabilitated at all.

One week out of getting out of prison, he has a knife he's carrying with him. He's on cocaine. And he has his mind set on payback. I wonder what he thinks now? The same motive that existed before, on April 7th, 2006, exists right now, the exact same motive, except now it's worse because he's looking at a whole lot more time.

Not only is the motive still there, but it's been multiplied tenfold, and he can't be rehabilitated. What's the appropriate sentence to give?

Think about this. What do you think Mr. Morrison's going to do when he gets out?

What do you think he's capable of? Nothing's changed except he has every reason in his own mind to be even more angry and vengeful and full of hate.

I'm going to please ask you to give [Sharon] the peace of mind that she can live the rest of her life without having to worry, without having to look over her shoulder. I implore you please, please, please give Mr. Morrison the maximum sentence allowed by law. Please give him the sentence of life. Please give Sharon that peace of mind. Please do that. Thank you.

Eardley delivered his earnest plea, wrapped up this case and sent the jury out knowing they had the power to right a wrong.

Despite the many potentially fatal errors made by Eardley, the failing to correct the 911 tape, failure to correct false statements by Arnett, failure to prepare me for trial, failure to enter evidence correctly, failure to present evidence . . . I was thankful for that moment. The closing. I was praying the jury would see past all the mistakes.

The court recessed for the jury to deliberate the sentence.

Hours later, the bailiff called the court to order and my stomach lurched. This was it. This was the end. I was about to learn what the rest of my life would look like and how long it might last.

I was more confident as I sat beside my brother, squeezing his hand until both of our hands were purple. I could feel his strength pouring into me.

I was focused on the foreperson and heard her say the jury recommended a sentence of five years. A five-year sentence in prison. I panicked. I told Rick, "I'll have to move, I'll have to move in five years, I can't live here."

Rick shook his head, no. "I think you misheard. It's life."

I sat eighteen inches from the jury. My body flopped forward onto Rick, and a tumult of searing grief exploded from me.

I unloaded the years of fear and the entire room heard it. I couldn't move as the judge dismissed the jury. I wanted to thank them, to run hug them all, but I sat crying and squeezing my brother's hand.

In the hallway, a female juror approached Carolyn and said, "We hope she gets her life back."

I hugged my brother and family and realized what I was really feeling was . . . empty. This process has burned everything out of me. It had been five years of my life with this singular focus, and now it was over. For now.

The next day I got on my phone to check messages. Two calls had come in during jury deliberation from *Larry Morrison*. I couldn't believe it! He called me while the jury was deliberating. Rick had told me he saw Morrison grab a legal pad and furiously scribble down my cell phone number as the 911 operator repeated it on the recording in court. Rick told me to change my number, but I hadn't had time. I couldn't believe he had the chutzpah to call me. Thankfully he couldn't leave me a message. All I could hear was the automated program spelling out his name asking if I'd accept a call from. L-A-R-R-Y-M-O-R-R-I . . . . then the voicemail cut off.

MARCH 9, 2011

Formal sentencing, when Judge Johnson would sentence Morrison considering but not obligated to follow the jury's recommendation, was scheduled for March 9, 2011. I had planned to go alone, but Marti called and asked if she could go with me. I was grateful.

Marti and I entered the courtroom that we were both very familiar with by now, and the proceeding started with defense objecting to my many victim impact letters. They wanted to review them prior to sentencing so they could object or ask for certain language to be redacted. Morrison would get to filter my statements?

Having Morrison sit with his defense team poring over the intimate details in my victim impact statement (VIS) was like having him worm his way inside my head to see my life from the most intimate perspective. Neither the prosecutors nor the victim advocate told me Morrison would read these. I felt violated and exposed. Was there going to be a time during this process that I didn't feel violated and exposed?

The judge retired to his chambers during a recess to give defense time to read my statement and those of my friends and family.

While we waited, the news reporters informed me they would be filming my face today since Morrison was acquitted on the sex abuse charge. Usually I could hide my face behind my mound of hair, but today I'd worn it half up, half down. My pride still got triggered at the thought of strangers seeing me plea for my future through tears as they ate their dinner watching the news.

I resented the defense team ruminating over my statements. The longer they took, the angrier I became. As they huddled around their table, I drew close, fully intending them to hear me, and spoke to Marti. "If I had known a bunch of public defenders were going to read my impact statement, I'd have used smaller words." For the record, some of the brightest and most passionate advocates I know are public defenders. I'm ashamed I said it but I didn't stop there. "I don't have to worry about when Morrison gets out of prison. After this I'll be fourth on his list. At least I did a good job for him." Not my best moment.

After the first trial in 2007, I approached Brian Canupp, Morrison's second attorney, and thanked him for doing his job well. I meant it. He managed to represent Morrison zealously while not attacking me. I had enormous respect for him. I didn't feel the same way about this group of attorneys. That didn't justify my being nasty. But I did wonder if there might be some truth to my now being number four on his list. I still do.

The bailiff announced court was back in session. All parties walked the well to stand in front of the judge's bench in lieu of sitting at our respective tables.

I looked around for Keith, and he wasn't there. But for the first time the victim advocate was. I never quite knew who was going to show up in court. As we gathered to take our positions, the bailiffs and victims' advocate stood speaking to each other, and Morrison took advantage of it. I stood less than eight feet from him at the bench while we waited for Judge Johnson to enter from his chambers. Morrison waived his arms, and I instinctively looked his direction as he started to threaten me. I knew that when the judge was in chambers, he could see and hear what was happening in the courtroom on his monitor, so I shouted, "Hey, are you all going to let him talk to me like that?"

Everyone startled and raced to create more space between us.

The bailiffs grabbed him and said, "Don't talk to her at all. Don't look at her."

I hope Judge Johnson heard that.

I had told Gordie about Morrison's calls to my phone hoping he would bring it to the Court's attention. Instead, he relayed that to Mr. Hart prior to the hearing.

FORMAL SENTENCING

MR. HART: Well, I would state for the record there's some allegations of some phone calls made during the trial. Mr. Morrison was locked in the cell without a phone so I would just like to point out that he had no access to a phone so I would certainly refute those ch—allegations.

Before the judge could speak, I leaned close to Gordie and said, "I have the recordings on my phone if you want to hear them." He didn't respond, but that didn't matter. I knew the judge heard me.

FORMAL SENTENCING CONTINUES

JUDGE JOHNSON: Okay. Does the defendant wish to say anything at this time?

MR. MORRISON: I'd just like to let Ms. Muse know that I'm truly sorry for everything that I've caused her over the past five years. After reading what she had written, I know she don't have no faith in me, and she don't believe I could change, but I know I've changed. In the last year and two months almost, I got myself together. I got saved. I even have people that comes, and I do Bible studies once a week. I attend all the church services. And I've grown to learn what love means instead of hate and dishonesty.

And I'm still growing and—and I'm going to keep growing regardless of this situation I'm in right now. I know that God's forgiven me and—and I ask Ms. Muse for forgiveness. I've never had a godly life. It's always been a criminal life for things that Larry could get. It was never nothing that—what Larry could give. It was always what Larry could get. And—and I thank God, and I thank Jesus that come and died for my sins to show me that He loves me enough to forgive me if I'll just come forward and—and march with Him and that's what I intend to do, you know.

I help people. I watch people that—if they get to where they're wanting to commit suicide, I talk to them, and I've talked to a lot of people at the jail since my incarceration. And all I can do is—is continue to walk in faith and continue to learn God's word.

As Ms. Muse mentioned, you know, it—I'm—I'm hurt, you know, to know what I have caused because of my drinking and—and abuse of drugs. You know, I've hurt this woman for no reason, none at all. I have no reason to—to hurt this lady. She was good to me, and she got me out of jail, and my wife had went and got her to—to help get me out of jail. So I'm truly sorry, Ms. Muse, for everything and—and all I can do is ask that you would have forgiveness for me in your heart regardless of what the punishment is today that you would have peace and know that you have no fear of me or no fear of me wanting to hurt you and just know that I'm on the page that you're on. I'm loving God and learning what His word means and how to love other people.

And, Judge, that's where I'm at now. I want to continue to keep learning and continue to love and grow regardless of what time you pass down. I do ask for forgiveness and—and ask that you recognize that this is my new life and you're welcome to verify with the jail or anybody there what I've been doing, who I've been talking to, the Bible studies that I go through thoroughly, and—and all the *Watchtower* books and things that I've been reading that's helping me to grow. And so it's been an educational part spiritually for me to learn and love and grow and not be selfish and all about Larry. It's about what Larry can do for somebody else now.

So I thank the Court for their time and—and I—and I—and I prayed several nights that Ms. Muse would have peace at all times and know that she don't have to fear me. And so I want to thank the Court and say I'm sorry for everything that I've caused.

JUDGE JOHNSON: Anything further?

MR. HART: No, Your Honor.

Listening to Morrison made me furious, but I was mindful of my body language and expressions since the TV cameras were focused on me. He'd blathered on about how he saved someone's life in jail, how he found Jesus. Sometimes I think Jesus has already returned and is living among the prison population since every single one of those guys seems to have met him when it comes time to stand and wait for their punishment to be meted out by a judge. Morrison's spurious comments about his good works while awaiting trial were too much for me to ignore. Before I could stop myself I turned to Marti, who stood between the cameras and me, and said, "Really? He's reading *Watchtower*? He's a Mormon now?" She rolled her eyes sharing my disgust. On the drive home we laughed at how of all the things he said, that was the thing that irritated me. And, *Watchtower* is Jehovah's Witnesses, not Mormon.

Then it came my turn to address the court. When Gordie said to speak from the heart, I took it literally. I didn't write notes to speak to the jury or for the judge. I didn't need them. It felt like the syllables tumbled over my tongue to rush out of my mouth. This wasn't as hard as the first time, but it was still a far cry from easy.

JUDGE JOHNSON: Mr. Shaw.

MR. SHAW: As far as on the Commonwealth's behalf, the jury recommended the sentence of life. I think they recognized the danger done and the danger imposed in the future. And unfortunately, the words at sentencing when somebody's facing life in prison, we've got to take them at face value, but the jury understood the nature of the offense and made the recommendation. The Commonwealth would ask that the Court impose that life sentence and now so allow Ms. Muse to speak and address the Court with regard to her concerns.

JUDGE JOHNSON: Okay. Ms. Muse.

MS. MUSE: Thank you for letting me speak. It's been a long five years, and it's nice to feel like I have a voice that I can share things with you and tell you what this is like. I would ask you to sentence him to—to life, and I don't know if it's possible, but—if there's anything you could do so he could never have parole, I would ask that you do that.

And it's not a lack of forgiveness. It's not vengeance or hatred. It's just that I—I miss—I miss living without fear. I don't—I don't remember what that was like. I know that you heard me speak to the jury about what it feels like always having a gun in my purse or in my car or sleeping with a loaded gun by my bed and just not being able to enjoy simple things like keeping my doors open and enjoying a breeze or walking around outside by myself.

I hope that what Mr. Morrison said is true. I hope that he found God, and I hope that he feels forgiveness, and I do believe that God forgives anyone and anything and—and has the ability to love us deeply. But we don't get to ignore the consequences of our actions just because we find Christ, and Christ would not ever suggest that. I hope for his sake that he does live a different life, but the life that he has lived up to this point has yet, to my knowledge, done anything to contribute to society other than to take from society and to hurt people. I was his tenth felony conviction. There's a long line of victims before me, and there will be a long line of victims after me if he's released. Ever. Ten years, twenty years, it doesn't matter. He doesn't have any skills to live in society.

Six days he waited, bought illegal drugs and got [a] weapon and formulated a plan. [He] came to my office, and he kidnapped me. I am certain that his goal was to stab me to death after he raped me, and I am certain that he will do that if he ever gets the opportunity. I wish that I could live and think that he doesn't want to hurt me. I wish that I could live that way because it is—it is so painful and so difficult to live your life every day knowing that someone else doesn't just want to hurt you, but they planned it, and they tried, and only by some miracle I survived. I wouldn't be here if it was up to him. This would be a murder case, not a kidnapping case. And the risk is too high.

His entire adult life has been felony after felony after felony, and he's been given opportunity after opportunity to be put back out into society and to be productive, and he chooses not to. Those are his choices. I've had no choice in any of this. The only choice that I have had is to learn how to fight and learn how to shoot a gun and learn how to make sure that the day he gets out that I am ready to fight back, harder than I fought back last time. That's my choice—to work and to constantly be prepared to plan my entire life around his. This man has total control over my future. He and this trial [have] dictated whether or not I become a mom, whether or not I move to Georgetown and live on my family farm—all these things that I want to do that I don't do because I can't. And there is nothing that he can say today to give me any confidence that he will ever be anything other than what he has been his entire life. I hope for him—I do hope for him that he changes, but I don't believe, and I don't think this Court can believe, that I'm somehow safe now just because he says he's read some Mormon literature and he's found God.

I am asking you to honor the jury's recommendation. I know they deliberated for a long time, and I know that they think this is the right thing to do, and if you would please, Judge Johnson, you're the only person who can give me the safety and peace and hope for a future and time that I can recover and take a

deep breath and learn how to live and—and move forward. Every moment that he's in prison is a moment
that I get back. This is technically—maybe it's his
sentencing date, but this is mine too. I have been
living for this day for five, long years. And I can-
not wait to hear what you have to say because then I
get to know what my future looks like. Do I have the
rest of my life to enjoy? Do I have ten years or fif-
teen years? I literally beg you to please sentence
him to life and give me mine.

Part of me felt Judge Johnson was going to sentence Morrison to life—he already
had in 2007. Even knowing that, I stood in front of him with my body quivering,
voice shaking, listening to every word. As he walked through the basis for his ruling, I held on to every syllable.

JUDGE JOHNSON

JUDGE: Mr. Morrison, you're before this Court after
having been found guilty of kidnapping first degree
and persistent felony offender first degree. Is
that your understanding of why you're before the
Court?

DEFENDANT: Yes, Your Honor.

JUDGE: It's my understanding that you've had the
opportunity to speak with your attorney about your
current legal situation?

DEFENDANT: I have.

JUDGE: You've had the opportunity to address the
Court regarding your particular sentence in this
case. Is there anything about this proceeding that
you don't understand?

DEFENDANT: No.

JUDGE: The jury in this case, based upon the kidnapping first degree enhanced by the persistent felony offender first degree, recommended life in this case. I've had a chance to listen to the testimony during the course of this case.

I've also had the opportunity to review your prior criminal history which indicates you've been found guilty of burglary third degree, criminal possession of a forged instruments, theft by unlawful taking, criminal mischief, alcohol intoxication, persistent felony offender, terroristic threatening, exploitation of an adult.

There are different reasons for incarceration in our system and it looks like up to this point, the reasons for incarceration for you have been in hopes that you'd be rehabilitated.

Due to the amount of time each charge has carried, everyone understood you would be back out in society and you would have the opportunity to make the changes that would be necessary to live a normal life within this society. The Court finds those opportunities have failed. I heard testimony from your expert who came here to testify that you manipulated police officers, Ms. Muse, and you even attempted to manipulate your own expert. That was his clear testimony and not only was he an expert in his field, he was an expert in his mini field of manipulation. And his expert testimony was that you attempted to manipulate him. Quite frankly, Mr. Morrison, I find that you are the most manipulative person that's been in my court.

DEFENDANT: Yeah. I can believe you would say that.

JUDGE: Excuse me.

DEFENDANT: I said I understand.

JUDGE: You've made statements today you have real-ized everything is not about Larry. Now how much you believe that I don't know. The crime in this case is one in which you've taken a great deal out of the victim. Obviously, the crime is very seri-ous. I truly believe the jury weighed the testimony and took time to deliberate what the sentence should be. I agree with the jury that life impris-onment is warranted not only for this charge but because of your long history of not being able to be a productive citizen. A citizen that is not going to continue to violate the rights that each of us are supposed to be able to enjoy. You've taken those rights away from Ms. Muse and from many victims in the past and it is going to stop. And it is going to stop here today. I am going to impose the sentence of life. I will recommend to the parole that they think very seriously and deliber-ate as to whether or not you should be entitled to parole. The testimony I've heard tells me very clearly that you are manipulative, and you intend to harm other people. My recommendation to the parole board is they seriously consider that any decision they make regarding probation—when you qualify for it- may come back to harm the victim or other people that took place in this process.

Is there anything else that needs to be taken care of at this time?

MR. SHAW: No, Your Honor. Thank you.

MR. HART: No, Your Honor. Thank you.

JUDGE: Thank you all.

When he pronounced the life sentence, I immediately turned to Marti, buried my head in the crook of her neck, and openly sobbed.

MARCH 25, 2011

Morrison's appellate lawyers filed his appeal directly to the Kentucky Supreme Court which is a matter of right for any sentence twenty-years or greater. I wasn't in the courtroom during the trial for anything other than my testimony and the closing arguments, so I had no idea how strong the appeal might be. More waiting. The legal system rarely resolves a case like this. You may get a reprieve, but there are always appeals, parole, probation, but rarely an end. Not until someone dies.

Two weeks later, I woke up to notice a giant patch of gray hair on my hairline. My weight plummeted, I had flu-like symptoms, and I was weak. Somehow I had survived five years in the legal system, but now that the trial was over, my body began to fall apart.

CHAPTER 26

THIRTEEN CALLS

JUNE 20, 2012

I logged onto the Kentucky Supreme Court website to check for a ruling in my case. Over the past two months, I'd periodically checked the website to see if the decision on Morrison's appeal had come down. Nothing yet, but I knew it could be any day.

My friend Vickie called from New York City, and we discussed plans for a visit. She asked what I was doing, and I told her a quick check to see if the ruling had posted online. We continued talking as I scrolled down the page and saw the styling of my case under the newly released cases section. I stopped listening—and breathing—at the same time. I clicked to open it and barely whispered to Vickie, "It's here." She immediately stopped talking.

I opened the document and read, "Memorandum Opinion of the Court Affirming." I gasped, held my breath and moved the mouse to the end of the document to confirm I understood it correctly. "Appellant's convictions and sentence are affirmed." My mouth fell open, and I dropped the phone. Somewhere my mind registered Vickie was still on the other end of the call, but it didn't matter. Everything went limp. My body fell forward, off the couch and onto the floor. Tears, sobs, and pain roared out, purging six years of living in fear. The sounds that erupted from me were indescribable. It sounded like I was dying. But actually I was living.

I eventually made my way back to the phone. Vickie cried and celebrated with me.

After I settled down, I read the opinion in its entirety. It was a unanimous decision, but the justices cited several issues that would otherwise constitute reversible error, including how the prosecution used Arnett to enter my drug tests into evidence instead of someone from the lab. Since West didn't object and acknowledged the drug allegations were lies, the Kentucky Supreme Court decided it was harmless error. They found several other instances of appealable error by the prosecutor but labeled them harmless error only because West failed to preserve the issues. Judge Johnson was unable to respond to these errors at trial due to West not raising the issue. I had a new appreciation for Mr. West. Maybe now I liked West a little more. Maybe he really didn't want Morrison back on the street. But I was speculating.

I thanked God for this outcome, for a break from the system until he is up for parole in fourteen years. Then it starts again.

After the Kentucky Supreme Court handed down their decision, I started living my new normal, but in many respects, it looked and felt like my life before. I was always mindful of my surroundings and prepared to address a threat, but since it had become second nature, it didn't feel much different than how I had navigated life before. At least I didn't carry a gun to take my trash out or go to the grocery anymore. I had traveled to Indianapolis, one of my favorite places to get away for a quick trip, but this time it was for work. It was a gray day in March with the nights coming far too early. After my meetings, I grabbed some takeout and headed back to my hotel to avoid the cold weather.

I sat in my room, finishing up a project, and clicked the remote to turn on a news channel. That was unusual for me since I prefer to work in quiet. A local crime report caught my attention. Something in the story triggered my intuition, and I moved the mouse off my work document to open the Internet.

I did a quick search for Morrison—and found that, according to a website run by the Department of Corrections (DOC), he was scheduled for early release in 2016.

I scoured the page, looking for anything that might indicate a glitch. Nothing. He was parole eligible ten years too soon!

How did this happen? I had no idea. Thank God the news program spurred me to check. I started calling. No one would be in their office after hours, but I left messages everywhere I could. I called the prison and then each department within the prison. I called the administrative office of the courts. I called the DOC.

Too many thoughts ran through my mind for me to sleep. I called the front desk to request a late checkout. I knew I had to get this resolved before I drove home. As soon as the clock showed 8:00 a.m., I made all the same calls again.

Not one person would help me. Everyone I reached said if he was scheduled for release, then it must be accurate. I firmly but politely explained that a life sentence means more than ten years. They were releasing him ten years too early by anyone's calculation.

Shocked by how many calls I had to make, I started to keep count. By my twelfth call, my voice was clearly stressed. I started with, "I know I sound upset, and I am, but not with you. I need your help. Please." Then I described what was going on.

This particular man was not helpful at all. He just kept repeating what was on his screen.

"Can I send you a copy of the court order and sentencing documents?" I asked, thankful I had copies on my computer.

"No, I can see them on my end." He was unwavering in his refusal to resolve this problem.

"How does it make sense that someone sentenced to life is scheduled to be released after serving only ten years?"

He responded as if bored and speaking to a small child. "Ma'am, sentencing guidelines are very complicated."

"I am willing for you to explain it to me." The tension in my voice expanded.

"Like I said, it is very complicated. I had to attend a two-week class to understand how it works," he said, as if believing this would shut me up.

"That's great. With all that training, you are the perfect person to explain this to me." I deliberately curbed the sarcasm that dangled precariously on the tip of my tongue.

"You won't be able to understand it," he said, very matter-of-fact.

Now I was done. "I'm a practicing attorney. I read and comprehend the tax code, secure transaction statutes, and have yet to be stumped, so I am confident that I can understand the sentencing guidelines," I said in my God-to-Moses voice I use when training my dog. Finally, I asked for a supervisor and got a contact number. That was the most help this guy had given me.

I called the supervisor, praying he would think this through with me, not just dully repeat what was on the screen in front of him. I started by telling him I was in need of his help, that this was my thirteenth call with no resolution. I explained the problem and offered to send him a copy of the court order and the sentencing documents. He started saying the exact same things the twelve prior employees had told me. I could hear his keyboard clicking as he pulled up the same documents. I was explaining to him that a life sentence demands at least twenty years before they were parole eligible when I heard . . .

"Humph." Then a longer, "Huummmph," followed by a long exhale. Pause. "You are right."

Longer pause. Neither of us spoke. I could picture this man, staring at his screen in disbelief, while I waited quietly.

I heard more clicking of the keyboard. Then, "You're right. I've got the court documents in front of me."

"Thank you for taking time and looking at this. You are my thirteenth call, the seventh at the DOC, and no one else has helped me."

"I've reviewed the documents, and Morrison should not be eligible for parole until March 2026." He sounded like he couldn't believe what he was saying.

"What happened? Why was he scheduled for release?" I asked, hoping to figure this out to make sure it didn't happen again.

"Data entry error. Someone put in the wrong date." His voice was flat as he grasped the significance of the mistake.

"None of the twelve people I called before you took the time to figure this out. Do you know that a lot of people would have stopped at call ten or eleven? Why did I have to push so hard to get someone to listen to me? Were you going to notify me of his release?"

"Yes, of course. We would mail you a letter."

"To what address?" I asked.

He recited an address with no connection to me, not even in the same city, not even the same county. "That isn't my address. Where did you get that address?"

"The prosecutor's office," he answered.

Unbelievable. He asked for my correct address. When he did, I realized there must have been a mix-up. The prosecutor's office wouldn't just make up a random address—they must have given the DOC another victim's address.

"Don't delete that address. Have you already?"

"Yes, why?"

"I'm thinking the address you gave me is the address of another victim. If you had their address, we could track them down and make sure the proper address is connected to their case. Now, we have no idea who they are, and I bet they won't get notification when *their* predator gets out of prison."

Silence. This was so frustrating. I was relieved I'd solved my problem—but it didn't make me feel much better knowing someone else was likely to get caught off guard.

The supervisor assured me things would be corrected on his end. My gut told me to take a quick screen shot with the wrong release date. I still have it. I doubted people would believe me otherwise.

It is interesting to note that Morrison got a life sentence from a jury in an area of Kentucky that doesn't often hand those down. I needed him behind bars, and I got it. Now, I'll fight, push, double-check, and do whatever I have to do to keep him there. I have no choice since life means eligible for parole in twenty years. Each time he is up for parole, I'll be there, pleading with the parole board not to release him. This is how it is for any victim who wants to keep a perpetrator away.

As I reviewed the court record to finish this book, I saw that Morrison had filed an additional appeal that wasn't resolved until 2016. Ten years to come to a temporary conclusion. Do you know what else I found out? Shortly after receiving the case, Judge Johnson imposed a one million dollar full cash bond. Morrison would never have been able to make bail under those circumstances. One more reason to be thankful he was my judge. *But the prosecutor's office never told me, not Gordie, not Keith, and not the victim advocate.* Can you imagine the difference that knowledge would have made? I was consumed with terror that Morrison would return. I almost killed him to prevent his coming back for me when I had nothing to fear. If only the prosecutor would have taken the time to make a five-minute phone call.

Years of my life would have been different. Of course, I could also have had faith and trusted God to keep me safe, but instead I relied on myself.

Despite all I have been through in the years following the kidnapping, it hasn't defined me. It has shaped me, but it will not define me. I won't let it. I can name far more interesting things about me than having been the victim of a crime.

However, a date on my calendar may change my life forever. March 2026—the month Morrison is eligible for parole. Will he stay in prison? I'll know in 2026. Will my life end violently? I'll know in March 2026. Does that date define what I do now? Absolutely not.

Honestly, it doesn't matter what we have accomplished or not accomplished in our lives. The bottom line is someone or something else doesn't get to define us. Cancer doesn't, crime doesn't, and bad decisions don't. We all have a future and a hope, and I find mine in my faith. I would not have survived without it. We get to define our lives and rise above anything that may shape us. We are free to take anything that happens to us and use it for good. This is the real healing. That is clear to me now. But when I was in the middle of my case, I could hardly see past the fear to imagine a life without the constant threat of Morrison and his plans for me.

Morrison kidnapped me, assaulted me, and tried to kill me. He wanted to rape me and then dispose of my body. He told me he was going to kill me. I knew he would leave my body behind the barn, allow Mother Nature to do her damage, and drive away in my car.

When I tell you he will find me and try to kill me if he's released, I know that to be true in my heart. He has not been rehabilitated or found Jesus. He's a violent man, driven by obsession, and for some reason, I'm it.

I wonder what he has in store for me now. He was angry before. Now he will have another twenty years to blame on me. I don't even want to think about that.

My story is a lesson to people who ignore the hair-raising on the back of their necks because they don't want to be rude. We need to trust our intuition and take action immediately if something doesn't feel right. But most of us are not taught this. Nor are we used to giving ourselves freedom to violate social norms and be rude, loud, or do whatever we have to do to present ourselves as hard targets and stay safe.

More so, my story is a lesson for anyone who's been the victim of a crime, cried out in relief when law enforcement showed up, and then sat back, trusting them to take care of things. I hope you understand that even the most passionate detective, attorney, and judge will be limited by the system. You must fiercely advocate for yourself. Don't be afraid to get involved. You have to live with the consequences—they don't.

I am in no way suggesting that law enforcement agencies and court officers, en masse, aren't doing their jobs conscientiously, but I find it frightening how many cases are handled, or mishandled, like mine. Employees of the justice system are overworked, from clerks to judges and everyone in between. These people, like all of us, can become overwhelmed, bogged down in minutiae, or simply incompetent or lazy. It is not a system you can rely on to protect you. You need to do everything you can, within the bounds of the law, to keep yourself safe. Work to make sure the defendant gets as much time as possible, life if warranted, so you can have yours back.

I've included resources in the back of this book and updated on my website, www.OwnYourMoment.org, that may help. I started OwnYourMoment as a movement to help create fewer victims and equip those who have been victimized. A damaged crime scene, a mishandled piece of evidence, or an error on an official form may be the result of an accident or ignorance, but intentional or not, the fallout is the same. A violent felon may be released, and someone will pay the price for it.

Everyone seems to understand why defendants have rights—they stand to pay the ultimate price, their freedom. While losing freedom as a victim may look different from that of a defendant since we are not literally put behind bars, what is taken from is just as significant. This is my frustration with the system. It was created without thought for victims. I believe we can bolster the victim without impinging upon the rights of the defendant. I'm pleased there are groups and legislatures that are moving in this direction by amending their state constitutions to create rights for victims. I hope we start to see a change in how the system overall treats crime victims. Maybe you can be part of that with me?

As for the end of my story, I don't know what that is. Check back with me in March 2026. I may be here.

And I may not.

EPILOGUE:

THE CAMPAIGN

Be the change you want to see in the world.

—Unknown

JANUARY 30, 2018

I drove to Frankfort, Kentucky, with a stack of papers in hand. My mind was racing as I made the drive. I was as excited as I've been in a long time. Today was the result of twelve years of prayers coming to fruition. As I neared the Frankfort exit, I noticed my gas light was on. I'd been so wrapped up in my thoughts, I hadn't noticed the yellow warning light letting me know the tank was almost empty. I started to sweat. I had a deadline to make it to the Capitol, or I'd forever lose this chance. This chance to fight for others the way nobody fought for me—the chance to change a generation of how criminal cases are prosecuted, to collaborate with law enforcement, and to give victims more hope.

If I didn't get there on time, nothing would change.

I coasted into the parking lot on fumes, found a place to park, and raced to the Secretary of State's Office (SOS). After trying to slow down my thundering heart, I walked into the SOS office and filed my papers to run for Commonwealth's Attorney for Bourbon, Scott, and Woodford Counties, Gordie's elected position for which Keith Eardley was now running.

I'm running for this office for a long list of readily apparent reasons: giving victims a voice, working a case from the beginning, preparing law enforcement and victims for trial, not offering minimum sentences to violent offenders, and vigorously prosecuting sex crimes.

As a courtesy, I called Keith to thank him for everything he did and let him know I wanted to run for that office and make sweeping changes. I want to reform the system in my small part of the world and set an example of how it can work. The system is only as effective as those who manage it, and I'll make it effective. I am praying that if it is God's will, I will win. And if I don't, I pray that Keith will consider my ideas, policies, and protocols that will change the lives of those who come in contact with the criminal's justice system in the 14th Judicial Circuit.

My research established that this specific office has never been a held by a female or person from my political party. Just a bunch of good ol' boys. The odds are stacked against me, but that's never stopped me before.

NOVEMBER 6, 2018. ELECTION DAY.
RESULTS:

OFFICE OF COMMONWEALTH'S ATTONREY
14TH Judicial Circuit (Bourbon, Scott and Woodford Counties)

	SHARON R. MUSE	J. KEITH EARDLEY
Bourbon Co:	4.486	3,178
Scott Co:	12,434	8,665
Woodford Co:	6,193	5,940
TOTAL VOTES:	**23,113**	17,783

APPENDICES

A CONVERSATION WITH
SHARON R. MUSE

Beth Tribolet is the founder of Reel True Stories, a film and television development company. Previously, Tribolet ran the Law & Justice Unit at ABC Network News, a high-performing specialized reporting team that won two Emmy Awards under her leadership. She lives in the San Francisco Bay Area with her husband and daughter. This is my interview with her.

Beth Tribolet: Was your family prepared for what happened—did they have a frame of reference for the violence you encountered?

Sharon R. Muse: Yes and no. This came in like a tornado. It was shocking, hard to comprehend and harder to process. This is why I wanted to keep it from my family. I was stunned and pleasantly surprised at how well my parents responded at the hospital. They reacted much better than I would have if roles had been reversed. Although we weren't specifically prepared for it, we were prepared in that I have a very strong family—strong in our faith in God, strong emotionally, strong mentally, and we love each other. We may pick at each other, but heaven help the person who tries to hurt any of

us. They rallied around me, fought for and protected me. My parents wrote letters to the State
Police post commander, to the prosecutor, to poli-
ticians. They didn't feel that I was being protected by the system, so they fought back in their
own way. Having a history of a personal relationship with Jesus means He provides what you need
when you need it. But not a minute before. Were
they the type of people who could endure it and
rise above it? Yes. And that was primarily because
of their strong faith. And being hard working persistent people who have a strong sense of justice,
they won't shy away from something difficult. We
did it. We survived it all together as a family. We
are warriors.

BT: You had to overcome the nice manners you were
taught as a child. Did you realize you had to coun-
terprogram some of the kindness your family
instilled?

SRM: I'm not sure if it is counterprogramming or
just adding boundaries to it. We have talked about
this as a family and with others, including pastors
and teachers. We can't teach loving and serving
others as a blanket statement. In Matthew 10:16,
Jesus states to be wise as a serpent and gentle as
a dove and you are sheep among wolves. We have to
acknowledge wolves exist so we can be prepared to
stay safe when they show up in our lives. Not living in fear but living with a filter. I got the
message about being nice. I didn't quite get the
message about wolves. Now I know, now we all know,
and I want to share that with other people.

BT: Your encounter with Morrison that day unalterably changed the direction of your life. Can you explain how your hopes and dreams have changed?

SRM: In 2018 I closed my private practice to campaign for the Office of Commonwealth's Attorney. I ran against Keith Eardley and won the election. Now I have Gordie's former position. I am grateful for what actions Keith and Gordie took on my behalf, but what they failed to do was so significant I felt compelled to be part of the solution to the problems I experienced as a crime victim. What I found in that office, well that is a book of its own. It was far worse than I would have imagined. Sex crimes against children going untouched for more than 5 years, cases backlogged having never been worked, hundreds of cases not yet brought to grand jury (meaning the suspects are out continuing to commit crimes). Many victims of adult and child rape, attempted murder, kidnapping had never been contacted—until I won. No electronic organization of files-evidence and case files missing etc.. Now everything is different. I am blessed to have a hard working and passionate team. We work with law enforcement from the beginning of the case to ensure we have the evidence we need to succeed at trial. We attend trainings, we are working the old cases that have been ignored, and we share information with law enforcement to help maximize sentences for repeat and violent offenders. We spend significant time with our victims and host a retreat for them annually. Our victims are given my personal cell phone number along with other prosecutors in the office and our victim advocate. Our team, Brooks Frye, Aubrey McGuire, Cheryl Winn, Pat Foley, Hannah Bernard and Kathy Gregory and Mitch Talaki work diligently for our community. The final member of our team is one familiar to the reader. It is Judge Rob Johnson. After my trial he moved to the Court of Appeals. He left the Court of Appeals in November of 2018, when I won my election, so I asked him to join me as a prosecutor. I only knew him in his capacity as a judge but knew he had extensive experience and vast knowledge that would benefit our office and more importantly our victims. He is a fierce and compassionate advocate. He is no longer just my judge but rather a trusted colleague and dear friend. And to answer the question from chapter 24, yes, he is single. I am very proud of what we have already done and will continue to do for the safety of our community.

BT: What happened ultimately revealed a very brave woman. Look what you are doing now. It doesn't seem to me to be your style to look backward. You are moving forward in so many ways. Is this book part of your moving forward?

SRM: Yes. This book comes from a deep place in me passionate about helping others. It has been hard to write at times but healing as well. I hope it is a blessing to those who read it, a comfort and encouragement to victims, a challenge for those in the system to do their best, and inspiration for anyone hurting from the senseless acts of others—whether it was labeled a crime or not.

BT: That comes through in your decision to write this book. Why did you decide to write a book based on these experiences?

SRM: After the kidnapping, I hated that anyone knew about it. I tried to keep it from my parents, hoping it would be a quiet little secret that I could make go away and move on, so it may seem odd that I'm telling the world about it now. There is a part of me that has been taught since I was a child that if you are able to help someone, you should. As I was trying to get a grip on what had happened, I searched everywhere, the web, victims groups, therapists, and I desperately wanted to speak to someone or read something written by someone who knew what I was feeling. I just felt so alone. I was desperate to speak with someone who knew what it felt like to be hunted. We all experience tragedy, disease, divorce, death, but I wanted someone who could say I know what it is like to be hunted, I know what it is like to feel you are going to die a violent death.

Clearly I'm not the only person who has lived through something like this. Statistically, it happens every day. I just couldn't find someone with whom I could identify. It would have been comforting for me to know that all the things I was experiencing were normal. For someone to say, "I did that, too." So part of this is to fill in the gap for other people to have what I needed but couldn't find. Part of it is to be a warning, to be an alarm to people not to make the choices I made. To encourage people to pause and take the time to learn a few new things to help keep them safer.

I'm not sure if the world we live in is becoming increasingly violent or if we're just more aware of the violence due to access to media. It's hard to escape the stories of people being injured, and I wonder, if those people had been better equipped, could that have ended differently for them.

Another reason was to help friends and family know how to support victims. It's hard to know how to help someone in great pain and hard for the victim to know what to ask for. It isn't like Hallmark has a violent crime section in the anniversary aisle where you can pop in for a card. Showing up, being present, and loving are the best things to do.

BT: I gather your family has always played a really big role in your life. What kind of family did you come from?

SRM: We have our quirks like every family, but it was very stable and nurturing. I felt very safe. I was very blessed to be raised on a horse farm in rural Kentucky, taken to church every time the doors were open. In summer, you wake up early to hoe out tobacco before going to cheerleading camp, school, work, or to help your neighbors. All-American kind of family.

Dad was an engineer with more than sixty patents, Mom was a registered nurse and later real estate agent, and we lived and worked on a horse farm. My brother Rick was my best friend. My sister, Lisa; Rick; and I were all involved in sports and activities. Faith was a huge part of family life. We prayed before bed and were taught to memorize Scriptures. We lobbied for the right to sleep with my Grandma Toney when she spent the night. My parents went out of the way to teach us hard work and a deep sense of providing for people that don't have what you have. You aren't blessed with a good life to keep it all for yourself. We had advantages many people didn't, and it was ingrained that we needed to help provide for those who didn't. This is why I got into mission work, started a nonprofit for orphans, and did a lot of pro-bono work for kids. You are here to make the world a better place, not grab all you can on your way down the path.

BT: How would you counsel a person in similar circumstances? What are the most important things to get his/her life back together?

SRM: Two things immediately come to mind that are imperative. Forgiving yourself and forgiving the person who did this to you. You tend to spend a fair bit of time in your head being angry at yourself for being manipulated or not identify the warning signs earlier. I would encourage him/her to realize that we aren't predators and our minds don't see the world the way they do. Give yourself grace and embrace that nothing you did made the predator hurt you.

It may sound strange for forgiveness to be the first thing that comes to mind, but it is crucial to forgive the person who hurt you. As you read in my story, the inability to forgive caused me more harm and more hurt and stole more peace and joy from my life than anything Morrison did to me. Playing tapes in my head of what happened, blaming him for everything that was different and how much he had taken from me, grinding my teeth, hating him—every time I felt something different in my life, my anger toward him increased. That didn't help me. That kept me stuck. It didn't only keep me stuck, it started to drown me. The most growth, freedom, and healing I experienced were when I was able to truly forgive him and release the hatred I had for him. My hating him didn't affect him at all. It didn't change his life or his day while it was destroying me. My hatred toward him sucked the life out of mine. It affected every part of me: how I saw the world, my sleep, my spiritual life, my mood.

This person has already taken enough from you. Let's not voluntarily give him anything else. Fight hard to take your thoughts captive and be mindful of what you are saying to yourself. Don't allow that person to continue to steal your joy. That would be priority.

BT: God was key to all of this. Did you come to this understanding in prayer?

SRM: Yes, it was like God showed me I was making my situation worse. I was making choices that increased my pain instead of decreasing it. The choice to hold on to all this hatred was what was destroying me. I remember feeling like my soul had been charred. If you can envision what our souls look like, mine was different after the incident. It was charred black like a piece of charcoal, flaky and without life in it, and would never be the same. I would never be the same. I believed that was because of what Morrison had done to me in that car, as if I had been in the presence of evil and it had touched me.

When I decided I wasn't going to hate him anymore—when I was no longer consumed with killing him—everything I lost returned to me. I still had a lot of fear and struggles, but now I could face those fears as a whole person. I was me again—my soul wasn't broken. I was going to respond to this from a healthy place. The hatred and revenge had depleted me of anything good inside me. I don't think I was able to receive what God wanted to give me because I was so eaten up with hatred I couldn't see or hear anything but fear or hate. He ultimately gifted me with the ability to forgive. Rescuing me again.

BT: You said at one point that the only thing worse than being wrapped in fear was being consumed by so much hatred.

SRM: Yes, I think the hatred caused me more damage than the fear ever did.

BT: Does Morrison occupy any part of your brain today?

SRM: No, not unless I am talking about the book or website. Now and then, I'll consider how much time I have before he is up for parole. But fear looks different now. If I suddenly get spooked or feel afraid, it's not Morrison's face I see. It isn't related to him at all. I respond differently to a perceived threat. If I don't feel safe, I employ what I've learned, assess the threat, and move forward accordingly.

In the months following the incident, he was always in the front of my mind, until I forgave him. Every creak at night, every car driving too slowly by my home, every knock at the door was him. He was inextricably intertwined with me. Not anymore.

BT: It was a serious issue for you that you felt the criminal's justice system was not protecting you. Can you explain how you felt betrayed by that?

SRM: It wasn't protecting me. That is why I call it the criminal's justice system instead of the criminal justice system. I realized it was never intended to protect me at all. It isn't even an afterthought. It wasn't part of the formula or concern when our rules of criminal procedure were created. The entire reason for its existence is to protect the rights of the defendant, and that is where it ends.

Initially, I felt betrayed by the weak charges. Kidnapping was great, but sexual assault and resisting arrest didn't carry much time, that is what I mean by weak. We had evidence to charge Morrison with more significant felonies but they never did. That was one of the biggest betrayals. Then not to have any evidence proffered to support the sexual abuse charge was horrifying.

BT: Why is it so important to get a good set of multiple charges?

SRM: Each charge against the defendant is more possible prison time if convicted. The average group of twelve law-abiding citizens will be hesitant to put someone in prison for life. Remember, all twelve jurors must vote to convict on each charge. In my case, they did not convict on two of the three charges. No evidence was presented to them so they couldn't. It wasn't their fault. (The trial jury had no way of knowing Morrison stood up and pled guilty to all charges years prior.) Keith failed to even mention the other charges during closing arguments. If there is evidence to support more than one charge, then the jury has more charges to vote on. If the prosecutor provides evidence to support each charge the odds are increased for a guilty verdict. If the prosecutor loses the case then the defendant will walk. And the victim's life may change forever. Or even end.

BT: Was it personally disappointing to you because you worked in this small legal community and knew some of the other lawyers?

SRM: Yes, very. I knew everyone involved, except Trooper Arnett and Detective Murrell. We all worked in the same small community. I wasn't expecting special treatment, but I thought they would give me or any victim a small voice. As hard as I pushed and was still ignored, I've often wondered how "outsiders" survive the system.

My friends kept telling me that if they were in my situation they would have no idea what to do or how to fight for themselves. They would not know to call the Attorney General's office asking for a special prosecutor or be able to write a memorandum of law for the prosecutor telling him how to get evidence entered. Or to keep a log of evidence and push for it to be collected or pass notes to prosecutors during hearings asking them to ask certain questions.

That's what bothers me.

BT: To what do you attribute the way they mismanaged your case?

SRM: I have no idea. Even today it makes no sense to me.

BT: Should a woman carry firearms?

SRM: Absolutely, if she is trained and comfortable with it. Merely owning a gun isn't a panacea. If you're scared of it or won't take the time to train with it, don't have one. It certainly won't be part of a useful safety plan if you aren't skilled with it. If you pull a gun out, everything will escalate exponentially so don't carry one if you aren't trained.

BT: Do you think people underestimate the amount of time and energy it takes to become proficient and safe with a gun?

SRM: Yes. I would no sooner buy a gun and not train to use it than I would give the keys of a car to a twelve-year-old and say, "Enjoy the car." Guns are not inherently unsafe; they are just tools. The hand and head on the other end of the gun is the concern.

BT: Do you still carry your gun to church?

SRM: No, not while Morrison is in prison.

BT: When could he be released?

SRM: He qualifies for parole March 2026.

BT: What does that mean to you?

SRM: Everything. Morrison will speak to the parole board and ask to be released. I'll speak and submit as many letters as I can to encourage the parole board to keep him in. If they release him, life as I know it will be over.

BT: What does that mean?

SRM: It means I'll have to decide what to do then. I don't want to run or hide. And I won't be hunted. I don't know. Maybe I can challenge him to a duel? Wait, I can't do that since that was included in the oath I took when I was sworn in as an attorney, so a duel is out.

BT: Did you get any variant treatment in the legal system as a female?

SRM: I don't think the treatment was because I was a female but because of the charges that were filed as a result of being a female. A lot of prosecutors don't like trying sex crimes, and most reported sex crimes are committed against females. In the defense closing in sentencing phase, the attorney thanks the jury for not convicting Morrison of sex crimes, and he notes no such evidence was proffered to them nor was it mentioned in closing. They charged him with it and then didn't prosecute it or present any evidence. For some reason, they did nothing with the charge. Since I've taken over the office of the Commonwealth's Attorney I've noticed that was the norm with sexual assault cases. But it is different now with us.

BT: How do you feel about the social movement #MeToo and other sex crime awareness?

SRM: These women are using their notoriety to bring critical issues to the forefront. I applaud their bravery. They are fighting back, and I love it.

Crime victims publicly sharing the truth about abuse, unsure how their vulnerability will be received, takes great courage and strength. I'm amazed by them. It is one thing to be violated by the perpetrator and another to be betrayed by your colleagues, friends, and society who blame you or don't take you seriously. They risked everything by stepping forward, yet they did it anyway. Note here for the skeptics concerned with false allegations: I do understand that those do happen. That is tragic, and it undermines the validity of those of us with real claims. I understand research has established that the number of false allegations is rare.

This movement has helped make it clear that society has been asking the wrong questions all along: *Why didn't she report it earlier? Why was she there? What did she have on? Was she drinking?* The questions need to be: *Why did a man rape a woman? Force a woman to watch him shower or masturbate?* If society sees how frequently these things happen and how victims respond differently—many freezing or doing nothing at all—it may help decrease the victim blaming that many victims and prosecutors have to overcome at trial and change the conversation.

My concern is that this won't be sustained long term and society will revert to victim blaming with incidents unreported, and the ones that are reported going unprosecuted. So I hope they—we—remain relentless.

BT: What are you mobilizing with OwnYourMoment.org, and what does it mean to you?

SRM: OwnYourMoment.org was created to help people: learn a new mindset and basic proactive self-defense moves; quickly asses a threat; and develop confidence to respond in the moment. This creates an awareness, mindset, and tactics to stay safer. You can't control what someone else brings to you, but you can control how you respond—you can Own Your Moment. We are creating discussion, training, thoughtful interactions through expert information and community.

I've included simple tactics to deter a predator, and information about the legal system and advice for surviving it, along with posts from profession-als on safety, trauma, and grieving.

BT: What is being a "hard target"?

SRM: Hard targets carry themselves with a certain amount of confidence, use situational awareness (no headphones with head down texting), and stay alert, appearing ready to respond.

BT: How are you sharing this knowledge of yours with others?

SRM: Primarily through this book and www. OwnYourMoment.org, which took years to develop along with incredible input from professionals and experts. I am doing a lot of interviews, public speaking, meeting with corporations, and working with individual victims to help guide them through the system.

TOPICS FOR DISCUSSION

1. Was Morrison a product of his upbringing? Do you think he is a violent person because his environment made him violent? Do you think he had violent/antisocial tendencies since birth? Any explanations for his choices?

2. How would you have handled the kidnapping if you were me? Honestly imagine how you feel when a family member or friend asks you to help them with something you don't really want to help them with. Do you have a tendency to help anyway, to try to get out of it, or to be honest and say I really don't want to? Then, ask yourself if you would have made the same choices I made. If not, what would you have done differently, and when would you have done it?

3. Do you believe Morrison planned to murder me? Rape me?

4. If Morrison had not been caught, do you think he would have come back to kill me? How do you think his life would have turned out?

5. Did the extreme terror I lived in make you question how you'd react in a similar situation? If you are a polite, do-unto-others type of person, has this book changed the way you view interacting with others?

6. What do you think about how the brain responds to trauma? Do you believe a violent crime might happen to you? Do you believe one's response to a traumatic event is a choice or a primal brain function? Could it be both? Have you ever experienced a traumatic event and responded in a way that surprised you?

7. Do you have a plan for dealing with a threat, be it a tornado, burglary, carjacking, mugging, or worse? Why, or why not?

8. To what lengths would you go to keep your children, spouse, mother safe from a predator who had targeted him/her? What do you think about why I felt driven to kill Morrison? Do you believe you would ever plan a murder?

9. Who is the person who has hurt you more than anyone else?

10. Do you understand "rape culture" as it exists today? Do you agree society tends to ask all the wrong questions, questions about the victim's behavior instead of questions about why the perpetrator felt he/she could violate someone else? Are you doing something to change it?

11. Before you read this book, did you believe that victims had legal rights? If so, did reading this book change that? If yes, what steps can you take to do something about it?

12. Would you encourage a crime victim to fight back, push, and work the system for themselves as much as possible? Would your decision be based on what the crime is: rape, burglary, kidnapping, etc.?

13. Has your confidence in, or opinion of, the criminal justice system changed?

14. Do you believe God loves you, and He sees you? If so, do you believe He is in the miracle business? Do you believe God intervened in my situation? Do you believe God cares about your situation?

15. How do you view forgiveness? Is it a spiritual obligation? Duty? Is it for the benefit of the receiver or the giver? Can you imagine the freedom of walking in forgiveness every day as a choice or a lifestyle? Is there something stopping you from forgiving? Have you forgiven the person you thought of in question nine above? If not, what is stopping you?

RESOURCES

OWN YOUR MOMENT www.OwnYourMoment.org A purpose-driven movement to empower others by addressing: personal safety and learning how to thrive in a system designed to protect the rights of criminals.

You may learn how to avoid a threatening situation or step into one with more confidence and awareness when it cannot be avoided. The resources may help you become a "hard target" with the ability to quickly identify a predator and develop a self-protection, not a self-defense mindset. You may increase your situational awareness and create specific boundaries in advance of a threatening situation by learning to "draw the line." You may learn tactics in prevention, de-escalation, and survival of a threatening situation, surviving the legal system and caring for victims both in and out of the courtroom.

VINE www.vinelink.com If the perpetrator has been arrested and is in custody, you can get custody status and/or sign up to be notified if he/she is released through the VINE program. You can also register to be notified of any changes in the court case: VINE (Victim Information & Notification Everyday), 800-511-1670.

THE GIFT OF FEAR, **BY GAVIN DE BECKER.** A seminal writing on the mindset of predators and how victims respond by a former FBI profiler. I have given countless copies of this book to family, friends, and clients. I encourage everyone to read it.

ACKNOWLEDGMENTS

First, I want to thank God. Not in a polite way but rather in a face down, completely humble, and unsure why you chose to rescue me way. Repeatedly. But I know you did. What I do with the rest of my life is an offering to you and I pray will bless the lives of many.

Mom, your constant support, late nights reading chapters, and prayers have gotten us here. Thank you for being part of this. Your help and the constant companionship of my Golden Retriever, Coby, who sat at my feet patiently waiting for me the throw him a ball got me through.

Beth Tribolet, thank you for investing in me and this story before anyone else. Tracy Crump of Tracy Crump Editing services. Without you there would be no book. Literally. Thank you both for the countless hours of prayers, brainstorming, hand holding, tears, encouragement. I'm sure you never imagined the long ride down a wild path you took with me when you agreed to come on board. You have both been more than mentors but have become trusted friends and earned my deepest respect. I've seen firsthand the depth of your genius and passion for those you serve.

Eric Jensen, gifted editor and grammar-obsessed bestie who helped shape this book from the beginning. I couldn't have made it happen without your enthusiasm, sense of humor, and prayers. Not to mention your special love of the Oxford comma.

Ruth Schenk and Katie Price, thank you for reading and re-reading my chapters and giving me courage to include the hard stuff.

Debbie Broadfuehrer for helping me see how to paint a picture and having a more curious mind than my own.

Judge Tony Saragas for helping me to "just keep swimming."

Kevin Taylor, thank you for patiently supporting me in writing this and in helping to create the ending.

Karen Taylor Richardson, for getting me started on this path.

To Judge Tamra Gormely, for a strategically timed phone call and believing I could be the first to beat a political machine of good old boys.

To Dave Stone, Kyle Idleman, and Debbie Carper at Southeast Christian Church—for being part of a loving, welcoming church that isn't afraid of the raw ugly stories and for teaching me to face the giant of fear.

Dina Stickle and your cadre of Indiana teachers, thank you for reading and commenting on the book.

Keith, Cheryl and all of Clan Otto, thank you for everything!

Carolyn Carroway, Kim Unfried, Judy Chase, Hope Hudson, Rachel Loy, Beth LeHue Cox, Marti and Darin O'Neal, Stephanie Love, Angeleta Hendrickson, Heather Adkins, David Stevens, Dale Muse, Tom Pelt, Lia Vassiliades, and the Faces of Christ ladies. Thank you for being my strength when I didn't have any, for being hands and feet when I needed them.

Special thanks to Amy Lusk. I can't begin to thank you for pouring into me, sacrificing for me, and loving me through the insanity of it all.

Ray Larson, Lana Stephens, Gail Whitt, Lisa Fath, Heather Adkins, Jackie Kidwell, Kathleen Smith Logsdon, Linda Knapp, Beth Stone, Beth Sharpe, Abigail Sharpe, Missie and Brian Hickey, Wade and Anna Calvert, Beth Wilson Smith, Jennifer Pursel Fain, Katie Price, Katie Cook, and Julia Jaddock for the significant investment in me and my pursuit to change things for victims.

And for Rob Johnson, Brooks Frye, Cheryl Winn, Aubrey McGuire, Hannah Bernard, Mitch Talaki, and work mom Kathy Gregory for choosing to go on an overwhelming journey of righting the wrong that has taken place in our community. For fighting for those without voices. For taking less pay for more work but making a real impact on the 14th Judicial Circuit. I couldn't do what I'm led to do without you.

Micheal Canale for connecting me to Beth Tribolet and for having passion to help a stranger with a cause.

My precious small group, April Whilhoite, Jessica Hockensmith, Nicole Sparkman, Brenda Washburn, Sheri North, Katie Price, Rene Swizegood, Melanie Butler, Karen Cook, Susan Killeen Jones and Christina Morreale Janisch—thank you for always being one text away with prayers and love.

To the countless friends and family that supported me—and still do—I love and appreciate you.